Sin against the Innocents

Recent Titles in
Psychology, Religion, and Spirituality
J. Harold Ellens, Series Editor

Married to an Opposite: Making Personality Differences Work for You
Ron Shackelford

SIN AGAINST THE INNOCENTS

Sexual Abuse by Priests and the Role of the Catholic Church

Edited by Thomas G. Plante

Psychology, Religion, and Spirituality
J. Harold Ellens, Series Editor

Westport, Connecticut
London

Library of Congress Cataloging-in-Publication Data

Sin against the innocents : sexual abuse by priests and the role of the Catholic Church /
edited by Thomas G. Plante.
 p. cm.— (Psychology, religion, and spirituality, ISSN 1546–8070)
 Includes bibliographical references and index.
 1. Child sexual abuse by clergy. 2. Catholic Church—Clergy—Sexual behavior. I.
Plante, Thomas G. II. Series.
BX1912.9.S56 2004
261.8´3272´088282—dc22   2004000064

British Library Cataloguing in Publication Data is available.

Library of Congress Catalog Card Number: 2004000064
ISBN: 0–275–98175–4
ISSN: 1546–8070

First published in 2004

Praeger Publishers, 88 Post Road West, Westport, CT 06881
An imprint of Greenwood Publishing Group, Inc.
www.praeger.com

Printed in the United States of America

The paper used in this book complies with the
Permanent Paper Standard issued by the National
Information Standards Organization (Z39.48–1984).

10 9 8 7 6 5 4 3 2 1

Copyright Acknowledgment

The editor and publisher gratefully acknowledge permission to reprint the following:
"Perpetrators of Clergy Abuse of Minors: Insights from Attachment Theory" by Donna J.
Markham and Samuel F. Mikail as published in *Studies in Gender and Sexuality,* 5/2.
Copyright © The Analytic Press, Inc. Reprinted with the permission of the publisher.

Dedicated to the memory of Curtis Bryant, S.J., Ph.D., friend, colleague, and contributor to this book. He helped so many people troubled by clergy sexual misconduct.

ADVISORY BOARD

CONTENTS

SERIES FOREWORD

The interface between psychology, religion, and spirituality has been of great interest to scholars for a century. In the last three decades a broad popular appetite has developed for books that make practical sense out of the sophisticated research on these three subjects. Freud expressed an essentially deconstructive perspective on this matter and indicated that he saw the relationship between human psychology and religion to be a destructive interaction. Jung, on the other hand, was quite sure that these three aspects of the human spirit—psychology, religion, and spirituality— were constructively and inextricably linked. Anton Boisen and Seward Hiltner derived much insight from both Freud and Jung, as well as from Adler and Reik, while pressing the matter forward with gratifying skill and illumination. Boisen and Hiltner fashioned a framework within which the quest for a sound and sensible definition of the interface between psychology, religion, and spirituality might best be described on expressed.[1] We are in their debt.

This series of general interest books, so wisely urged by Greenwood Press, and particularly by its editor, Debbie Carvalko, intends to define the terms and explore the interface of psychology, religion, and spirituality at the operational level of daily human experience. Each volume of the series identifies, analyzes, describes, and evaluates the full range of issues, of both popular and professional interest, that deal with the psychological factors at play in the way religion takes shape and is expressed, in the way spirituality functions within human beings and shapes both religious formation and expression, and the ways that spirituality is shaped and expressed by religion. The primary interest is psychological. In terms of the rubrics of the discipline and the science of psychology, this series of superb volumes investigates the operational dynamics of religion and spirituality.

The verbs *shape* and *express* in the above paragraph refer to the forces that prompt and form religion in persons and communities, as well as to the manifestations of religious behavior in personal forms of spirituality, in acts of spiritually motivated care for society, and in ritual behaviors such as liturgies of worship. In these various aspects of human function the psychological drivers are identified, isolated, and described in terms of the way they unconsciously and consciously operate in religion and spirituality.

The books in this series are written for the general reader, the local library, and the undergraduate university student. They are also of significant interest to the informed professional, particularly in corollary fields. The volumes in this series have great value for clinical settings and treatment models, as well.

This series editor has spent an entire professional lifetime focused specifically upon research into the interface of psychology in religion and spirituality. These matters are of the highest urgency in human affairs today when religious motivation seems to be playing an increasing role, constructively and destructively, in the arena of social ethics, national politics, and world affairs. It is imperative that we find out immediately what the psychopathological factors are that shape a religion that can launch deadly assaults upon the World Trade Center in New York and murder 3,500 people, or a religion that motivates suicide bombers to kill themselves and murder dozens of their neighbors weekly, or a religion that prompts such unjust national policies as preemptive defense; all of which are wreaking havoc upon the social fabric, the democratic processes, the domestic tranquility, the economic stability and productivity, and the legitimate right to freedom from fear, in every nation in the world today.

This present volume, *Sin against the Innocents: Sexual Abuse by Priests and the Role of the Catholic Church,* so carefully researched and crafted by editor Thomas G. Plante and his coauthors, addresses issues equally global but at the same time more personal and close to home. They have seen that it is urgently necessary to discover without any lost time what the psychological factors are that shape a distorted spirituality which can permit trusted and highly esteemed religious leaders to fall into horrendous behaviors that deeply wound and often destroy the lives of innocent and unsuspecting children. This is an urgent and timely work, the motivation for which is surely endorsed enthusiastically by the entire world today, as we increasingly witness the progressive unfolding of this horror of child abuse by religious practitioners. What is going on in these cases? How are we to understand, stop, and heal this lethal epidemic? The scholars who have prepared this volume have found some answers and share them with us in remarkably readable fashion.

Of course, not all of the influences of religion now or throughout history have been negative. Indeed, most of the impact of the great religions upon human life and culture has been profoundly redemptive and generative of great good. It is just as urgent, therefore, that we discover and understand better what the psychological forces are that empower people of faith and genuine spirituality to give themselves to all the creative and constructive enterprises which, throughout the centuries, have made of human life the humane, ordered, prosperous, and aesthetic experience it can be at its best. Surely the forces for good in both psychology and spirituality far exceed the powers and proclivities toward the evil that we see so prominently in our world today.

This series of Greenwood Press volumes is dedicated to the greater understanding of psychology, religion, and spirituality, and thus to the profound understanding and empowerment of those psycho-spiritual drivers that can help us transcend the malignancy of our pilgrimage and enormously enhance the humaneness and majesty of the human spirit, indeed, the potential for magnificence in human life.

J. Harold Ellens
Series Editor

NOTE

1. Aden, L., & Ellens, J. H. (1990). *Turning points in pastoral care, The legacy of Anton Boisen and Seward Hiltner.* Grand Rapids, MI: Baker.

PREFACE

Few subjects have received the kind of constant media attention and heated debate than the topic of sex-offending clergy in the Catholic Church. Behind the headlines and media frenzy are too many stories of vulnerable children and teens being sexually exploited by Catholic priests. Furthermore, bishops and other religious superiors have too often failed to protect vulnerable others from abusive clergy and have tried to cover up, deny, or minimize this problem. It is a story about too many bishops (and priests) behaving badly when they are purported to be the moral, religious, and ethical leaders of society. It is a remarkable story. However, it is a complex story that has had little thoughtful, civil, and data-driven scholarship and discourse.

The purpose of this book is to bring together some of the best minds in the world on this topic in order to shed some light on the problem of clergy sexual abuse in the Catholic Church. The book is a companion to an earlier book on this topic which was published by Greenwood Press and edited by me in 1999 titled, *Bless Me Father for I Have Sinned: Perspectives on Sexual Abuse Committed by Roman Catholic Priests*. In that book, leading mental health professionals from the United States and Canada came together to provide a state-of-the-art understanding of priest sex offenders and their victims. In the current volume, we expanded the group to include journalists, theologians, canon lawyers, ethicists, victim advocates, and mental health professionals from the United States, Canada, England, and Italy to better understand the challenges of clergy sexual abuse in the Roman Catholic Church following the crisis of 2002 in the American Church.

Contributors met for several days during May 2003 at Santa Clara University in northern California to reflect on and discuss the topic and provide feedback to one another regarding their chapter contributions. We hope that this effort resulted in a richness and seamlessness not usually experienced in other edited volumes.

Clergy sexual abuse in the Catholic Church is a complex issue with few simple and straightforward answers. This book hopes to provide a thoughtful reflection among leading professionals who are very much involved and concerned with various aspects of this problem. We hope that this book will make an important contribution to understanding clergy sexual abuse and perhaps improve the odds that it might become a problem of the past.

ACKNOWLEDGMENTS

Many people other than the author or editor assist in the completion of a book project. Some contribute in a direct way while others help in a more supportive manner. I would like to acknowledge the assistance of the people who worked to make this book idea a reality.

First and foremost, I would like to thank the contributors to this volume. Not only did they complete their chapter contributions in a timely manner but they also traveled to Santa Clara University in California from as far away as Rome to participate in a conference that I hosted on this important topic. The contributors also read one another's chapters and offered feedback to all. Thus, the influence of the group can be seen throughout the book.

Second, it is important to recognize the wonderful people at Greenwood who published this book. Most especially, many thanks go to Debbie Carvalko, our editor at Greenwood.

Third, I would like to thank Santa Clara University for its support of the project and for funding the international conference to allow all the contributors a chance to meet and discuss their work. Funding for the project came from the President's Office (Father Paul Locatelli), the Bannan Center for Jesuit Education (William Spohn, Ph.D., director), the College of Arts and Science (Atom Yee, Ph.D., acting dean), the Markkula Center for Applied Ethics (Kirk Hanson, director), and the Moran Family Trust. Additional in-kind support came from the Santa Clara University Center for Professional Development and the Psychology Department.

Fourth, I would like to thank David DeCosse, Ph.D., editorial consultant, for his outstanding editing work with the chapters and filling in for me while I was out of town. I'd also like to thank administrative assistants Jane Najour, Henrietta Matteucci, Patricia Brandt, and Nicole Dutemple for their assistance with the conference.

Fifth, I would like to acknowledge the anonymous victims and clergy referred to in this book who have allowed their life experiences and traumas to become an instrument for learning and reform. Finally, I would like to thank my wife, Lori, and son, Zachary, for their love and support while I worked on another compelling book project.

INTRODUCTION

Thomas G. Plante

The year 2002 was *not* a very good year for the Roman Catholic Church in the United States. In fact, it was probably the worst year for the American Catholic Church in memory. Each day throughout the year, beginning with the January 6, 2002, investigative report published on the front page of *The Boston Globe* (*Boston Globe* Investigative Staff, 2002), was greeted with headline stories in newspapers across the country of allegations, convictions, resignations, and cover-ups of priest sex offenders. Just about every newspaper, magazine, and television news program across America (and in many parts of the world) reported on the numerous cases of Catholic priests who sexually abused children and teens during the past several decades. Few stories have had that kind of laser beam of attention by the mass media for so long. For example, the sexual abuse crisis in the Catholic Church was *New York Times* front-page news for 41 consecutive days in 2002. Many people called for the resignation or defrocking of not only the priests accused of sexual misconduct but also of the various bishops, cardinals, and other religious superiors who were responsible for supervising these men and assigning them to their priestly duties. Countless lawsuits were filed on behalf of the victims and victim groups totaling over a billion dollars in claims. Church dioceses, such as the one in Boston, threatened to go bankrupt by filing for Chapter 11 protection. Of course, many potential victims have likely not come forward and thus have not engaged in litigation yet. Laws were altered in numerous states to extend the statutes of limitations so that additional victims could come forward.

One of the major focal points of the anger, resentment, and upset by the public regarding the clergy sexual abuse crisis centered on Cardinal Bernard Law of Boston. Remarkably, 58 Boston-area priests (Paulson, 2002a, 2002b) as well as the 25,000-member, Boston-based Catholic reform organization, Voice of the Faithful, demanded that Cardinal Law resign (Mehren, 2002). Cardinal Law was responsible for supervising several priest sex offenders who apparently abused hundreds of victims over many years. Finally, on December 13, 2002, Pope John Paul II accepted Cardinal Law's resignation. Catholics and non-Catholics alike have been furious with Church leaders for not better protecting unsuspecting children and families from sex-offending priests. Many have felt that the Church considered itself above the law and arrogant in the manner in which it handled this issue over the years. Many have suggested that the Church has lost its moral compass and authority on all topics (e.g., unjust wars, the gap between rich and poor, sexuality) due to the sexual abuse scandals. Calls for reform have also been voiced about other challenging and controversial issues within the Roman Catholic Church such as the prohibitions against female, married, and homosexual priests. It is unlikely that the American Catholic Church has experienced a more difficult crisis in our lifetime (*Boston Globe* Investigative Staff, 2002; United States Conference of Catholic Bishops, 2002a). The Catholic Church in the United States has experienced a major earthquake with its epicenter in Boston and yet, many months following the initial quake, the earth still shakes violently.

The problem of clergy sexual abuse among Catholic priests is not a new problem at all. In fact, media attention has centered on this problem in the past. Prior to the crisis of 2002, it was quite well known that a sizable percentage of priests had sexually abused minors (e.g., Plante, 1999a, 1999b; Sipe, 1995). Books and articles on this topic, outlining a variety of problems with priest sex offenders, had been published in both professional and popular press outlets. Several notable and sensational cases have dominated press attention in the past. These include the exploits of Father James Porter in New England as well as Father Gilbert Gauthe in Louisiana. Furthermore, comments about clergy sexual abuse were recorded hundreds and even well over 1,000 years ago.

For example, St. Basil (330–379 c.e.) stated, "A cleric or monk who seduces youths or young boys...is to be publicly flogged...For six months he will languish in prison-like confinement, . . . and he shall never again associate with youths in private conversation nor in counseling them."

Therefore, sexual abuse committed by Catholic priests is not a new story that only became public in the media storm of 2002.

Research from a variety of reliable sources across North America suggests that six percent or fewer of Roman Catholic priests or other male Catholic clergy such as brothers have had a sexual experience with a minor (e.g., anyone under the age of 18). On the high-estimate side, Sipe (1990, 1995, 1999) states that two percent of priests are pedophiles (i.e., sexual involvement with prepubescent children) and an additional four percent are ephebophiles (i.e., sexual engagement with postpubescent teens). Since there are approximately 46,000 active Catholic priests in the United States, Sipe's figures suggest that approximately 2,700 Catholic priests have been sexually involved with minors. If we include the additional 15,000 retired priests and other male Catholic clergy such as brothers, this figure swells closer to 3,600. Plante (1999a) brought together leading clinicians and researchers from across North America (including Richard Sipe noted above) to participate in an edited book on this topic and in a professional conference held at Santa Clara University. This group agreed that, based on their collective research findings and both clinical and consultative experiences, up to six percent of priests appear to have had sexual experiences with minors. This conference was held in 1998, long before the sex abuse crisis in the Church during 2002.

Other researchers and sources disagree with Sipe's findings. For example, Loftus and Camargo (1993) carefully examined the histories of 1,322 priests over 25 years who were hospitalized at Southdown (a private Canadian psychiatric facility specializing in the diagnosis and treatment of clergy). These researchers reported that 2.7 percent of the treatment population had been sexually engaged with minors. Rossetti (2002a) reports that about one percent of Catholic priests have had a sexual experience with a child and an additional one percent have had a sexual experience with an adolescent, totaling two percent of all Catholic clergy, based on his work at the St. Luke's Institute (the largest American psychiatric facility that evaluates and treats clergy). Jenkins (2001) reports that of the 150,000 active and retired Catholic priests in the United States since 1960, approximately 800 (less than one percent) have experienced credible accusations of sexual abuse of minors. *The New York Times* conducted an evaluation of the available data and published a series of articles starting in January 2003 (Goldstein, 2003). Their research found that 1.8 percent of priests ordained between 1950 and 2001 had credible accusations regarding sexual abuse of minors. The report also found that most of the abuse occurred during the 1970s and 1980s and that most abusers were ordained during the early to mid-1970s. Of course, the figures published by *The New York Times* and others do not represent all of the potential cases that have not yet come to public attention. The potential for additional cases that are unreported is currently unknown. Since the recent media attention on this topic erupted during 2002, approximately 300 to 400 American Catholic priests and brothers have had credible accusations brought against them (Robinson, 2002). Curiously, the best available data before the crisis of 2002 suggested that up to six percent of priests have had a sexual experience with a minor while the best available data after the 2002 scandals suggest that about two percent of priests (but perhaps as many as six percent) have had these experiences. Remarkably and contrary to what most people might think, the best estimates of the percentage of clergy sexual offenders in the Catholic Church have not gone up after the 2002 crisis. However, no one knows for sure exactly how many cases of sexual misconduct by priests in fact exist.

Tragically, we know that sexual abuse of minors is also not limited to the behavior of Roman Catholic priests (Francis & Turner, 1995; Ruzicjka, 1997; Young & Griffith, 1995). Although solid and reliable statistics are not easy to obtain, it is very clear that sexual abuse committed by male clergy is certainly found among Protestant, Jewish, Muslim, and other religious leaders (Francis & Turner, 1995). Of course, reasonable estimates are the best we can do at this point in time. While the Roman Catholic Church has easily received the most media attention, sexual abuse of minors exists at alarming rates among others who have easy access to minors and who are usually trusted with the welfare of children (e.g., physicians, psychologists, social workers, school teachers, Boy Scout leaders, coaches, and school bus drivers). For example, it has been well established that, in mental health professions, between one to seven percent of female professionals and two to seventeen percent of male professionals sexually exploit their patients (Gonsiorek, 1995; Schoener, Milgrom, Gonsiorek, Luepker, & Conroe, 1989). These figures, however, predominantly reflect adult victims, and the prevalence of child and adolescent victims among these professions is too poorly researched to draw confident conclusions. Sexual abuse committed by people in the helping professions is too common. Sadly, sexual abuse of children and adolescents can be found in every area of the world and in every profession. Those who have trusted relationships with children and ready access can do the most harm. Those with a great deal of power and authority with little accountability can do enormous harm to many.

Furthermore, it has been well established from a wide variety of solid research studies that approximately 17 percent of all American women and

12 percent of American men report that they have had an unwanted and abusive sexual experience with an adult while they were still minors (Laumann, Gagnon, Michael, & Michaels, 1994; Rossetti, 2002a). Amazingly, about one in six adult Americans report that, as children or adolescents, they were sexually abused by an adult. Sadly, there is a great deal of sexual exploitation of minors by adults regardless of religious persuasion, profession, and role. Of course, we'd expect much better behavior from clergy than the general population.

Contrary to media portrayals and public perceptions, the majority of Catholic priests who sexually abuse children victimize postpubescent adolescent boys rather than latency-aged prepubescent children or young girls (Haywood, Kravitz, Grossman, & Wasyliw, 1996; Plante, 1999a; Plante, Manuel, & Bryant, 1996; Robinson, 1994; Robinson, Montana, & Thompson, 1993; Rossetti, 1995, 1996, 2002b; Rossetti & Lothstein, 1990). Therefore, the notion of sex-offending priests primarily targeting young, latency-aged altar boys is clearly a myth. In fact, the best data suggest that 80 percent to 90 percent of sexual abuse of children perpetrated by Catholic priests is directed toward adolescent boys (Bryant, 1999; Haywood, 1994; Haywood et al., 1996; Jenkins, 2001; Plante et al., 1996). Therefore, pedophilia among Catholic clergy appears to be very rare with ephebophilia being much more typical. It has been reported that about 50 percent of members of clergy-victim abuse support groups are female (Clohessy & Wegs, this volume). It may be that females are more likely than males to come forward as well as join victim support and advocacy groups.

Of course, sexual abuse of young, prepubescent children as well as abuse against teens is both illegal and immoral. However, it is important to distinguish the fact that most sex-offending clergy do not target young children. This distinction can help with both the evaluation and treatment of sex offenders as well as with being more aware of at-risk populations. For example, parents of teens might be more concerned about the possibility of sex-offending clergy than parents of young, prepubescent altar boys.

If this growing body of research is in fact correct, then why has there been so much relentless attention on sexual abuse committed by Catholic priests and little if any attention to abuse perpetrated by other male clergy members or other respected members of society? This is not an easy question to answer at all. However, there are a variety of important factors that most likely contribute to the attention the American Catholic Church has received about this terrible problem. First, about 25 percent of the American population identify themselves as being Roman Catholic (Association of Statisticians of American Religious Bodies, 2000). Additionally, numerous people (both Catholics and many non-Catholics alike) have received elementary, secondary, and/or university education through Catholic schools and universities (McDonald, 2002). Furthermore, each year over seven million Americans receive social and medical services from Catholic Charities while Catholic hospitals are the largest nonprofit healthcare providers in the United States with over 800 facilities treating over 70 million patients each year (Catholic Charities USA, 2000; Flynn, 2000). This figure alone represents almost one-third of the entire American population! Therefore, an enormous subset of the American population have had or continue to have direct contact with priests, other Catholic clergy such as religious sisters and brothers, and the Catholic Church in general at least in some capacity regarding education, health care, or spiritual activities. Because of the large number of people affiliated with the Catholic Church and their social, educational, medical, and religious services, many people either personally or professionally interact with the Catholic Church and Catholic clergy, including priests.

Second, the current crisis in the American Catholic Church is a crisis of priests (including religious superiors such as bishops making decisions about wayward priests under their charge) behaving very badly. This includes the behavior of priests and other male Catholic clergy (e.g., brothers, deacons) who have sexually abused minors, and Church leaders such as bishops for inadequate supervision and decisions regarding how to best manage priests who behave in problematic ways. The problem seems, on the surface, so easily preventable since it is a behavioral problem that is obviously wrong, immoral, illegal, and against priestly vows. Additionally, no one would expect this kind of horrible behavior to occur among moral and religious clergy members and leaders in the community. Before the media attention regarding sex-offending clergy, priests were the last people on earth one would expect of being sex offenders. I suppose we also would expect better behavior from them than clergy from other faith traditions who might be perceived as being more "like us" in terms of being likely to be married with children and mortgages. Priests appear to be much more removed from everyday life due to their commitment to chastity, poverty, and obedience and seem to maintain a special calling or relationship with God that would likely prevent them from engaging in sexually abusive behaviors with children or anyone.

Third, the Catholic Church has certainly had a history of acting in a highly defensive and arrogant manner regarding this issue. This has clearly contributed to people (both Catholics and non-Catholics alike) becoming furious with Church leaders. In so many cases, church leaders have not treated victims and their families with understanding, concern, and compassion. This behavior has led victims and victim groups to become enraged with the Catholic Church and its leadership. Many religious superiors such as bishops have not managed many of these cases very well. For example, Cardinal Bernard Law of Boston was accused of allowing priests who have allegations brought against them to continue to serve in the church in a variety of parishes for years without informing these churches of the allegations (*Boston Globe* Investigative Staff, 2002).

Fourth, unlike most other religious traditions and most organizations in the United States and elsewhere, the Catholic Church does not use lay boards of directors to hire, fire, and evaluate priests or other Church officials. Local bishops (as well as other religious superiors) do not have to answer to local boards, community members, or even to one another. They individually must answer to the Vatican personnel, who are thousands of miles away and who are preoccupied with the world's one billion Catholics in just about every spot on the globe. Furthermore, bishops and other religious superiors are not elected to their posts in the Catholic Church but are assigned. These assignments do not come with term limits and are not subject to renewal by the lay community. Therefore, if a particular religious superior such as a bishop makes bad decisions about how to manage problematic priests or others, the checks and balances associated with most organizations that might help to nip potential problems in the bud do not exist. Bishops do not get fired or recalled for poor performance. Other than legal limits imposed by the state, church leaders do not have to please a variety of groups in order to remain in their positions of power and influence. Each bishop must please his boss who is located in Rome and who will likely not be in touch with the day-to-day operations and decisions of bishops across the globe. Therefore, problems can easily spread like a virus out of control without these useful checks and balances.

The Catholic Church is by far the largest continuously operating organization in the world representing about 20 percent of the 6 billion people on the planet. It is not a small, insular, and obscure cult or church. It influences billions of people. The Catholic Church has also tried to be the ethical voice of moral authority for about 2,000 years. The Church's often-unpopular positions and standards on sexual behavior associated with contraception use, sexual activity among unmarried persons, homosexuality, and divorce make sex crimes committed by their priests even more scandalous and remarkable (Cozzens, 2002). When priests err, sin, and fall from grace, it is a much bigger drop for them than for ministers from other religious traditions who are much more like the general population. The intriguing secrecy and inner workings of the Catholic Church also make the story of sexual abuse committed by priests fascinating and of great interest to the media and the general population (Wills, 2000). Finally, many of the 25 percent of Americans who identify themselves as being Catholic, have mixed feelings about the Church. Many of the millions of Americans who have experienced Catholic education or were raised in the Church have stories of priests and nuns who were very strict and difficult to deal with. Many have felt that they couldn't measure up to the impossibly high standards of the Church. Perhaps the gospel verse attributed to Jesus—"He who is without sin may cast the first stone"—is a poignant perspective on the media and public's view on clergy sexual abuse.

Church leaders could certainly have done more over the years to prevent sexual abuse committed by priests. This is clearly true in the now famous Boston case that sparked the current attention on this problem. Victims and their families could have been treated with more respect and compassion as well. Offending clergy could have been treated quickly and relieved from duties that placed them in contact with potential victims. Change will likely occur gradually over time through grassroots efforts by Church members, victims, and religious, mental health, and legal professionals. Furthermore, the American bishops, with Vatican approval, have policies in place to better respond to allegations of clergy sexual misconduct and to prevent at-risk clergy from having access to vulnerable children and others (United States Conference of Catholic Bishops, 2002a, 2002b). The recent media spotlight on sex-offending clergy has acted as a catalyst to examine this problem more closely and to develop interventions at both individual and institutional levels. The problem of sex-offending clergy is certainly complex and lacks simple answers. Yet, at stake is the moral and spiritual authority of the Roman Catholic Church as well as the health and well-being of countless priests and laypersons.

Although the popular media has provided a great deal of attention to this topic, little scholarly activity has been associated with clergy sexual abuse. Most of the books published on this topic have been written by either victims or journalists who tell the story of individual or a variety of specific and especially egregious cases. An earlier edited book on clergy sexual abuse committed by priests (Plante, 1999a) was published long before the most recent crisis and only focused on mental health-related issues among abusive priests and their victims.

In this book, we have assembled many of the leading figures in this area including mental health professionals, canon lawyers, journalists, moral theologians, ethicists, and victim-group advocates. The purpose of this collaboration was to reflect on the problem of clergy sexual abuse through the lens of a variety of disciplines and perspectives following the remarkable year of constant attention and crisis in the American Catholic Church.

These contributors met during May 2003 in order to work together in a collaborative effort to help fine-tune one another's thinking about this problem. Each contributor read the drafts of the other contributors and offered reflection and feedback. The result of this collaborative work is this book. The concluding chapter is my reflection on all of the chapters and conference discussions, which then offers some thoughts about future directions for research, prevention, policy, and procedures to minimize or eliminate this problem in the future.

The sexual abuse crisis in the Roman Catholic Church has affected countless numbers of people across the United States and elsewhere. This not only includes victims and their families but also clergy, rank-and-file Catholics who are demoralized about what has happened to their church. The best available data, reason, and compassion can help to avoid hysteria about this issue. Steps can and should be taken to minimize this problem in the future. Collaboration between the Church leadership, laypersons, and appropriate professionals is needed to avoid future sin and victimization of innocents. We hope that this book will productively help in this important process.

REFERENCES

Association of Statisticians of American Religious Bodies. (2000, September 18). Religious congregations and membership in the United States: 2000. Washington, DC: Author.

Boston Globe Investigative Staff. (2002). *Betrayal: The crisis in the Catholic Church.* New York: Little Brown.

Bryant, C. (1999). Psychological treatment of priest sex offenders. In T. G. Plante (Ed.), *Bless me father for I have sinned: Perspectives on sexual abuse committed by Roman Catholic priests.* (pp. 87–110). Westport, CT: Praeger/Greenwood.

Catholic Charities USA. (2000). *Annual report.* Alexandria, VA: Author.

Cozzens, D. (2002). *Sacred silence: Denial and the crisis in the Church.* Collegeville, MN: Liturgical Press.

Flynn, T. (2000). Can secular patients survive Catholic hospitals? *Free Inquiry, 20,* 32–34.

Francis, P.C., & Turner, N.R. (1995). Sexual misconduct within the Christian church: Who are the perpetrators and those they victimize? *Counseling & Values, 39,* 218–227.

Goldstein, L. (2003, January 12). Trail of pain in Church crisis leads to nearly every diocese. *New York Times.*

Gonsiorek, J.C. (Ed.). (1995). *The breach of trust: Sexual exploitation by health care professionals and clergy.* Newbury Park, CA: Sage Publications.

Haywood, T.W. (1994). Cleric misconduct with minors: Minimization and self-reported sexual functioning. Paper presented at the 13th annual conference of the Association for the Treatment of Sexual Abusers, San Francisco, CA.

Haywood, T.W., Kravitz, H.M., Grossman, L.S., & Wasyliw, O.E. (1996). Psychological aspects of sexual functioning among cleric and noncleric alleged sex offenders. *Child Abuse and Neglect, 20,* 527–536.

Jenkins, P. (2001). *Pedophiles and priests: Anatomy of a contemporary crisis.* New York: Oxford.

Laumann, E.O., Gagnon, J.H., Michael, R.T., & Michaels, S. (1994). The social organization of sexuality. Chicago: University of Chicago Press.

Loftus, J.A., & Camargo, R.J. (1993). Treating the clergy. *Annals of Sex Research, 6,* 287–303.

McDonald, D. (2002). Annual statistical report on schools: Enrollment and staffing research. Washington, DC: National Catholic Educational Association.

Mehren, E. (2002, December 13). Expectation grows that cardinal will resign. *Los Angeles Times,* p. A28.

Paulson, M. (2002a, February 10). Catholics favoring priesthood changes. *Boston Globe,* p. A1.

Paulson, M. (2002b, December 10). 58 priests send a letter urging cardinal to resign. *Boston Globe,* p. A1.

Plante, T.G. (Ed.). (1999a). *Bless me father for I have sinned: Perspectives on sexual abuse committed by Roman Catholic priests.* Westport, CT: Praeger/Greenwood.

Plante, T.G. (1999b). Sexual abuse committed by Roman Catholic priests: Current status, future objectives. In T.G. Plante (Ed.), *Bless me father for I have sinned: Perspectives on sexual abuse committed by Roman Catholic priests* (pp. 171–178). Westport, CT: Praeger/Greenwood.

Plante, T.G., Manuel, G.M., & Bryant, C. (1996). Personality and cognitive functioning among sexual offending Roman Catholic priests. *Pastoral Psychology, 45,* 129–139.

Robinson, T. (1994). Shadows of the lantern bearers: A study of sexually troubled clergy. Paper presented at the 23rd International Congress of Applied Psychology, Madrid, Spain.

Robinson, T., Montana, S., & Thompson, G. (1993). A descriptive study of sexually abusing clergy. Paper presented at the 12th Annual Association for the Treatment of Sexual Abusers Conference, Boston, MA.

Robinson, W. V. (2002, February 24). Hundreds now claim priest abuse. *Boston Globe,* p. A1.

Rossetti, S. J. (1996). *A tragic grace: The Catholic Church and child sexual abuse.* New York: Liturgical Press.

Rossetti, S. J. (2002a). The Catholic Church and child sexual abuse. *America, 186,* 8–15.

Rossetti, S. J. (2002b). The Catholic Church and child sexual abuse. Paper presented at the 21st Annual Conference of the Association for the Treatment of Sexual Abusers, Montreal, Quebec, Canada.

Rossetti, S. J. (Ed.). (1995). *Slayer of the soul: Child sexual abuse and the Catholic Church.* Mystic, CT: Twenty-Third Publications.

Rossetti, S. J., & Lothstein, L. M. (1990). Myths of the child molester. In S. J. Rossetti (Ed.), *Slayer of the soul: Child sexual abuse and the Catholic Church* (pp. 9–18). Mystic, CT: Twenty-Third Publications.

Ruzicjka, M. F. (1997). Predictor variables on clergy pedophiles. *Psychological Reports, 81,* 589–590.

Schoener, G., Milgrom, J., Gonsiorek, J. C., Luepker, E., & Conroe, R. (Eds.). (1989). *Psychotherapists' sexual involvement with clients: Intervention and prevention.* Minneapolis, MN: Walk-In Counseling Center.

Sipe, A. W. R. (1990). *A secret world: Sexuality and the search for celibacy.* New York: Brunner Mazel.

Sipe, A. W. R. (1995). *Sex, priests, and power: Anatomy of a crisis.* New York: Brunner Mazel.

Sipe, A. W. R. (1999). The problem of prevention in clergy sexual abuse. In T. G. Plante (Ed.), *Bless me father for I have sinned: Perspectives on sexual abuse committed by Roman Catholic priests* (pp. 111–134). Westport, CT: Praeger/Greenwood.

United States Conference of Catholic Bishops. (2002a). *Charter for the protection of children and young people.* Washington, DC: Author.

United States Conference of Catholic Bishops. (2002b). *Essential norms for diocesan/eparchial policies dealing with allegations of sexual abuse of minors by priests or deacons.* Washington, DC: Author.

Wills, G. (2000). *Papal sin.* New York: Doubleday.

Young, J. L., & Griffith, E. E. H. (1995). Regulating pastoral counseling practice: The problem of sexual misconduct. *Bulletin of the American Academy of Psychiatry & the Law, 23,* 421–432.

Chapter 1

SCANDAL: THE *BOSTON GLOBE* AND SEXUAL ABUSE IN THE CATHOLIC CHURCH

Michael Rezendes

On December 13, 2002, Cardinal Bernard F. Law resigned as archbishop of Boston, his embattled leadership in America's most Catholic major city no longer viable. "To all those who have suffered from my shortcomings and mistakes, I both apologize and from them beg forgiveness," he said.

Law's public act of contrition was a dramatic departure from the imperious pose he often struck as the nation's senior prelate and its most influential Catholic. And he stepped down only after a yearlong exposé of clergy sexual abuse by a team of reporters at the *Boston Globe*. That journalistic endeavor differed markedly from previous efforts by the *Globe* and other newspapers to report on abuse in the Catholic Church. In the summer of 2001, the *Globe*'s Spotlight Team was asked to investigate Law's role in the reassignment of a notorious pedophile, the Rev. John J. Geoghan. But after learning that Geoghan might be only the most obvious sign of a larger problem, the team of reporters also set out to measure the full extent of clerical abuse in the Archdiocese of Boston, and the response of Law and his bishops.

By the time Law resigned, the *Globe* had published more than 800 stories. Characterized by escalating revelations of sexual misconduct, the stories cited thousands of pages of the Church's own records to reveal institutional forgiveness of abusive priests, consistent indifference to victims, and compelling evidence of a decades-long cover-up by a succession of cardinals and their bishops. Today, the number of priests accused of sexual misconduct in the Boston archdiocese during the last four decades exceeds 150. Twenty-four priests have been suspended from active ministry. More than 500 people have filed clergy-abuse claims. And donations to the Church have dropped by about half, leaving the archdiocese in fiscal free-fall.

The implosion has reverberated far beyond Boston. News organizations across the country and throughout the world have used the *Globe*'s reporting as a template and have launched investigations of their own. Since January of 2002, when the *Globe* published its first stories on the cover-up in Boston, more than 450 priests in the United States have been forced from their jobs because of sexual misconduct allegations. And four bishops, including Law, have resigned after being accused of abuse, admitting to sexual misconduct, or acknowledging they failed to remove known child molesters from active ministry.

Meanwhile, the United States Conference of Catholic Bishops has adopted a Charter for the Protection of Children and Young People. It has also established a Vatican-approved system of church tribunals to hear allegations of sexual misconduct against priests. And several states, including Massachusetts, have approved new child protection legislation and other laws requiring clergy to report knowledge of child sexual abuse to civil authorities.

But the complete story of clerical abuse in the Catholic Church has yet to be told. And in the absence of further reporting, and desperately needed clinical studies, the Church and its critics will continue to debate whether the number of accused priests points to a crisis in the Catholic Church and its celibate clergy, or merely reflects the prevalence of child sexual abuse in the American population.

Nevertheless, it's clear that the number of accused priests revealed thus far is only a fraction of the whole, and that the true extent of clergy abuse in the Catholic Church remains unknown. Complete Church records on allegations of clergy sexual misconduct have been aired in only a few of the 195 dioceses in the United States. And even in those instances, the number of accused is nothing more than a measure of those whose victims had the courage to step forward and identify their abusers. It also appears that Church officials at the highest levels have underestimated the problem. In November 2002, Cardinal Joseph Ratzinger, the Vatican official now in charge of overseeing the new Church tribunals hearing cases of clergy abuse, said that "less than one percent" of priests had sexually molested children. But a survey by the *New York Times* found that, in the few American dioceses where Church officials have released the names of all accused priests, or where judges and prosecutors have forced the

Church to air the information, the estimates range from 5.3 percent in the Boston archdiocese to 6.2 percent in Baltimore and 7.7 percent in Manchester, New Hampshire (Goldstein, 2003). And that survey, completed at the end of 2002, undercounted the total number of accused priests that have come to light in the Boston archdiocese, meaning that the percentage of abusive clerics in Boston is higher than 5.3 percent.

Although some Church officials have suggested that Boston, the fourth-largest diocese in the nation, is an aberration, it is just as likely that it is representative of the American Church as a whole. Its lay population of two million Catholics is nothing if not diverse, ranging from highly educated third- and fourth-generation Irish and Italians now serving in the region's power elite, to recently arrived immigrants from Latin America and Southeast Asia who are working in entry-level jobs while filling parishes in cities such as Boston, Lawrence, and Lowell. And leaders of the archdiocese—the bishops who served under Law for a generation—have been exported to dioceses across the country. Indeed, seven of the bishops who worked under Law were given their own dioceses, including Bishop Thomas V. Daily of the Brooklyn diocese and Bishop William F. Murphy of the Rockville Centre, New York diocese, two of the most populous dioceses in the country.

Moreover, it's not clear that the Church will voluntarily disclose what it knows about sexual abuse by its own priests any time soon. As this was being written, American bishops had reached an agreement to provide information about abusive priests—without disclosing their names—to a lay board appointed by the United States Conference of Catholic Bishops. But the agreement was brokered only after the board's chairman, former Oklahoma Governor Frank Keating, compared U.S. bishops fighting to prevent the disclosure of Church records with members of "La Cosa Nostra," the mafia. And despite the accord, bishops facing criminal investigations, civil lawsuits, and the prospect of paying victims hundreds of millions of dollars in out-of-court settlements continued to use a variety of legal strategies to prevent additional disclosures of Church records. Of course, without the information in Church files, reporters and clinicians, not to mention parents and parishioners, will be unable to accurately gauge the problem of sexual abuse in the Church.

And yet, both the Church and its critics have said the unprecedented scandal erupting in the wake of the *Globe*'s reporting has had one overarching benefit: Thousands of victims who suffered in silence and now call themselves survivors have been freed from the secrecy and shame of sexual abuse and are able to live more fulfilling lives. At the same time, it seems reasonable to believe, or at least hope, that countless children entering the Church under new child protection policies are being spared the debilitating abuse that too often characterized the past.

The *Globe*'s investigation was triggered by a routine court filing by Cardinal Law in June of 2001. That document—Law's response to the allegations in 84 lawsuits filed by victims of John Geoghan—contained a brief yet startling admission: in 1984, Law had assigned Geoghan to a suburban parish knowing that Geoghan had been accused of molesting seven boys in the same extended family. Law, writing in the archdiocesan newspaper, *The Pilot,* (Law, 2001) later explained that the church, like the larger society, knew little of the intractable nature of child sexual abuse when he assigned Geoghan to St. Julia's parish in Weston, where Geoghan went on to molest more children. And Law's attorney, Wilson D. Rogers Jr., writing in the same edition, assured parishioners that each of Geoghan's assignments following the first complaint of abuse had been approved by Geoghan's physicians (Rogers, 2001).

The *Globe* Spotlight Team—editor Walter V. Robinson and reporters Matt Carroll, Sacha Pfeiffer, and myself, Michael Rezendes—began to test those assertions. In particular, we wanted to know how Law had been informed of Geoghan's molestations, who had informed him, and exactly how much he knew about Geoghan's pedophilia when he gave the predator priest another church assignment and continuing access to children.

Working under the direction of special projects editor Ben Bradlee Jr., we found, within a matter of days, that Geoghan was only one of a large number of priests who had sexually molested children and been given new assignments. In fact, we were told, Church officials had been quietly settling claims against sexually abusive priests for at least a decade, often with "hush money" and terms that prevented the victims from ever speaking about the abuse or the settlements. It was an efficient arrangement that seemed to serve the interests of all involved: Victims received financial compensation, although often quite modest, and were spared public embarrassment. Their lawyers received one-third or more of the settlements, for minimal labor. And the Church avoided scandal.

But proving that the transactions had taken place was another matter. The Church, unlike government agencies or publicly traded corporations, operates with virtually no public disclosure requirements. The Constitutional guarantee of freedom of religion gives Church officials significant insulation from civil oversight. And in Catholic Boston, decades of deference to Church officials had discouraged criminal prosecutors from prying into Church affairs. And when it came to the Geoghan case, 10,000 pages of Church records that had accumulated in the course of the 84 lawsuits against Law and other Church officials had been sealed by a highly unusual confidentiality order issued by the state's Superior Court.

Martin Baron, the *Globe*'s newly named editor, decided to challenge that order. Given the newspaper's large Catholic readership, it was a bold decision likely to have far-reaching consequences, whatever the outcome. Indeed, the *Globe*'s relations with Law and conservative Catholics were already strained because of the newspaper's editorial support for abortion rights and its reporting on another pedophile priest, the Rev. James R. Porter, during the early 1990s. Although Porter had attacked more than 100 children in the nearby Fall River diocese, most Catholics believed Law when he insisted that Porter's crimes amounted to "an aberrant act." And many were persuaded when Law said that coverage of the Porter case was not only exaggerated but also evidence of media bias against the Church. "By all means," Law said at the time, "we call down God's power on the media, particularly the *Globe*."

A decade later, on September 6, 2001, more than a half-dozen lawyers were calling on the power of a judge as they made their arguments on the *Globe*'s motion to lift the confidentiality order in the Geoghan case. Attorneys for the archdiocese, standing before Superior Court Judge Constance M. Sweeney, made several points. Citing the Constitution's guarantee of freedom of religion, they asserted a right to keep church records private. They also argued that the *Globe* had no standing in the case and said that lifting the order would imperil the ability of Church officials to receive a fair trial. Representing the *Globe,* attorney Jonathan M. Albano noted that the public is routinely granted access to evidentiary files in civil lawsuits, and argued that the public's overall interest in child sexual abuse should prevail over the privacy concerns of Church. Attorneys for the victims backed Albano.

Judge Sweeney, the product of 16 years of Catholic education, peppered all sides with questions. At one point she asked Church lawyers for a more complete rationale for setting aside the customary rules of evidence in keeping Church records in the Geoghan case from the public. But she also told the *Globe*'s lawyer that her "bottom line" would be a fair trial for Law and his assistants—offering not a clue about what her final ruling might be.

The next day, September 7, the Spotlight Team learned the names of more than 30 priests who had been accused of sexual misconduct. While awaiting Sweeney's decision, the four reporters established a two-track reporting process. One was an attempt to pierce the secrecy surrounding

the out-of-court settlements involving accused clergy, while trying to measure the extent of abuse in the archdiocese and the response of the Church
leaders. The other was an effort to learn everything possible about
Geoghan's career, the scores of victims he had left behind during three
decades as a priest, and, most important, the evident failure of Church officials to stop him.

Both tracks yielded more clues than we had imagined. While combing
through the public records in the Geoghan lawsuits, we discovered documents revealing Church knowledge of Geoghan's early molestations that
had been previously overlooked. We also discovered that some of the files
listed on the public court docket were missing—a not uncommon occurrence in the often-chaotic Suffolk County Courthouse—and set out to
have them restored to the public record.

Meanwhile, we had learned through interviews the names of most of the
attorneys in the Boston area who accepted clergy abuse cases. Using a
public computer data base, we called up all of the lawsuits involving those
attorneys, as well as those involving local church lawyers, then sorted out
the cases that appeared to involve clergy sex abuse, and compiled a list of
priests who had been publicly accused of child sexual misconduct. In several instances, however, the computer would only tell us that no information—no public file—was available in a particular lawsuit. These cases
turned out to involve clergy sex abuse claims where a judge had granted a
Church request, often joined by the victim, to have the records impounded,
or sealed from public view. Additional court motions filed by the *Globe* in
two counties later resulted in court orders opening these files.

To identify the still larger number of priests who had been privately
accused, without leaving a paper trail in the courts, we turned to the
Church's own official directories. These annual listings, available at local
libraries, specify the assignments of each of the approximately 900 priests
in the Boston archdiocese. It was the Boston Catholic Directory of 1985,
for example, that told us that Geoghan, when he was assigned to St. Julia's
parish despite a long record of child abuse, was put in charge of the altar
boys.

But in many other instances the names of priests were followed by nota-
tions such as "sick leave," "in between assignments," or "lend-lease." All
of these, we believed, were often euphemisms reserved for clergy who had
been accused of sexual misconduct, shelved and then, in many cases, reassigned to active ministry. In a tedious, time-consuming process, we examined directories going back 19 years and catalogued every priest who had
been listed with one of these non-assignments and built a computer data-

base of more than 100 priests. Several of them were on our list of priests who had been publicly accused in civil lawsuits. Others were on a separate list of the 30-plus priests who, we were confidentially told, had been involved in secret Church settlements.

While working on the data base, we also fanned out to interview priests and victims of clergy abuse to learn more about how the Church dealt with allegations of sexual misconduct by its clerics. What we learned was often devastating: The Rev. Ronald R. Paquin was at the wheel during a car accident—possibly involving alcohol—in which a Haverhill teenager entrusted to his care was killed. The Rev. Paul R. Shanley, a celebrated street priest during the 1970s, seduced sexually troubled teenagers during counseling sessions. And the Rev. Paul J. Mahan, a popular priest in a working class section of Boston, molested young boys during boating trips off Boston's affluent North Shore.

When we compared notes, a disturbing pattern emerged: Many of the victims were from large, lower-income families with absent fathers and overburdened mothers grateful for the help and attention of a Catholic priest. Patrick McSorley, for instance, described how Geoghan molested him after dropping by his apartment in a public housing project to offer condolences following his father's suicide. Predator priests, by zeroing in on lower-income, fatherless boys, were sexually exploiting children most in need of fatherly attention. They were also targeting families most likely to remain silent—and least likely to be believed if they talked.

In late November of 2001, nearly four months after the Spotlight Team began its investigation, Judge Sweeney ruled in favor of the *Globe*'s motion to lift the confidentiality order in the Geoghan case, saying that the public's interest in child sexual abuse outweighed the privacy claims of the archdiocese.

The Church appealed. But by that time Sweeney had also directed attorneys in the Geoghan case to re-submit the records that were missing from the public file. Those records contained startling revelations about Church knowledge of Geoghan's abuses. They included excerpts of a deposition taken from Joanne Mueller, a single mother who said she complained to Church officials after a horrific evening in the early 1970s, before Law arrived in Boston, when her four sons, aged 5 to 12, tearfully confessed that Geoghan had been molesting them. It was just one of at least six documented instances where adults—in one instance a fellow priest—had complained about Geoghan's molestations, all to no avail. The re-filed records also included a 1984 letter to Law from one of his top deputies, Bishop John M. D'Arcy, protesting Geoghan's assignment at St. Julia's because of the priest's "history of homosexual involvement with young boys." Geoghan had not slipped through the cracks, as Law implied in his column in *The Pilot*. To the contrary, his assignment had been contested at the highest levels of the archdiocese after decades of complaints.

With these records in hand, the *Globe* received another Church document, one of more recent vintage and addressed to the newspaper's lawyer. "It has been brought to my attention that certain reporters of your client, the *Boston Globe,* have been making inquiry of a number of priests of the Archdiocese of Boston," wrote Wilson D. Rogers Jr., the lead attorney for the archdiocese. Rogers claimed that the interviews were based on information we had obtained from the confidential Geoghan files. "In the event that the *Boston Globe* in any way further disseminates these materials, either by way of inquiry or publication," Rogers continued, "I will seek appropriate sanctions against both your client and Bingham Dana [the paper's law firm]."

In fact, Mitchell Garabedian, the attorney for Geoghan's victims, had excerpted portions of the confidential files and inserted them into the public record as exhibits attached to various legal motions. It was a tactic that, in effect, made portions of the confidential documents public. In any case, the *Globe* ignored Rogers's letter and, in late December, the Appeals Court upheld Judge Sweeney's decision to lift the confidentiality order. Rogers never followed up on his threat.

The court gave attorneys in the case 30 days to publicly file the 10,000 pages of previously sealed documents. In the meantime, we quickly prepared a two-part series about Geoghan. Part one would be built on a foundation of records we had culled from the public files; part two on some of Geoghan's psychiatric records, which would be delivered to the plaintiffs after the Appeals Court ruling but before the release of the 10,000 pages of previously filed documents. Weeks before publication, we also requested interviews with the Cardinal and other Church officials, even offering to submit questions in writing. But, with only two days remaining before publication, Law's spokeswoman said the archdiocese would not even consider our questions.

The Geoghan series was published on January 6 and January 7, 2002 (*Globe,* 2002a, 2002b), and the effect was like setting a match to gasoline. Two days later, on January 9, Law held an extraordinary news conference where he issued the first of several apologies, fielded questions from reporters, and assured parishioners that no priest accused of sexually abusing a minor remained in active ministry. But unlike a decade earlier, when his stern denunciations of news coverage of the Porter case helped assuage a restive laity, Law's words did little to quell the outrage of Boston Catholics. To help cover the quickly spreading conflagration and continue the investigation into the Church, the four Spotlight Team reporters were joined by religion reporter Michael Paulson and investigative reporters Stephen Kurkjian, Thomas Farragher, and Kevin Cullen.

Law, while issuing his apology for assigning Geoghan to St. Julia's, echoed the remarks his attorney had made in *The Pilot* the previous year, saying his decision was based on "psychiatric assessments and medical opinions" that such assignments "were safe and reasonable." But only a week later, on January 16, we reported that these assessments were highly suspect. One medical evaluation stating that Geoghan was "fully recovered" was written by a family physician and longtime friend with no qualifications to assess sexual disorders. Another was written by a psychiatrist who had twice been accused of sexually molesting his own patients. And, once again, his qualifications did not include expertise in treating or evaluating sexual dysfunction.

Then, on January 24, we reported on the contents of the 10,000 pages of Church records. The documents included sympathetic letters from Law to "Jack" Geoghan expressing admiration for his ministry. They also contained records strongly suggesting that the archdiocese had influenced doctors at The Institute of Living, a Connecticut mental health facility, to approve Geoghan for active ministry after those same doctors had expressed reservations about Geoghan's fitness.

Finally, on January 31, we published the results of our five-month investigation of clerical abuse in the archdiocese (*Globe,* 2002d). It was another bombshell. Over the previous 10 years, the church had secretly settled sexual abuse allegations against 70 of its priests. The story undermined what remained of Law's credibility: Geoghan was no aberration, only a symptom of a much larger problem.

Yet the Cardinal's credibility was eroded still further on a Saturday in early February 2002, when he abruptly removed two pastors—one a regional vicar with oversight of 19 parishes—after reviewing evidence in the Church's own files showing that they were accused of sexually molesting minors in the past. Five days later, Law removed six more in a process that would continue, leading to the suspension of a total of 24 clergymen over a 12-month period.

Our reporting might have trailed off there. But the Spotlight Team stories were accompanied by the *Globe* telephone numbers and e-mail addresses of the reporters, and an invitation to contact the paper with more information about abusive priests. Scores of victims responded, frequently with tales of abuse they had never before revealed, not even to spouses or other family members. In the meantime, the state attorney general and five district attorneys launched criminal investigations that would lead to charges against a half-dozen priests. But the vast majority of allegations against Catholic clergy fell outside the criminal statute of limitations. So it was the victims stepping forward to tell their stories, and the lawsuits many of them would file, that drove our stories through the remainder of 2002.

In the civil lawsuits filed by alleged victims of the Rev. Paul Shanley, plaintiff's attorney Roderick MacLeish Jr. argued that, in order to determine whether Law and his bishops had engaged in a pattern of negligence, he would need to examine all of the internal Church files on all priests of the Boston archdiocese who had ever been accused of sexual misconduct. Judge Sweeney agreed, triggering the periodic disclosure of thousands of pages of additional Church files, more embarrassment for the Church, and Law's resignation.

Like Cardinal Law in the early 1990s, many Catholic officials today persist in the belief that the problem of clergy sexual abuse has been exaggerated by critics of the Church. At the June 2003 meeting of the United States Conference of Catholic Bishops, Archbishop Gabriel Montalvo, Pope John Paul II's representative to the United States, said, "We all know that we are going through difficult times and that some real problems within the Church have been magnified to discredit the moral authority of the Church."

But the laity might have a different view. When the *Globe* published its first stories on the cover-up of clergy sexual abuse in January 2002, we expected some Catholics to take offense. But for the most part there was no blaming the messenger. Time and again, devout Catholics called to thank us for exposing a horrendous wrong, often directing their anger at Law and his bishops.

More than a year later, the number of Catholics who blamed Law for the scandal continued to grow. A *Globe* poll taken in May 2003 showed that nearly 90 percent of the estimated two million Catholics in the Boston area—and more than 80 percent in every Catholic demographic group—approved of Law's resignation. Fifty-seven percent said he should be criminally prosecuted.

Of course, true leadership is not a popularity contest. But as this was being written, it was difficult to find solid evidence of decisive leadership in the Church. Former Oklahoma Governor Keating's resignation as head of the bishop's lay review board, after a dispute with Los Angeles Cardinal Roger M. Mahony over Keating's "La Cosa Nostra" remark, and Mahony's refusal to deliver Church records to local prosecutors (Lobdell, 2003) were blows to the credibility of all Catholic bishops.

Many Catholics were hoping that newly named Boston Archbishop Sean Patrick O'Malley would be able to settle 500 outstanding abuse claims and lead the archdiocese—and by extension the Catholic Church in America—out of the clergy sexual abuse crisis. Indeed, O'Malley, a Franciscan Friar, had received much credit for his work following abuse scandals in the Fall River, Massachusetts, and Palm Beach, Florida, dioceses. But he was also criticized by Bristol County District Attorney Paul F. Walsh Jr. in September of 2002 for failing to give law enforcement officials the names of priests accused of sexual misconduct in Fall River earlier.

In June 2002, at the height of the clergy abuse scandal, American bishops meeting in Dallas approved their *Charter for the Protection of Children and Young People*. Article seven of the Charter says "each diocese will develop a communications policy that reflects a commitment to transparency and openness," and that dioceses "will deal as openly as possible with members of the community." A few bishops followed through. In Baltimore, for instance, Cardinal William H. Keeler released the names of all priests accused of sexual misconduct in the archdiocese over the previous seven decades (Rivera, 2002).

But Keeler's gesture was an exception to what was fast becoming the rule. In Los Angeles, Cardinal Mahony tried to withhold Church records from criminal prosecutors in two counties, citing the First Amendment's guarantee of freedom of religion. And in dioceses including Cincinnati, Cleveland, and Bridgeport, Connecticut, bishops also cited the First Amendment or other privacy grounds in attempting to keep Church files out of the hands of prosecutors and civil attorneys. No one has said the Church has an obligation to forfeit its right to a vigorous legal defense, but its commitment to openness remains largely unfulfilled.

The *Globe* Spotlight Team's investigation into sexual abuse in the Catholic Church affirmed the right and responsibility of a free press to question authority. That may be an uncomfortable notion for a hierarchical institution unaccustomed to public scrutiny. But the moral corruption known as child sexual abuse is no different from the political corruption more often investigated by news reporters in one crucial respect: It thrives in secrecy. Spotlight editor Robinson has said that in 2002, the *Boston Globe* shined a light on a very dark place. The Church has a duty to keep it on.

REFERENCES

Globe Spotlight Team. (2002a, January 6). Church allowed abuse by priest for years. *Boston Globe,* p. A1.

Globe Spotlight Team. (2002b, January 7). Geoghan preferred preying on poor children. *Boston Globe,* p. A1.

Globe Spotlight Team. (2002c, January 24). Documents show church long supported Geoghan. *Boston Globe,* p. A1.

Globe Spotlight Team. (2002d, January 31). Scores of priests involved in sex abuse cases. *Boston Globe,* p. A1.

Goldstein, L. (2003, January 12). Trail of pain in church crisis leads to nearly every diocese. *New York Times,* p. 1.

Law, B. (2001, July 27). Restoring hope to broken hearts and lives. *The Pilot,* p. 2.

Lobdell, W., & Winton, R. (2003, April 2). L.A. archdiocese seeks to withhold files in sex cases. *Los Angeles Times,* p. B1.

Rivera, J. (2002, September 25). Keeler letter reveals abuse. *Baltimore Sun,* p. 1A.

Rogers, W. (2001, July 27). A letter to the editor of The Pilot. *The Pilot,* p. 1.

Chapter 2

CLERGY SEXUAL ABUSE IN THE AMERICAN CATHOLIC CHURCH: THE VIEW FROM THE VATICAN

John Allen Jr.

Just before the war began in Iraq, I paid a visit to a senior cardinal, an Italian, in his apartment inside the Vatican city-state. This is a man who has been at the nerve center of Vatican policy for the better part of the last half-century, a cosmopolitan and polyglot, who reads six newspapers in five languages before breakfast. The agenda was to discuss the Vatican's diplomatic press against the war. After 45 minutes of rather intense conversation about the Middle East, Islam, and the Vatican/American relationship, our focus drifted to other matters. It emerged that I was the first American journalist with whom the cardinal had spoken about the sex abuse crisis that has gripped the U.S. Catholic Church.

The cardinal had a question he had been wanting to ask: "Is it true what they say here—that the Masons and the Jews are behind it all?"

I didn't press the cardinal on who "they" were, because I already knew two things. First, I knew that some influential people in and around the Roman Curia held this idea. Italian journalist Orazio Petrosillo, correspondent for the Rome daily *Il Messaggero* and a man with impressive connections in the Curia, had asserted at a December 4–8 Vatican conference that "Masonic lodges," "Jewish lobbies," and "groups of free thought and free morals" had targeted the Catholic Church in the United States. Second, I knew that many others in the Vatican, undoubtedly a solid majority, do not subscribe to this view. I knew, in fact, that the mythical entity called the "Vatican" that haunts the popular Catholic imagination—an organism that thinks, moves, and acts in monolithic, lockstep fashion—

doesn't even exist. Different departments and different officials within the Holy See have widely varying assessments. Given this diversity, it's almost meaningless to ask what "they" think about a given topic. To adapt Gertrude Stein's famous quip about Oakland, one might say there is no "they" there.

Yet the assertion that Jews and Masons somehow engineered the American scandals, even if it's a minority view, illustrates something critical in trying to understand how the Vatican reacted to the American crisis. There is a widespread sense in Rome that there is something more than meets the eye to the American situation, that the incidents of sexual abuse, however repugnant, and the failure of bishops to intervene when they should have, do not by themselves explain the meltdown in American Catholicism. Since the revelations from Boston began to emerge in January 2002, I have had hundreds of conversations with Vatican officials, including virtually all of those responsible for setting policy on the issue of sexual abuse. If there is one constant to their reactions, it is this: they find the pummeling the American Church took in the court of public opinion hard to understand. Given that whatever the actual figure (two percent? six percent?), it's a small number of priests who are guilty of sexual abuse, and given that most sexual abuse of minors occurs within the family, many Vatican officials remain puzzled as to how the problems of the Catholic Church ended up on page one of *The New York Times* 41 days in a row. How, to put it simply, did sex abuse of minors in the United States become a Catholic story? The Jewish/Masonic theory is one of the more irrational attempts to respond to this rational question.

The puzzlement of Vatican officials, which led to a nagging sense that the Church was being treated unfairly, helps explain some of the ambiguity or hesitation many American Catholics detected from the Holy See as the dramatic events of 2002 unfolded. Many Vatican personnel had, and still have, the conviction that some of the pressures underlying the sexual abuse crisis arise from forces hostile to the Church.

A SLOW RESPONSE

Probably the most common criticism American Catholics voiced of the Vatican's response as 2002 unfolded was that "they don't get it,"—that engagement from Rome was too slow and too halfhearted. Why, American Catholics wondered, was there no public statement from the Holy See between January 6, 2002, when *The Boston Globe* first began reporting the cover-up of clerical sexual abuse, and March 22, 2002, when the pope issued his Holy Thursday message to priests? (Even that text, of course, was indirect and promised no new plan to solve the problem.) Why did the pope not take any action until April 15, when he summoned the American cardinals plus the president and vice president of the bishops' conference to Rome for a summit? Why did the Vatican stand by as the American bishops crafted a new set of standards for sexual abuse in Dallas in June under intense public pressure, only to turn them down in October? (It was crystal clear in Rome from the very beginning that the approach adopted in Dallas, which relied on an administrative rather than a judicial process to adjudicate accusations of sexual abuse, would never be approved on the basis of due process concerns.)

Two hypotheses to explain this inaction, frequently floated in the American press or in Catholic conversation, can be dismissed out of hand. No one in the Vatican, for example, is "soft" on the sexual abuse of minors. In scores of conversations with personnel in a dozen Vatican offices on the issue, I have not found one person who was anything less than horrified by the revelations. John Paul II gave voice to an overwhelming Vatican consensus when he said in his statement to the American prelates on April 15: "There is no place in the priesthood and religious life for those who would harm the young." Because senior officials in the Vatican tend to have a high theological understanding of the clerical state, they are among the most scandalized when priests betray their vows. There is no one in the Holy See who would defend the conduct of John Geoghan or Paul Shanley, nor for that matter are there many who would excuse Cardinal Bernard Law's failure to intervene with these offenders swiftly and surely.

Nor does the Vatican believe that sexual abuse by priests is an "American problem." In recent months, the evidence has been too overwhelming to the contrary. In January 2002, religious orders in Ireland agreed to pay $110 million to settle sex abuse claims. In March, Archbishop Juliusz Paetz of Pozanan in Poland, a former prelate of the antechamber in John Paul II's own papal household, stepped down under accusations of sexual abuse against seminarians. In April 2002, French Bishop Pierre Pican received a suspended three-month jail sentence for failing to report the conduct of a priest who was allegedly engaged in sexual abuse. In October, Archbishop George Pell of Sydney, Australia, was cleared after being suspended on charges of sexual abuse. More than 90 priests and church employees have been convicted of sexual abuse in Australia over the last decade. Examples could be multiplied all over the world. My newspaper, the *National Catholic Reporter,* broke a story two years ago concerning the sexual abuse of nuns by priests in Africa and elsewhere. No one whose eyes are open can pretend that the phenomenon of sexual abuse within the Catholic Church is restricted to American airspace. Few in the Vatican suffer from this delusion. The notion that the Holy See believes sexual abuse by priests is an "American problem" is part of the unhelpful, and inaccurate, mythology generated by the scandals.

Yet it is nevertheless true that the Vatican was slow, at least by American standards, to respond in the early stages of the crisis, when crucial public opinion was formed. Its public statements, when they finally began to arrive, often seemed halfhearted and grudging. When the American cardinals came to Rome in mid-April, Vatican officials largely refused to make themselves available to the press, reinforcing (albeit perhaps unintentionally) the image of an institution that did not consider itself answerable to its people. How to explain this attitude, if Vatican officials are indeed horrified by the sexual abuse of children, and are resolved that the Church must eradicate such conduct from the priesthood?

The answer lies in three other factors that many Vatican officials believe are underneath the American crisis.

First, many Vatican officials believe that much of the legal action against the Catholic Church related to the sex abuse crisis amounts to a rather crass financial shakedown. There is no concept of corporate liability in most systems of European tort law, so victims in Italy, for example, have no legal mechanism to force the institutional Church to pay compensatory and punitive damages when they are abused by priests. Unlike in the United States, there are no big financial penalties for juries to levy, no multimillion dollar settlements to negotiate. Many non–Anglo Saxons in the Vatican struggle to understand the logical connection between an employee committing a crime that is manifestly against company policy, and his or her company being forced to pay for that crime. Since the Catholic Church teaches that sex abuse is sinful, and swears its priests to celibacy, how can one reasonably blame it when individual priests choose to violate those teachings and vows? Even if a bishop turned a blind eye, that is the moral and perhaps criminal responsibility of the bishop, not the Church as such. (It is worth recalling that according to the traditional Catholic moral theology still held by most in the Holy See, guilt and sin are always individual, never corporate.) Some Vatican officials thus conclude that lawyers, and perhaps even some victims, who are dusting off long-forgotten charges from 30 or more years ago are "in it for the money." The fact that there are now whole law firms in the United States whose practice is dedicated to clerical sexual abuse fuels the suspicion that lawyers will pursue any charge, however outdated or undocumented, that might wring dollars out of a vulnerable Church.

Second, many Vatican officials believe there is a streak of anti-Catholicism in American culture that has resurfaced in the sexual abuse crisis. In part, this is the historical product of the fact that Catholicism is a minority religion in the United States, frequently disdained by Protestant elites on the East Coast, and seen as the agent of a foreign power with suspect loyalties to the American nation. There is, in fact, a long and ugly history of accusing priests of all sorts of sexual misconduct in anti-Catholic polemical literature, so the recent crisis tapped a deep vein of prejudice. To some extent this suspicion and dislike of Catholicism has never gone away; as the subtitle of Philip Jenkins's May 2003 book *The New Anti-Catholicism* suggests, it is America's "last acceptable prejudice." In part, modern anti-Catholicism is also a byproduct of the nasty "culture wars" of the 1980s and 1990s, in which the Catholic Church has become identified with strong conservative positions on abortion, birth control, and gay rights. These views, seen by critics as intolerant and repressive, have earned Catholicism an army of cultured despisers. Given that many newsrooms in the United States tilt to the left, it's easy for Vatican officials to conclude that the press campaign against the Church has been led by people already inclined to be hostile to Catholicism for other reasons.

Third, Vatican officials also believe that interest groups inside the Catholic Church, of both left and right, have manipulated and exacerbated the sexual abuse crisis in order to grind their ideological axes. Vatican officials noted with growing irritation throughout 2002 that on virtually a daily basis left-wing pundits such as Fr. Richard McBrian, Eugene Kennedy, and Gary Wills were publishing op-ed pieces and appearing on television talk shows to catalog the ills of the Catholic Church. Similar exposure was being showered upon conservative spokespersons such as Fr. Richard John Neuhaus and William Donohue to criticize what they saw as cowardly and compromised U.S. bishops. Groups such as Call to Action or Catholics for a Free Choice on the left, and Catholics United for the Faith and the Catholic League on the right, were doling out their programs for reform before vast national audiences. A sense grew that these activists liked the spotlight, because they were suddenly playing on a public stage not previously available to them. They thus had an interest in making the crisis seem as deep as possible, in not letting up on the throttle, because as soon as the media moved on to another subject, their high profile would evaporate. (Some of these commentators won an unexpected reprieve from the 15-minutes-of-fame rule when the Catholic Church turned out to be a major player in the next media obsession, the war in Iraq.)

Hence when Vatican officials size up the American situation, they see a genuine pastoral crisis that requires engagement from all levels in the Church, including their own. They also, however, see a legal industry hustling to cash in on the Church's weakness, a residual anti-Catholicism kicking the Church when it's down, and an industry of self-appointed Catholic pundits exacerbating the crisis to peddle their own magic cures, whether it's eliminating celibacy or driving out gay priests. Vatican officials are quite reluctant to feed what they consider negative energy, and thus they weigh every public statement, every proposed intervention, with this in mind. The result has been a degree of caution and of compromise that has frustrated some Americans seeking dramatic action, but that also reflects a good deal more reflection than the apathy or ignorance some critics have suggested.

CULTURAL GAPS

Making the matter more complicated is the fact that decisions concerning the American situation were being made in the Vatican largely by non-Americans. Aside from the Polish pope, the other senior officials most involved included a German (Cardinal Joseph Ratzinger, Congregation for the Doctrine of the Faith); a Colombian (Cardinal Dario Castrillón Hoyos); an Italian (Cardinal Giovanni Battista Re, Congregation for Bishops); and a Spaniard (Archbishop Julian Herranz, Council for the Interpretation of Legislative Texts). This meant that European and Latin American cultural experiences loomed large in the evaluation of the American crisis.

This revealed itself, for example, in a tendency to regard the intense media criticism in America as "manufactured" by enemies of the Church. In both Eastern Europe under Communism and Latin America under the police states of the 1970s, it was standard operating procedure for hostile regimes to use accusations of sexual abuse against priests as part of anti-clerical smear campaigns. Because of his vow of celibacy, nothing strikes at the identity of a Catholic priest more directly than accusations of sexual misconduct. Over the years, many high-profile priests now recognized as heroes have faced this sort of scurrilous accusation. At least one man now recognized by the Church as a near-saint, Cardinal Alojzije Viktor Stepinac of Croatia, was accused of sexual misdeeds by the Communist rulers of his country during show trials in the 1950s. Even the famous Capuchin mystic Padre Pio, canonized by John Paul II on June 16, 2002, had been the object of a fierce whispering campaign suggesting untoward relations with some of his female devotees. Upon inspection, such charges proved to be groundless, rooted in the malice some detractors felt for the Church. Hence, Vatican officials, including the pope himself, were prepared by their own cultural experience to distrust some of what they saw coming out of the American press, especially in the early stages of the crisis.

The cultural divide was also clear in the evaluation of the new legal norms governing cases of sexual abuse by priests adopted by the U.S. bishops in Dallas in June, which were rejected by Rome, then revised by a special "mixed commission" of four Vatican officials and four U.S. bishops. They were approved again by the U.S. bishops in Washington in November, and quickly accepted by the Vatican. The most troubling aspect of the Dallas norms, from the Vatican's point of view, was the use of an administrative rather than judicial process as the ordinary means of removing priests guilty of sexual abuse from ministry. The American bishops opted for this solution because they wanted to ensure swift and sure justice. Since the mid-1980s they had experienced Church tribunals as slow and expensive, especially when an accused priest appealed to Rome, as is his right under the *Code of Canon Law.* Moreover, the bishops knew the benefit of the doubt in the Vatican often went to these accused clerics, which in at least a few cases had led to orders of reinstatement from Rome for priests that bishops wanted desperately to remove.

From the European and Latin American perspective of the Vatican, however, the vocabulary of "administrative procedure" dependent upon the whims of the bishop smacked of royal star chambers, or of kangaroo courts in police states. For John Paul, the parallel with the lack of due process in the Soviet bloc was too close for comfort. Informed observers sensitive to this cultural reality knew there was never the slightest possibility that the Vatican would sign off on the Dallas norms, and in due course a "mixed commission" revised the document to specify that ecclesiastical tribunals will be the ordinary means for dealing with sexual abuse cases. The clear intent was to preserve the due process rights of accused priests.

The Dallas norms also envisioned a quasi-automatic process of relaying accusations of sexual abuse to the police and other civil authorities, under which bishops would have little discretion about what to report and what to withhold. This too was alarming to many in the Vatican, who see the bishop's relationship to his priests on the model of the ancient Roman concept of the *paterfamilias.* The bishop is supposed to be a father to his priests, the head of the ecclesiastical household. He should have a relationship of intimacy and confidence in which priests feel comfortable confiding their weaknesses and failures, in order to receive paternal counsel. What does it do to that atmosphere of trust, Vatican officials wondered, if bishops are required to call the police if a priest acknowledges a certain kind of wrongdoing? This is not to say that most acts of sexual abuse do not merit immediate reporting, merely that Vatican officials would prefer discretion for bishops to make the tricky calls in borderline situations, as a father would do with his sons.

Finally, many American Catholics became steadily more furious in the months between January and December 2002 as no bishops were "fired" for failing to stop sexual abuse by priests when they should have known better. There could be no healing, these Catholics insisted, without accountability, which to them meant that episcopal heads should roll. But in the culture of the Vatican, there is a different understanding of accountability. It begins from the premise that the life of a retired cleric, and above all a retired cardinal, is a comfortable one. The retired prelate enjoys all the benefits of office, but none of the burdens. Hence "allowing" a man to retire is considered a reward for good behavior (this notwithstanding the fact that some cardinals stay on long beyond the retirement age of 75, because they feel they can still make a contribution). Thus when a cardinal is in trouble, the way to hold him accountable in the culture of the Vatican is to refuse to lift him out of the mess he has made.

THE LAW CASE

Cardinal Bernard Law of Boston came to symbolize the national crisis. As long as Law remained in power in Boston, many American observers felt, there could be no healing. Yet Law survived 11 months of devastatingly bad publicity, a deep crisis of confidence among his faithful, and a diocese pushed to the brink of bankruptcy, before his resignation was finally accepted on December 13, 2002. Why did Rome not move against Law sooner? Aside from the different understanding of accountability outlined above, there were three other factors.

First, there is the deliberate slowness of the Vatican, especially when facing a major decision. The unhurried approach is intended to foster calm, objectivity and serenity, so decisions will be driven by good judgment rather than crisis and haste. In part, Vatican officials are hesitant to move swiftly to take action for which people are clamoring because they don't want to encourage the impression that the Church can be held hostage to public pressure. The Catholic Church carries with it a culture, the product of 2,000 years of history and the mission it was entrusted by Jesus Christ, and this must be protected from transitory political impulses. Indeed, the most frequently heard criticism in the Vatican of the U.S. bishops during the crisis is that in Dallas they "caved in" to public pressure, adopting a punitive set of norms that did not reflect the discipline of the universal Church.

Second, there was fear of a "domino effect." The concern was that if Law were to resign under pressure, other Church senior officials could be brought down in his wake. This was a special concern in Law's case since several of his former aides, men who were involved in personnel decisions on abuser priests such as Geoghan and Shanley, went on to become bishops themselves. The list includes John McCormack of Manchester, New Hampshire; Thomas Daily of Brooklyn, New York; William F. Murphy of Rockville Centre, New York; Daniel A. Hart of Norwich, Connecticut; Alfred C. Hughes of New Orleans, Louisiana; and Robert J. Banks of Green Bay, Wisconsin. Moreover, there are other prelates in the United States facing charges analogous to those that brought Law down. They include high-profile Cardinals Roger Mahony in Los Angeles, California, and Edward Egan in New York (related primarily to Egan's tenure in Bridgeport, Connecticut). When the situation was at its most volatile, one could imagine a scenario in which a significant portion of senior figures in the American Catholic hierarchy could have been wiped out. To Vatican officials seeking to restore stability, this seemed a decidedly unappetizing prospect.

Third, there is the strong personal bias of Pope John Paul II against bishops resigning when things get tough. The pope himself has in recent years faced persistent calls to resign on the basis of an alleged incapacity to lead, due to his physical weakness and age. His response? "Jesus did not come down off the cross," he once said to Chilean Cardinal Jorge Medina Estevez. The point is that one does not walk away when suffering comes, but it is precisely by bearing suffering in faith that one follows Jesus Christ. Moreover, John Paul takes seriously the traditional Catholic understanding of the bishop's office. A bishop is a spiritual father to his people, not a corporate CEO who can be sacked when earnings projections are not met. A father does not abandon his family in moments of crisis, even if that crisis is of his own making. It is precisely in those moments when the father's calling is to acknowledge his mistakes, buckle down, and do whatever it takes to make things right.

The intersection of these factors explains why, when Law first floated the idea of stepping down in April, word came from the papal household that his resignation would not be welcome. In the end, of course, the situation in Boston became so ungovernable that all of the usual logic had to be swept aside.

WHERE THINGS STAND

There have been several indications in recent months that the Holy See has, at least to some extent, grasped the depth of the American crisis and taken steps to address it.

First, after the Vatican declined in October to grant the *recognitio,* meaning formal approval, to the Dallas norms, the normal procedure would have been to remand the norms to the American bishops, who would go back to the drawing board and eventually re-submit something to Rome. On other matters, such as liturgical texts, this process took years. Instead, the Vatican formed a unique "mixed commission" composed of four Vatican officials and four U.S. bishops, which over the course of two days worked out a new proposal. It was ready for the mid-November meeting of the U.S. bishops in Washington. The revised norms were over-whelmingly approved and forwarded to Rome, and the *recognitio* was issued in December. By the normal pace of Vatican business, this was lightning speed.

Second, changes to a set of Vatican norms on sex abuse cases approved in secret by John Paul II February 7 were designed to speed up trials of priests accused of sexual abuse and make it easier to remove priests from the clerical state. The changes allow deacons and lay people to serve on criminal tribunals in the Catholic Church, even as judges. Under rules decreed by the pope in April 2001, those roles had been restricted to priests. The changes also drop the requirement that tribunal members have a doctorate in canon law, insisting only that they hold the lesser degree of a licentiate and have worked in tribunals for "a reasonable time." Both moves should expand the pool of judges and lawyers. In a notable depar-ture from canonical tradition, the changes also give the Congregation for the Doctrine of the Faith the power in "clear and grave" situations to dis-miss someone from the priesthood without a trial. That administrative power had heretofore belonged only to the pope himself. The congregation also acquired the power to *sanate,* meaning clean up, procedural irregular-ities in the acts of a local tribunal. That means that if a case comes to Rome on appeal, the problem can be resolved without remanding the case for a new trial. The pope's changes also permit a recourse, or appeal, only to the regular Wednesday assembly of cardinal members of the congregation. Other appeals are excluded, meaning that the congregation's decisions are final. All of this suggests the Vatican understands these cases must be han-dled in a manner that is swift, sure, and final.

Third, the Vatican held a private symposium on pedophilia April 2–5 featuring eight leading scientific experts, all of them non-Catholic, who offered "state-of-the-art" insight on sexual abuse to officials responsible for various elements of the Vatican response to the crisis. These experts told the Vatican officials that homosexuality is a risk factor but not the cause of the sexual abuse of adolescent males. They also questioned the wisdom of "zero-tolerance" policies, listing three criticisms: (1) the complexity of individual cases; (2) stress is a risk factor, and a priest stripped of his livelihood and support system experiences stress; (3) it is dangerous to "let loose" an abuser priest on the community. Vatican officials said this input might help shape a document currently in preparation concerning the admission of homosexuals to seminaries. It might also prompt a new set of guidelines on the Church's responsibility to men after they have been removed from the priesthood. The decision to hold this symposium, and to reach out for experts independent of the Church, was not business as usual.

Fourth, when a group of three sex abuse victims from Boston came to Rome in mid-March seeking an audience with the pope, they received a response that most uninvited visitors never do. A senior official from the Vatican's most powerful office, the Secretariat of State, visited the men in their Rome hotel for more than an hour, carrying a personal message from the pope. "The Holy Father realizes the seriousness of this problem, and is doing all he can," Gary Bergeron said he was told by Monsignor James Green, who added that Bergeron was free to share the message with other victims. "He will continue to do all he can to heal the church and to pray for the victims," Green said on the pope's behalf. "He will see that this doesn't happen again." Bergeron later said the meeting was "very intense, very emotional, very good." Green wanted to know what the three men— Bergeron, his father Joseph, and friend Bernie McDade, all of whom say they were sexually abused by priests—made of the U.S. bishops' new sex abuse norms. He also asked their views about Bishop Richard Lennon (the interim replacement for Law), and in general about the climate in Boston and the American church. "Everything was on the table," Bergeron said. Green's mission signals a high level of concern on the sex abuse issue, because most people who wash through Rome banging on Vatican doors do not get this treatment.

At the same time, there are areas where the Vatican still harbors doubts about the approach taking shape in the United States.

Many Vatican officials have deep reservations about the National Lay Review Board empanelled by Bishop Wilton Gregory to oversee implementation of the sex abuse norms. The board's job description could be read to suggest that these lay Catholics have a sort of informal supervisory power over bishops in their dioceses. For the Vatican, this is an ecclesiological enigma. Power in the Church flows from the risen Christ through the apostles to their successors in the episcopal college. Based on this theological framework, the idea of a layperson "supervising" a bishop is anomalous. Moreover, many in the Vatican would say the heart of the sex abuse crisis was a failure on the part of many bishops to take personal responsibility for overseeing the quality of priestly life, screening candidates for Holy Orders, and overseeing the implementation of existing sex abuse policies. Thus the idea of creating another way for the bishops to "pass the buck," in this case to lay boards (whether national or diocesan), is troubling.

Vatican officials also still have concerns about the protection of due process rights for accused priests in the United States. There is a sense in Rome that some American bishops are acting out of panic, removing men without a true preliminary investigation and stacking the procedural deck against them. There will be careful scrutiny of such appeals when they arrive at the Congregation for the Doctrine of the Faith. Ultimately, there may be Vatican pressure to soften the "zero tolerance" stance, at least as it refers to elderly priests facing a long charge distant in time, or a priest in religious community who can be assigned to a ministry in which there is little risk of a repeat offense. As noted above, the Vatican is also likely to push the bishops to continue to exercise some kind of responsibility for a man even if the evidence warrants his removal from the priesthood.

The story of the crisis of 2002 illustrates that after more than 200 years, the Vatican and the American Catholic Church still in some ways remain strangers to each other. Especially as American Catholics attempt to explain their needs, their frustrations, and their desires to their leaders in Rome, they would be well advised to learn something of the Vatican's culture and worldviews. Otherwise they risk attempting a dialogue without a common language.

Chapter 3

CANON LAW AND THE CLERGY SEX ABUSE CRISIS: THE FAILURE FROM ABOVE

Thomas P. Doyle

The Catholic Church has its own legal system, known as canon law. The word *canon* is derived from the Greek *Kanon,* which means a rule or straight line. Canon law is the oldest continuously functioning legal system in the world. Its roots go back to the fourth century when gatherings of bishops enacted rules or laws to deal with problems facing the infant Church.

Canon law took its definitive shape as a legal system in the twelfth century when Gratian, a Carthusian monk, composed a systematic compilation of the scattered Church laws. A decisive factor in shaping the Church's legal tradition was the rediscovery of Roman law in that same century. The basic Roman law system has been the most influential force in the development of both ecclesiastical and civil-law systems in western history. Canon law today is one of several legal systems that are based on the concept of codification. The basic source of Catholic Church law is found in the *Code of Canon Law.* The first actual codification was issued in 1917. It was in force until 1983 when the second revision, based on the decrees and spirit of Vatican Council II, went into effect (cf. Coriden, Green, & Heintschel, 1985).

Canon law, like any legal system, grew up in response to questions, disputes, and problems that the Catholic Church encountered. Unlike other ecclesial denominations, Catholicism is not only a religious entity but a secular political force as well. Throughout its history it has been a combination of a spiritual movement, a military power, a potent political body, and a significant economic power. All of these facets come into play when the Church is forced to deal with serious internal problems such as the misdeeds of its clerics.

Today's major challenge is the sexual abuse of children, minors, and adults by clerics. Clerics are members of the subcaste or subculture that comprises the primary functionaries of the Church. All receive the sacrament of Holy Orders. There are three classes: deacons, the lowest; priests, the most numerous; and bishops, the highest in rank and those who hold all major offices and possess the fullness of power in the church. "Pope" and "cardinal" are not sacramental orders but special offices held by the supreme leader of the entire church, the pope, and the most influential group of office holders and decision makers, the cardinals.

Generally clerics are bound by the law of celibacy, which is assumed at the time a cleric becomes a deacon. There are some exceptions. Married men may become permanent deacons but they never attain the higher ranks and never are eligible for the more important governmental offices in the Church. In the Eastern rites, priests have the option of marriage before their ordination. Yet the vast majority of the world's clerics, including all bishops, assume the celibacy obligation and are celibates at least in theory. The law of celibacy proscribes not only marriage, but also any kind of romantic or sexual relationship or sexual contact with any other person in any degree (cf. Canon Law Society of America [CLSA], 1983, canon 277).

The present canon law system and its predecessor, the 1917 *Code*, both have contained the legal means to effectively confront and deal with clerical sexual abuse. The contemporary scandal has focused on sexual abuse of children and minors. Such actions are specifically forbidden by the *Code*: "If a cleric has otherwise committed an offense against the sixth commandment of the Decalogue [a sexual offense] with force or threats or publicly or with a minor below the age of sixteen, the cleric is to be punished with just penalties, including dismissal from the clerical state if the case warrants it" (CLSA, 1983, canon 1395). Thus the violation of the obligation of celibacy under the conditions mentioned in this canon is also a significant crime in canon law. It has been specifically listed as such because history has shown that in spite of the noble ideals of the concept of celibacy, violations against it have been numerous and constant. The most serious are those that involve force or minors.

Canon law also provides a clear and detailed procedure for investigating allegations of sexual wrongdoing. Canon law contains its own procedural law with provision for a court or tribunal system. Like the civil courts of most countries, there are civil and criminal processes. The criminal law section of the *Code* begins with a section entitled the "Preliminary Investigation" (CLSA, 1983, canons 1717–1719). Herein we find the mandatory procedure for responding to allegations of any form of sexual offense by a cleric. The bishop does not have an option but is obliged to investigate any report especially if it concerns a matter as serious as the sexual abuse of a child or minor by a cleric (CLSA, 1983, canon 1717). If the investigation reveals that the offense possibly took place, the bishop then must decide whether to deal with the offender by means of a pastoral admonition, an administrative disciplinary process, or a full judicial trial. In a sense the preliminary investigation resembles the grand jury process found in common law. For proven instances of actual sexual abuse of whatever degree, a pastoral admonition is hardly appropriate. An administrative process can only impose a temporary suspension but cannot dismiss a cleric from the clerical state. Dismissal, the ultimate penalty that can be imposed on an errant cleric, amounts to the permanent termination of his ministry. Although Holy Orders, once validly received by means of a sacramental ceremony, can never be erased, this does not mean that a deacon, priest, or bishop is then free to function as such for the rest of his life. Dismissal from the clerical state or laicization as it is technically known, means that the deacon, priest, or bishop can never exercise his ministry.

Dismissal can be imposed by a canonical trial on the local or diocesan level. This has rarely been accomplished because of the complexities of the process and the stringent proofs required to convict. The pope can laicize a cleric if the cleric so petitions, which is the most common way of removing clerics from active ministry. The pope also holds the power to dismiss or laicize a cleric against his will, generally upon the request of the cleric's bishop. This route had rarely been followed until 1998 when the pope, in response to pleas from certain American bishops, agreed to impose dismissal on several priests who had proven to be especially egregious sexual predators. Nevertheless, forced dismissal of this type remains a rarity.

One would expect that Church authorities would reach out and provide comprehensive pastoral care to any person sexually abused by a cleric; however, the opposite has been true. Nevertheless the law itself contains provision for the "reparation of damages" incurred as the result of a clerical crime (CLSA, 1983, canons 1729–1731). This is in addition to the broad admonition given to all bishops that they be "concerned with all the Christian faithful" committed to their care (CLSA, 1983, canon 383, 1). Canon law does not specifically require a bishop to extend sincere pastoral care to the victims of sexual abuse for a very good reason: such a response is presumed based on the very nature of the bishop as pastor or shepherd.

With the above in mind, as we look back on this disastrous chapter of modern Catholic church history, we clearly see that the canonical system has been an abysmal failure at dealing with clergy sexual abuse. The law is impersonal and static. As with any legal system, it must be given life by those in charge of the community. The failure of canon law to prevent the widespread and horrendous damage wrought by sexually dysfunctional clerics is not due to the law itself but to those charged with implementing it, namely the Vatican bureaucracy and the individual diocesan bishops. The pope and the bishops are the primary leaders of the Church. Canon law has its relevance in the correct and honest application by the Church's leadership. It becomes trivialized when bishops ignore it or apply it dishonestly for self-serving purposes.

Yet the failure of the Church to respond to the contemporary sexual abuse crisis can be epitomized in the conflicts inherent in certain aspects of Church structure, set forth in canon law. The application of church law has not been uniform throughout the ages. In many ways the law's life depends on the influence of extant political, cultural, and even economic needs. Throughout its history, Catholicism has had to face the reality of clergy sexual abuse. It is not a new phenomenon, the result of infidelity to vows, the negative influence of a so-called materialistic generation, or rejection of traditional sexual morality by a post–Vatican II generation of maverick clerics. Those who promote such shortsighted excuses are either steeped in psychological denial or completely unaware of the historical roots of clergy sexual abuse.

There is abundant evidence that the institutional Church has grappled with the sexual sins of the clergy from its earliest centuries. At times the response was open and decisive and at other times, clandestine and ineffective. The earliest mention of clergy sexual abuse is found in the canons of the Synod of Elvira (309), which included mention of presbyters and bishops who commit sexual sins (canon 18) and "those who abuse boys" (Laeuchli, 1972, p. 47). The Penitential Books of the early Middle Ages mention sexual crimes committed by clerics against young boys and girls (Payer, 1984, pp. 40–44). It appears that clerics were not as protected by the Church as they are now since the canonical texts neither omit nor hide clergy sexual offences but include them with other instances of *sodomia,* the term used to denote homosexual acts (Doyle, 2003, p. 194).

One of the most vivid indicators of the problem is found in the *Book of Gomorrah,* authored by St. Peter Damien in 1051. This work decried rampant homosexual practices of the clergy as well as ecclesiastical superiors who failed to take decisive action. Peter ended his book with several recommendations to the reigning pope for decisive and stringent action. The pope's response rang a familiar chord in that he praised Peter's work but significantly softened the author's urging that offending clerics be dismissed. (Bullough & Brundage, 1982, p. 61).

The *Decretum Gratiani* is considered by canonical scholars to be the most important single historical source for canon law. It is a collection of canonical texts published in 1140, which contains specific reference to the sexual violation of young boys. In the section on penance, Gratian offers the opinion that clerics guilty of pederasty suffer the same penalties as laymen, including the death penalty. In another section he states that clerics who sexually abuse children should be excommunicated (Doyle, 2003, p. 196).

Five years after the momentous Council of Trent (1545–1563) Pope Pius V issued a papal decree entitled *Horrendum illud* (August 30, 1568) in yet another attempt to curb clergy sexual abuse. "Priests who abuse are deprived of all offices, benefices, privileges, degraded, and turned over to secular courts for additional punishment" (Gasparri, 1926, no. 128).

The historical texts, especially those from the Middle Ages, refer to homosexual activity involving clerics, often with young boys. There is no mention of true pedophilia; rather the problem appears to have been sex with young, adolescent boys, and was generally labeled pederasty. This canonical documentation clearly shows that sexual immaturity of the clergy has been a consistent problem and that throughout time, the solution was limited to punitive measures against erring clerics. There is little if any historical evidence of serious study into the etiology of the problem (Doyle, 2003, p. 197).

Returning to the failure of the canonical system to effectively address clergy sexual abuse, it is apparent that the impediment is in the very nature of Catholic Church governance. In short, there is no separation of powers, hence no checks and balances and no true accountability for Church leaders. The Church's governmental system is hierarchical. All power in ecclesiastical governance resides in individuals and not in collective bodies. The various councils, synods, and conferences have largely consultative roles. Any deliberative power is either given by canon law itself, which in turn is totally subject to the approval of the pope, or it is vested in a specific collective body by either the pope or a diocesan bishop. In any case, any regulatory activity undertaken by any of these bodies is subject to the ultimate approval of a diocesan bishop or the pope. Even the decrees of an ecumenical council, the highest collective body in the Catholic Church, are subject to the approval of the pope for their validity (cf. CLSA, 1983, canon 338).

The pope is the supreme authority for the universal church. His power even extends to each individual diocese and religious order (cf. CLSA, 1983, canon 333). Papal power is not merely executive in nature. The pope is the supreme lawmaker for the entire Church as well as the supreme judge. All Vatican subordinates who exercise any legislative, judicial, or executive power do so as delegates of the pope (cf. CLSA, 1983, canon 331). For centuries the Catholic Church has taught that this supreme power and the hierarchical structure are of divine origin (cf. CLSA, 1983, canons 330, 331, 333).

On the local or diocesan level, the bishop enjoys nearly total power. He is subject to the pope as his immediate superior. The diocesan bishop holds full judicial, legislative, and executive powers in his diocese (cf. CLSA, 1983, canon 391). Bishops are believed to be the successors of the 12 apostles. They are individually appointed by the pope who, it is believed, is guided in this task by the Holy Spirit (cf. CLSA, 1983, canon 375).

Traditionally all power in the Church has been held by clerics, the only exceptions being the power that religious women (nuns and sisters) hold over their subjects within their own religious congregations. There was some loosening up of this monopoly after Vatican Council II, allowing laymen and laywomen limited participation in specific areas of Church governance and liturgy. Yet the canons embody the clericalist tradition whereby the clergy consider themselves as somehow set apart, special, and above the laypeople. One need look no further than rampant clericalism for an explanation of the fear, secrecy, and arrogance so prevalent in the clerical elite's inadequate response to the sexual abuse crisis (Doyle, 2003, pp. 209–218).

The first collision between the institutional Church, with its clericalist attitude and the laity happened in Louisiana with the celebrated case of Gilbert Gauthe, a predatory pedophile from the Diocese of Lafayette. One family broke the mold of clerical control and brought suit against the diocese, charging intentional negligence and mishandling of the numerous reports received of Gauthe's pedophilic activity. This suit opened the gates for the thousands of others that have either been settled or brought to trial throughout the United States. In time nearly every diocese in the nation would face the problem of sexually abusing clerics. As one who has served as an expert witness and consultant in several hundred of the civil cases throughout the United States, I have testified in nearly every instance that the canon law requiring an investigation of alleged sexual abuse, appropriate disciplinary action against offending clerics, and proportionate pastoral relief for victims has been blatantly ignored. Bishops and their staffs were well aware of the demands of the law but, since there is no separation of powers in the diocese, the open due process required was replaced by a secretive solution to the problem that protected the bishops and the diocesan governing structure and neglected the search for justice for the victims and perpetrators alike. By sidestepping the required procedural investigation altogether or substituting a secret and perfunctory inquiry followed by a transfer of the offending cleric, the bishop effectively dispensed himself from the obligations of procedural and penal law, an action that is blatantly canonically illegal. The canons specifically state that a diocesan bishop cannot dispense from either type of law (CLSA, 1983, canon 87). What certain bishops have actually done has been to rewrite the canons to suit their own purposes while at the same time denying due process to the victims.

In addition to subverting due process, those who knew about almost-certain instances of sexual abuse of children or minors and simply transferred perpetrators elsewhere, actually cooperated in the crimes. According to the 1917 Code, if an ecclesiastical officeholder (bishop, pastor, vicar, etc.) neglected to act accordingly in the face of knowledge about an offense, he shared liability for the offense (1917 *Code,* canon 2209, 6 in Woywood & Smith, 1957, p. 454.) Those who sheltered, hid, or shielded a known offender likewise shared in the liability for the offense itself (CLSA, 1983, canon 2209, 7). Simply put, those Church leaders who shuffled abusing priests around, hid them from civil prosecution, or lied about their offenses when questioned, committed additional canonical offenses. Although the 1917 *Code* went out of use in 1983, there is similar legislation in the new *Code* (CLSA, 1983, canon 1329). The canons recognized the fact that Church leaders have covered up clerical crimes in the past and, to address similar actions in the future, pertinent laws have been enacted.

In a hierarchical system, overladen with the trappings and values of monarchy, accountability is painfully difficult. Basically it flows from the bottom up: the laity and lower clergy are accountable to the hierarchical leadership, the bishops to the pope, but there is no accountability to those whom the ecclesiastical leaders are supposed to serve. One way the canons try to promote accountability is by requiring that all due process procedures be recorded and preserved. Failure to find a written record of a canonical investigation almost always means that there was none. Such records are part of the *external forum,* the Church public forum for judicial acts. It stands in contrast to the *internal forum,* the forum of conscience that is never recorded in writing and is generally limited to sacramental confession. Discovery of Church documents in civil cases has revealed very rare instances of recorded canonical investigations, leading to the presumption that they either did not happen or were not conducted according to the prescribed format. Confidentiality of records has been a hot issue in civil litigation. Some Church leaders have tried to claim that such records are privileged and amount to *internal* forum information. This, of course, is untrue from a canonical standpoint. The records are written and, therefore, belong to the external forum. As such, they lack the privileged level of confidentiality accorded to confessional-type matter.

Had these laws been honestly and vigorously followed, one can only speculate how many young people might have been saved from the anguish of physical and spiritual abuse.

Faced with an ecclesiastical bureaucracy that responded to their anguished pleas with subterfuge, stonewalling, intimidation, and outright lies, the victims and their families overcame their fear and awe of the clerical elite and sought justice in the only place left to them: the civil courts of secular society. As the civil lawsuits unfolded throughout the United States and, in time, in other countries, the Church's canon law system became a major weapon used against the Church.

From a canonical standpoint, the liability has been configured from a number of directions. At the foundation is the essential obligation of the bishop for the pastoral welfare of all in his charge. The *Code of Canon Law* provides much more detail about the bishop's governmental rights and obligations than it does about his pastoral obligations even though these are far more important in the overall theological scheme of the bishop's ministry. The *Code* sums up his pastoral role by saying that he is to show concern for all those committed to his care (CLSA, 1983, canon 383). There is more specificity found in other sources, equally authoritative yet not enumerated in the *Code.* First among these is the *Directory for the Pastoral Ministry of Bishops,* published by the Vatican in 1973. The bishop's responsibility to young people is summarized thus: "A field of the apostolate that constantly preoccupies the fatherly heart of the bishop is youth: young people, especially students, in the crossroads of opinions, being aroused by the struggle of new ideas and social conditions and accustomed to a way of life that is outside or even contrary to good morals, are already at this early age very easily alienated from the Church.... Those who take part in the pastoral care of youth should try to interpret their hopes and encourage the new ways in which youth legitimately tries to feel itself concerned, but they should not in any way yield to the superficiality of thought and the contemporary errors to which youth is liable.... Finally they should guide their apostolic energies in such a way that the young people may see and actually experience themselves as sharing and shaping the Christian community, its living and conscious members, as it evolves day by day" (*Directory*, 1973, pp. 77–78).

Bishops and religious superiors have, with disturbing frequency, tried to claim before the civil courts that they have limited direct authority over their priests, alleging, among other things, that the priests are independent contractors or that they have no control over what they do on private time. This is totally false, of course, since the bishop has almost total power over a cleric subject to his authority. All clerics owe obedience and reverence to their bishop (CLSA, 1983, canon 273). The bishop's responsibility for his clerics is summed up in canon 384 which mandates that he protect their rights and see that they fulfill their obligations, which of course includes the obligation to adhere to the demands of clerical celibacy. The bishop also has direct control over all clerical ministry exercised for lay people. This power extends to any priest in a diocese, whether he is officially attached, a visitor, a religious order priest, or a priest from another diocese.

Lurking only slightly below the Church's canonical surface are the legal links to the overpowering emotional and spiritual duress that has enabled countless destructive relationships between clerics and layperson. This same duress, now commonly referred to as "religious duress" by plaintiff lawyers, has been the primary internal force that has prevented victims from disclosing their abuse, trapping them in a web of fear and false guilt. Convinced by traditional, though erroneous, teaching that priests and bishops are direct representatives of God, victims and their families have too often succumbed to this fear, brought on either by external intimidation and coercion or by their own misguided conviction that to expose a priest's sexual abuse is to invite God's wrath (Doyle, 2003, pp. 218–219).

Religious duress is a direct by-product of clericalism. Clericalism has its roots in the privileged place claimed and nurtured by the clerical establishment itself, a place solidly supported by the canon law tradition. In addition to the many canons that protect clerics, accord them special privileges, and admonish the laity to pay them special honor (CLSA, 1983, canons 273–289), the entire sacramental system is constructed in such a way that the sacraments, the traditional means of salvation for Catholics, are basically controlled by clerics who are their ordinary ministers and in many cases (as with baptism, confirmation, Eucharist, marriage, orders) the authority figures who control access to them.

The canons provide a framework for a host of cultural and psychological attitudes that give rise to several dark phenomena that have emerged from the sex abuse morass. Though considered here separately, they are intimately connected. Religious duress, already mentioned, supports the severe power imbalance between cleric-abusers and laypeople, especially young adolescents or women. The ensuing relationships are progressively more destructive wherein the lay victims lose control and become entrapped by the unique and powerful figure of the cleric. At the core of this sick relationship one often finds that a trauma bond exists (cf. Carnes, 1997, pp. 65–69). This bond exists in seminal form in the "awe" with which clergy are held by Catholics. These strong feelings, which mask religious duress, can prevent the victim from recognizing the seductive patterns of abusing clergy, from resisting sexual victimization once it has surfaced, from recognizing the abuse itself and any resultant harm, and, finally, from exposing the abuser after the fact (Doyle, 2003, p. 223).

Psychologist Leslie Lothstein of the Institute for the Living asserts that sexual abuse by a priest is more destructive with longer lasting negative effects than similar abuse by ministers of other denominations or even incestuous abuse. Victims see their abuse as "soul murder" and many can never recover. The reason lies in the victim's belief in the Church's assertion that the priest-abuser is the direct representative of Jesus Christ (DiGiulio, 2002).

Church law is supposed to be a concrete, practical expression of divinely revealed truths about God's people on earth. As Pope John Paul II stated in the *Apostolic Constitution* by which the *Code* was promulgated, "The *Code* is in no way intended as a substitute for faith, grace, charisms, and especially charity in the life of the Church.... Its purpose is to create such an order...that while assigning the primacy to love, grace, and charisms, it at the same time renders their organic development easier in the life of both the ecclesial society and the individual persons who belong to it" (Apostolic Constitution *Sacrae Disciplinae Leges,* in Coriden, Green, & Heintschel, 1985, p. xxv). Recent experience with clergy abuse alone, added to an honest consideration of the darker side of the Catholic Church's role in unfolding history, clearly illustrates that these lofty ideals have simply not come to pass. Why not? Because the transition from the ideal to the real in the lived experience of Catholicism has always been marred by the destructive force of power addiction, economic greed, and unsavory politics. The ordained leadership and middle management, a minuscule minority of the total Church population, have fallen prey to an error common to organizations. The power elite has identified its own needs as the needs of the Church in general. This reflects a distorted interpretation of canon 204 which refers to the "Church" as a society of the Christian faithful constituted as the "People of God," to use the classic phrase of Vatican II (cf. Vatican Council II, *Dogmatic Constitution on the Church*, November 22, 1964, in Flannery, 1988, pp. 359–369.) The Church consists of all the people and not only the hierarchy and clergy. Yet historical events, especially those surrounding the clergy sexual abuse scandal, lead to the distinct impression that the hierarchy act as if they believe that they are the essential and most important aspect of the Church. This entire multifaceted phenomenon, responsible in great part for the destructive forces that have destroyed rather than saved souls, has been propelled by clericalism.

The latest chapter in the abuse saga began on January 6, 2002, when *The Boston Globe* unleashed heretofore-dormant forces with its publication of documents related to the Geoghan case. One unforeseen result was the launching of two sets of values, both enshrined in the Church's canon law, on an inevitable collision course. Governmental and sacramental power, tenaciously held by the hierarchy and clergy, found itself challenged by the mandate for lay holiness, mission, and participation. These values are given practical force in the canons (cf. CLSA, 1983, canons 204, 212, 213). Their correct interpretation requires that the clergy understand that being set *apart* does not mean being set *above*.

Lay efforts at responding to the spiritual vacuum caused by the scandal were inevitable. The victims, generally from devout, faithful *Catholic* backgrounds, could hardly turn to the institutional Church for solace, relief, and spiritual guidance. The traditional sources of help were the very perpetrators, protectors, and enablers of the soul destruction. The shepherds' response to the wounded victims of clergy abuse has not been compassionate pastoral care but marginalization and further victimization by brutal legal tactics. Instead, the victims turned to each other and to non-victim supporters. The People of God have responded in ways consistent with the hope embodied in the canons. Challenged to "manifest to the sacred pastors their opinion on matters which pertain to the good of the Church, and they have a right to make their opinion known to other Christian faithful…" (cf. CLSA, 1983, canon 212, 3), laymen and laywomen supported by a few courageous clerics, have spoken directly and forcefully to the hierarchy. This rapid maturation of the laity from the spiritual infancy in which they were held to ecclesial adulthood has posed a significant threat to the power-holders. Donald Cozzens sums it up well: "*As the church's medieval clerical culture—a closed, male society of privilege, exemption, and deference—comes undone, the witness of lay leaders in the church is now emerging*" (Cozzens, 2002, p. 151).

The abuse crisis has revealed much about the beleaguered hierarchical superstructure. The question as to *how* the spiritual and ecclesiastical power, woven through the Church's canonical framework, has been wielded has been answered: monarchically! The age of monarchy has long passed yet the Church has been slow to catch up. If the lofty canonical ideals of the Church as "People of God" are to become real, there must be a new dialogue between bishop and priest and between clergy and laity. Any hope for success must be based on a new paradigm of power that incorporates respect for the laity, compassionate humanity, fundamental equality, and impartial justice. These are the foremost values to be faithfully guarded, not the traditional values that served almost exclusively to protect and expand clerical, hierarchical, and papal power. In short, the center of the law and the benchmark against which it is applied must always be the compassionate example of Jesus and not the tenaciously held power of the hierarchy.

REFERENCES

Bullough, V., & Brundage, J. (1982). *Sexual practices and the medieval church.* Buffalo, NY: Prometheus Books.

Canon Law Society of America. (1983). *Code of canon law* (Latin-English ed.). Washington, DC: Author.

Carnes, P. (1997). *The betrayal bond.* Deerfield Beach, FL: Health Communications.

Coriden, J. A., Green, T. J., & Heintschel, D. E. (Eds.). (1985). *The code of canon law: A text and commentary.* New York: Paulist Press.

Cozzens, D. (2002). *Sacred silence: Denial and crisis in the Church.* Collegeville, MN: The Liturgical Press.

Damian, P. *The book of Gomorrah: An eleventh century treatise against clerical homosexual practices* (P. Payer, Trans.). Waterloo, Ontario, Canada: Wilfred Laurier University Press.

DiGiulio, K. (2002, August 9). Interview of Dr. Leslie Lothstein. *National Catholic Reporter.*

Directory of the Pastoral Ministry of Bishops. (1973). Vatican: Polyglot Press, 1973.

Doyle, T. (2003). Roman Catholic clericalism, religious duress, and clergy sexual abuse. *Pastoral Psychology, 51,* 189–231.

Flannery, A. (Ed.). (1988). *Vatican Council II: The conciliar and post-conciliar documents.* Northport, NY: Costello Publishing Company.

Gasparri, P. (Ed.). (1926). *Codicis Iuris Canonici Fontes: Vol. 1. Concilia Generalis-Romani Pontificis.* Rome: Typis Polyglottis.

Laeuchli, S. (1972). *Power and sexuality: The emergence of canon law at the synod of elvira.* Philadelphia, PA: Temple University Press.

Payer, P. (1984). *Sex and the penitentials.* Toronto, Ontario, Canada: University of Toronto Press.

Woywood, S., & Smith, C. (1957). *A practical commentary on the code of canon law.* New York: Joseph F. Wagner.

Chapter 4

PLEDGES, PROMISES, AND ACTIONS: THE ROAD TO RESOLUTION OF THE CRISIS OF ABUSE OF CHILDREN BY CATHOLIC CLERGY

Kathleen McChesney

The meeting of the United States Conference of Catholic Bishops (USCCB) in June 2002 in Dallas, Texas, was primarily devoted to devising effective ways to address the problem of sexual abuse of minors by Catholic priests and deacons. Building on the *Restoring Trust* program developed by the Bishops' Ad-hoc Committee on Sexual Abuse in 1994, the bishops created the *Charter for the Protection of Children and Young People,* which was subsequently adopted by the bishops at the 2002 session.

An unprecedented document in the history of the Catholic Church in the United States, the *Charter* serves as a guideline for policies and procedures to be implemented in all of the Church's dioceses and eparchies. The *Charter's* core concepts deal with healing and reconciliation with victim-survivors, effective response to allegations of abuse, and prevention of future acts of abuse. To ensure fewer departures from settled experience, there is emphasis on consistency in implementation, compliance, and public accountability.

Several things bode well for the *Charter* and set it apart from the previously adopted principles and the *Restoring Trust* program. The spotlight created by the revelations of multiple cases of serial abuse drew the attention of Catholics across this country. Concerned faithful watching the process unfold came to realize that the *Charter* was, in effect, a universal framework for members of an organization (the bishops as members of the USCCB) that actually has no administrative or legal authority over

its members. By adopting the *Charter,* however, the bishops publicly affirmed their intention to comply with its provisions based on the premise
that to do anything less would not address this serious problem.

The Conference of Bishops published the *Charter* and posted it on its
popular Web site. It was widely reprinted in religious and secular periodi-
cals and eventually reviewed and analyzed by victim-survivors, lay-
Catholic groups, theologians, and canonists. Notwithstanding skepticism
from several quarters, many looked to the implementation of the *Charter*
as the beginning of the end of this crisis.

The *Charter* also differs from past attempts to prevent acts of abuse by
the creation of a national oversight board composed of lay Catholics.
These individuals bring professional experience, commitment, and broad
perspective to their unique role. This National Review Board provides
advice and guidance to the Conference of Bishops through Conference
President Bishop Wilton D. Gregory and oversees the work of the Office
of Child and Youth Protection, which was also created by the *Charter* as
another vehicle for protecting children.

The specificity of the 17 articles of the *Charter* is similar to those that
might be found in a business practices manual. This reduces the chances of
inconsistent interpretation and implementation of the required programs
and processes. In addition, as is common in more structured organizations,
the mandated compliance audits provide the appropriate level of scrutiny
of the work that is to be accomplished. This level of attention reinforces
the expectation that all that has been promised will be accomplished.

Establishing audit mechanisms for implementing the *Charter* is a key
responsibility of the Office of Child and Youth Protection. Following the
conduct of 194 on-site compliance audits, the Office will produce a public
report on the progress made by each diocese and eparchy. The report will
identify any diocese or eparchy that is not in compliance with the provisions and expectations of the *Charter.* An important part of the report will
include recognition of commendable actions taken by bishops that exceed
what is required by the *Charter.* This objective review is unique to the
operations of the dioceses and eparchies in the United States, and now distinguishes the commitment of the Church from other organizations facing
similar crises.

While neither the Office of Child and Youth Protection, the National
Review Board, or even the United States Conference of Catholic Bishops
can impose any penalty upon a diocese or eparchy that has not fully
adhered to the provisions of the *Charter,* the public nature of the audit
report creates a record that will be sought out by many—victim-survivors,

their families, interested laity, and, of course, the media. Raising the bar of transparency and openness in this manner is highly unusual and presents some risk of discomfiture to those who might choose to ignore the dictates of the *Charter.*

An even higher level of responsibility is provided for within the *Essential Norms for Diocesan/Eparchial Policies Dealing with Allegations of Sexual Abuse of Minors by Priests or Deacons.* Following the adoption of the *Charter,* the Conference of Bishops also requested "recognition" of the *Essential Norms* by the Holy See. The *Essential Norms* were so recognized on December 8, 2002, thereby creating particular canon law for the bishops of the United States. As a result, failure to comply with a specific norm could result in canonical penalties. It is important to recognize that the substance of each of the norms reflects the various articles of the *Charter,* thus strengthening the *Charter* as a guiding document for action.

Another unique aspect of the *Charter* pertains to its directives regarding the study of the problem of child sexual abuse within the Church. Recognizing that it is essential to know the magnitude of the problem and its causes, the authors of the *Charter* called for two major studies. The first is a descriptive study of the "nature and scope" of the problem within the Catholic Church in the United States, including such data as statistics on offenders and victims. The second study will identify the causes of the crisis and the context in which it exists. By determining the extent of abuse that has occurred, progress in eliminating these incidents can be measured. Information pertaining to the characteristics of the offenses, offenders, and victims will lead to a better understanding of child sexual abuse, which can be utilized to affirm prevention strategies or to suggest new approaches. Identifying the causes of abuse will contribute to the body of knowledge about this aberrant behavior that can be shared among the social science disciplines, other religious bodies, and institutions of learning. These studies will likely be the impetus for a greater search for answers to questions about these devastating acts and, thus, a major step toward the reduction of abuse in American society in general.

At the conclusion of the *Charter,* the bishops include four solemn pledges: to work for the protection of children and youth, to devote the resources and personnel necessary to accomplish this goal, to attempt to ordain to the priesthood and put into positions of trust only those who share a commitment to protecting children and youth, and to work toward healing and reconciliation for those sexually abused by clerics. Notwithstanding these public promises, some skepticism exists about the bishops' sincerity and the efficacy of the provisions of the *Charter.*

REASONS TO BE HOPEFUL

The Charter has been characterized by a few as a "public relations response," lacking substance or strength. Others believe the document does not provide enough oversight by the laity. Despite these criticisms, those responsible for its implementation and those responsible for over-sight have begun those processes with vigor and determination. As never before, the eyes of the faithful are carefully watching the actions being taken to meet the *Charter*'s requirements.

The goals of reconciliation and healing, effective response, and accountability are imperative, but it is protecting the young and defense-less in the future that concerns most Catholics at this moment. Priests describe encounters with parents, children in tow, who attempt to physi-cally shield a child from the cleric. Others tell of suspicious glances, cite demeaning articles, and tell of having become the subject of disparaging public humor. It is imperative to remove these incorrect characterizations of the overwhelming number of priests and deacons. Much more time and effort will be required to change these perceptions and to ensure that the Church is, indeed, a safe haven and a place of peace for everyone.

How then will the elements of the *Charter* truly protect those who are vulnerable to sexual assault within the Church communities? At the outset, it must be understood that no plan, however detailed or carefully crafted, can prevent all acts of abuse from occurring in the future. Were that the case, society could apply this magic potion and be rid of all evils that are committed by fractured human beings against one another.

The protection plan envisioned by the *Charter* describes a variety of actions that elevate the level to which this religious institution must go to protect children and young people. These actions form the substance of "safe environment" programs required in all dioceses and eparchies. A safe environment program begins with a "code of conduct" for all adults who interact with youth on a regular basis or who could establish a per-sonal relationship with a young person by virtue of private contact during a Church activity. Codes of conduct define expected behavior that is pro-fessional, responsible, and caring. Because instances of child abuse are sometimes committed by peers, codes of conduct are recommended for minors as well.

The other aspect of a safe environment program is a robust training pro-gram that involves parents, ministers, educators, church personnel, and volunteers. Most adults are ill informed about child abuse in general and sexual abuse in particular. By heightening awareness as to the existence or possibility of abuse, it can be dealt with more effectively and prevented in many situations.

Training programs for adults include information as to what constitutes child abuse, including sexual abuse. It identifies actions, procedures, and policies used to prevent child abuse. Adults are taught what signs to look for in a child who may be abused, as well as what characteristics to look for in a person who may be abusing a child. Information is provided as to what actions should be taken when it is believed that abuse may be, or has been, occurring. Finally, each training program must include instruction as to the relevant laws and policies regarding the reporting of abuse.

A review of some cases of abuse reveals that some offenders have a previous history of abusing children. Background checks to determine if an individual has been convicted for such an offense is a minimum standard to be followed in selecting persons for positions in which they will deal with young people. Additional investigation and screening of the applicant may reveal prior suspicious activity or unusual interest in children and young people. As past behavior is the strongest predictor of future behavior, persons with these types of histories should not be allowed to work where they may have unsupervised contact with children.

The *Charter* and the *Essential Norms* are very clear about transfers of clerics who have committed acts of abuse against minors. Priests and deacons who fall within this category may not be transferred for ministerial assignment to another diocese, eparchy, or religious province. Furthermore, before a priest or deacon can be transferred for residence, his bishop or eparch must forward to the local bishop, eparch, or religious ordinary of the proposed place of residence any and all information indicating that the cleric has been, or may be, a danger to children or young people. Significantly, this also applies even if the priest or deacon will reside in the local community of an institute of consecrated life or a society of apostolic life. These measures make firm earlier guidelines from the Conference on transfers and effectively bar the movement of offenders across diocesan boundaries.

Clearly, the bishops' efforts to select only those candidates for the priesthood who are committed to the safety and security of children are an important undertaking. No testing mechanism or predictor of future behavior exists that will identify all of those who might offend at some later time. Therefore, where not already established, each diocese and eparchy must develop systematic ongoing formation programs that will provide continual guidance to priests as to the limits of their personal contacts with others as well as sufficient oversight of their activities.

THE MANY FACES OF OUTREACH

Well-designed codes of conduct and educational programs have the potential for a high degree of success in obviating future abuse. For those who have suffered, however, sincere and straightforward outreach must occur. The *Charter* calls for pastoral outreach, competent persons to assist victims and their families, and frank and open communications with the public.

Pastoral outreach is defined as the attempt of the bishop, or his designee, to meet with victim-survivors and their families. During this contact, the bishop is to listen with patience and compassion, sharing solidarity and concern. This same pastoral outreach is to be extended to those in faith communities in which the abuse occurred.

The victim-assistance coordinator has a related responsibility in that he or she must coordinate immediate assistance for those who have been harmed. The coordinator must be a capable, caring, and committed person who has the communications and interpersonal skills necessary for this important role. Laypersons with experience in dealing with victims of trauma can be very effective in allaying the common fears associated with reporting offenses of this nature.

Outreach also includes attempts to communicate openly with the public about the actions the bishop has taken regarding offenders. In the interest of safety it is important for families to know of those who have abused and to know of the preventative measures that are in place to preclude further offenses. Transparency serves to comfort parents and caregivers and to accurately convey the fulfillment of the promise to protect.

IS RESOLUTION OF THIS CRISIS ACHIEVABLE?

Across the country this scandal rocked Catholics, regardless of their participation in Church activities or attendance at Mass. The initial responses of anger and shame seemed to evolve over time into sadness and despair. Concerned parishioners became activists seeking ways to help deal with the problem. Certainly, the problems were not created by the faithful, but because their character had been molded in large part by the teachings of the Church, there grew a great and sincere desire to participate in the correction. Members of the laity who willingly provide personal support to victim-survivors and their families, as well as those who provide moral support to all members of the clergy, are part of the process of change. The commitment of the people is deep, sincere, and rooted in their adherence to the principles of the Catholic faith. A National Review Board member explained this commitment to the Conference of Bishops recently when he said, "I want to help you and I want to help this Church. This is the Church that nurtured me as a child, and this is the Church that sustains me as a man."

The skepticism about the bishops' ability to effectively deal with what has occurred may last for several years. That skepticism is to be expected and will likely stimulate continuous attention to these issues. Nonetheless, all concerned are expecting substantial change and improvement over what has occurred in the past.

What might that substantial change look like? Without question, it will be a time of few, if any, new cases. Past offenses will be addressed with a new openness and transparent attitude. It will be a time when the stories about the ministries and charities of the Church are prominent once again. It will be a time when public perceptions of the clergy are no longer colored by scandal. Most important, it will be a time when victim-survivors and their families begin to heal and where there is no uncertainty about the potential for abuse within this Church.

The *Charter for the Protection of Children and Young People* is not a perfect document. It does represent, however, a sea change in the manner in which American bishops are attacking the problem of sexual abuse of minors. There is a great optimism among the clergy and the laity that the *Charter* will help the Church in the United States meet its greatest and most serious challenge.

Chapter 5

CLERGY SEXUAL MISCONDUCT OVERSIGHT REVIEW BOARDS

Nanette de Fuentes

Since June 2002, the United States Conference of Catholic Bishops (USCCB) has made concerted efforts to repair the breach of trust in the Church stemming from revelations of sexual misconduct by clergy and from the lack of leadership by the bishops to deal more openly and effectively with this shocking and horrible problem. The USCCB created national and diocesan initiatives resulting in the documents *Essential Norms for Diocesan/Eparchial Policies Dealing with Allegations of Sexual Abuse of Minors by Priests or Deacons,* and the *Charter for Protection of Children and Young People.* The norms are universal Church law for the U.S. dioceses and Eastern Catholic eparchies, which means that they must be implemented and followed. The "Charter" which the bishops approved June 2002 and revised in November 2002, represents the public commitment of the bishops to implement the norms (Feister, 2003). One of the bishops' methods for restoring trust is to require all of this nation's 195 dioceses and eparchies to respond to clergy sexual abuse allegations by creating oversight review boards composed primarily of laypeople as outlined in norms four and five. The Conference of Major Superiors of Men (CMSM), which is composed of the elected leaders of more than 20,000 vowed religious priests and brothers in the United States, has also followed suit and made a public commitment to honor the values and principles of the Charter (CMSM, 2002).

A variety of salient issues regarding these review boards were not addressed in the norms or Charter, and the dioceses, eparchies, and religious orders were left to interpret, develop, and implement this directive on their own by designing these important boards to match the unique needs and resources of each religious community and diocese. The purpose of this chapter is to provide an understanding of the background, workings, and limits of these review boards, as well as the dilemmas frequently faced by board members when making important decisions that affect not only the victim-survivors, their families, and the accused cleric but also the Catholic community as a whole.

Recommendations and insights are offered on making the clergy sexual misconduct oversight review boards more sensitive, effective, and independent. These recommendations are based on the concerns of victim advocate groups and the Catholic community, on the best of psychological research and standard practice, and on my own personal perspective and experience as both a clinical psychologist and a victim-survivor of clergy sexual exploitation. I have treated both victim-survivors and impaired clergy of several religious denominations, as well as have had the privilege of serving as a founding member on a Roman Catholic archdiocesan clergy oversight review board for many years.

The following definitions may be useful in guiding the reader's understanding.

"Victim-survivor": This term refers to individuals (adults as well as minors) harmed by sexual misconduct by clergy (bishops, priests, or deacons). By using this joint term, their woundedness is acknowledged, and at the same time they are urged on in the healing and recovery process (de Fuentes, 1999). "Sexual misconduct": This is a general term that describes a broad spectrum or continuum of behavior including gestures and speech as well as physical contact not limited to sexual intercourse. It includes sexual harassment, sexual exploitation, and sexual abuse (Catholic Diocese of New Ulm, 1994). "Eparch": This term refers to the dioceses of the Eastern Catholic Church.

BACKGROUND

The concept of these predominantly lay review boards, which deal with allegations of sexual misconduct and abuse by clergy, is not new. The United States Conference of Catholic Bishops recommended the use of these clergy oversight review boards since at least 1994 (USCCB, 1994). However, the USCCB had no real power to require all dioceses and eparchies to implement them prior to December 2002, when the norms were finally revised, approved, and given the Vatican *recognitio.*

Currently, the exact number of dioceses in compliance with the establishment of the review boards is not available. However, the USCCB reported that most dioceses had indeed developed these boards and would have them fully operational soon. These new review boards developed as a result of the Charter and norms and are to be audited by outside contractors primarily with a law enforcement background. These audits are part of The National Review Board's mandate to monitor the bishops' compliance with the Charter and the essential norms, and to learn more about the extent and pattern of the sex abuse problem in the Church. The National Review Board, created in 2002, has emphasized that they will make the results of the studies and audits known, no matter what the findings (Feister, 2003). The subject of the audits and the National Review Board is more fully addressed by Kathleen McChesney, chair of the Board, in this volume.

DESCRIPTION

Specifically, "the review boards" are mandated by the norms to function as a "confidential consultative body" to each bishop or eparch who appoints the review board members. The functions of these boards include advising in the assessment of allegations of sexual abuse of minors and in the determination of suitability of the accused cleric for ministry, reviewing policies for dealing with sexual abuse of minors, and offering advice on all aspects of the cases, retrospectively or prospectively. The review boards are to be made up of at least five people "of outstanding integrity and good judgment in full communion with the Church." Although most are to be laypersons not in the employ of that specific diocese/eparchy, at least one is to be a priest, specifically a pastor representing the diocese/eparch, and the other member should have "particular expertise in the treatment of the sexual abuse of minors." Appointments are to last five years but can be renewed. Although not mandated, it was considered desirable that the "Promoter of Justice participate in the meetings of the review board." The Promoter of Justice is one familiar with canon law. The procedures for those making a complaint should be "readily available in printed form and be the subject of periodic public announcements." Since the review boards are primarily only advisory in nature, the final outcome of the accused cleric's ministry mainly depends upon the process of the canonical trial or tribunals run by fellow priests.

Guidelines for these review boards provided by the essential norms are general and broad, and based upon each diocese/eparch having a developed written policy on the sexual abuse of minors by priests and deacons, and other Church personnel. On a positive note, the guidelines and mandates in norms four and five are more specific than ever before, and guarantee the input of laypeople and from appropriate professions (e.g., psychologists) on these boards. Despite the power of the tribunals and lack of clarity on their own relationship and coordination with the local review boards, many wise and responsible bishops have vowed to faithfully follow their local review board's recommendations regarding restricting ministry or removing abusive clergy to protect minors and vulnerable adults, regardless of the pending tribunals.

The review boards' input on "fitness for ministry" regarding clergy accused of abusing a minor may seem unnecessary as law enforcement usually becomes involved in these cases. However, criminal investigations frequently take many months or years to be complete prior to an arrest and or an indictment being made. As emphasized in the norms and Charter, Church leaders have a responsibility to act to protect the Church community as soon as a suspicion or allegation of abuse has occurred, especially when a minor has been abused. The pastoral judgment of bishops is different from criminal law or convictions, and bishops have frequently removed clergy from ministry even when law enforcement decided not to prosecute due to inadequate evidence. A lack of evidence needed for criminal prosecution does not mean that abuse did not occur nor will not occur in the future. An impartial, well-functioning lay review board can provide valuable insights, resources, and perspectives to overworked and understaffed Church officials as well as assure compliance with the norms and Charter.

RELIGIOUS ORDERS REVIEW BOARDS

The 317 Catholic religious communities of priests and brothers in the United States are not under the auspices of any dioceses, and the Charter and the norms do not specifically address the role or coordination with them. However, the norms and the Charter apply to all priests and Church personnel in public ministry in the Church. The CMSM stated that they "heard the call to accountability," apologized, and vowed to increase efforts to protect children and vulnerable adults (CMSM, 2002).

Currently, the superiors of religious orders have to petition the bishop of a particular diocese for a religious priest to have faculties to preach or to minister the sacraments in public (such as in a parish in that diocese). This permission often includes any history of sexual misconduct, and written assurances by the religious superior of the psychological well-being and safety on the part of the religious-order priest seeking faculties. Bishops should consult their own local diocesan review boards on petitions where some of these issues are in question.

Many of the larger religious orders have had their own sexual misconduct policies and separate clergy review boards for many years (e.g., Jesuits). Some of the smaller religious orders are only now developing their own sexual abuse polices and local lay review boards. Many choose to utilize the resources of the local dioceses' review boards. Some have established review boards that cover a particular geographical area while some pool resources with other religious orders. While the CMSM has no jurisdiction over the leaders of individual religious institutes, the Conference has offered to provide members "leadership and services," and to publicly monitor those institutes that subscribe to the issues raised in the Charter. The Conference members have also committed to creating their own "national review board" that evaluates the implementation of sexual abuse policies of men's religious communities and will publicly report on its findings in a way similar to the reporting practices of the bishops' National Review Board.

PUBLIC REACTIONS

The Catholic community, media, and public reaction to these clergy oversight review boards have been mixed. Some Catholic groups who are more predisposed to be patient and willing to give the bishops and religious superiors time to implement their new initiatives view the lay review boards as a very positive step in the right direction. They accept them as a clear manifestation of the bishops' taking responsibility and making a commitment to deal more openly, compassionately, and effectively with the clergy sex abuse problem within the Church. Many of these groups and individuals have been pushing for more lay involvement in Church decision making for many years.

Victim advocates groups (e.g., SNAP and Linkup) and groups wanting strong reforms in the Church (e.g., Voice of the Faithful, FutureChurch) have been very critical and suspicious of these review boards. Specifically these criticisms focus on the *advisory* nature of the boards; these groups are fearful that they will have no real power and that they will be "stacked with yes-men." These are legitimate concerns. The members of these review boards will probably be primarily Catholic, since they are appointed by the bishops themselves and the investigations of sexual abuse allegations are executed primarily by other priests. In addition, the major criticism is that the essential norms did not mandate or encourage membership of clergy sexual abuse victim-survivors or their family members on these review boards. Other criticisms include the issue that victims and their families are not themselves allowed to present their cases to the review boards and that the functions and recommendations of the boards are confidential and secretive. This all fuels the belief that the prejudice and resulting leniency will be towards the accused cleric.

Given the shocking revelations in 2002 of the extent of the sexual abuse problem in the Church, forced resignations of prominent bishops, high profile cases, resulting lawsuits, and millions of dollars spent to settle these lawsuits; one can hardly blame the victim advocate groups for their less than lackluster feelings towards the essential norms and review boards. These groups' wariness is reasonable since, as previously described, many dioceses and U.S. religious orders had utilized clergy review boards for several years. Some of the high-profile lawsuits in which confidential documents of dioceses and religious orders were made public revealed that, in some cases, the review board's recommendations were not heeded by bishops, or the review board (often made up primarily of Catholic clergy) gave the bishops or religious superiors bad advice on dealing with abusive clergy in ministry.

Some groups advocate for the members of the review boards to be elected directly by parish councils or by victim support groups, and that the review boards should have wider decision-making and investigative powers beyond their current role as outlined in the essential norms. Others call for complete outside "independent commissions, empowered to examine all the records, to issue public reports on cases, dispositions, and costs; and to explore the cases of the scandal and suggest reports." It was emphasized that these independent commissions should work closely with the National Review Board (O'Brien, 2003).

LACK OF NATIONAL PROTOCOLS

As previously described, the norms only provide a general description of the new review boards' functions and composition, and there has been little information available on how these boards functioned in the past. Currently, there are no national protocols (except for those mandated by canon law) for each board to follow on some very important issues. For example, there are no protocols for investigations of allegations of clergy abuse or for who should conduct these investigations (i.e., internal or external, priest, or retired law enforcement). Most of the diocese and religious orders rely on their own trained clergy (a practice that has been highly criticized and rightly so), while others utilize retired law enforcement or probation officers. These investigations are paramount to gathering information and are the basis upon which review boards make decisions and recommendations on fitness for ministry and rehabilitation plans.

There are no specific national protocols or list of "best practices" for each board to follow in decision making and adjudicating cases, especially when there is a lack of information from the victims. There are no standard methods of tracking cases and follow-up, preventing bias towards clergy among Catholic board members, and dealing with cases of criminal/law enforcement investigations and parallel civil lawsuits, and the use of sexual offender treatment experts. Most important is the ability to balance both the alleged victim's and accused clergyman's rights. Questions regarding victim-survivors also arise with regard to such issues as adult victim confidentiality, whether to contact other potential victims named in allegations, allowing victims to present to boards, and coordination with diocesan victim assistance programs and victim advocacy groups.

These issues can be somewhat addressed in the newly mandated sexual abuse policies (see norm two) of each diocese/eparch and religious order. However, the same problem of the lack of national protocols exists for these sex abuse policies as for the review boards. Many of the sex abuse policies are just being developed or are being completely revised to comply with the Charter and essential norms. As can be seen from the above, this nation's diocesan, eparch, and religious-order review boards are probably struggling with similar issues due to this lack of national coordination and information sharing, which was a major contribution to the sex abuse problem among the clergy in the first place.

CHALLENGES FOR REVIEW BOARDS

It would seem to a person on the outside that the issues that these review boards deal with are clear-cut when assessing an abusive cleric's fitness for ministry, especially regarding minors. When all of the information is available and the victim-survivor cooperates with the investigation, the course of action and recommendations by each board are clear—outlined by civil, criminal, and canon law, and by common sense. This is especially so if more than one victim comes forward. However, most cases presented to oversight boards for their review are often not this straightforward, and definitions of "credible" are not uniform and can differ for each board member across the country. Most often, situations presented to boards are of allegations of sexual misconduct against adults—a situation that is often minimized by board members unenlightened on the power dynamics between cleric and parishioner. In addition, many of the current cases and lawsuits are from alleged abuses 20–40 years ago—a span of time that makes finding corroborating evidence much more difficult.

Frequently, cases are presented in which very little information about the allegation is available, there is no corroborating evidence, and the person alleging the abuse is reluctant to provide more information or to speak with Church authorities or investigators. Given the Church's past response to victim-survivors and their families, this reluctance is understandable. In addition, there is often a credible denial by the accused clergy member who has many years of stellar ministry and service to the Church and no other allegations of sexual misconduct. A psychological evaluation may fail to reveal sexual offending tendencies or other psychological abnormalities in the accused cleric. The review board's recommendations have serious consequences. Under "zero tolerance" in norm eight, any clergy member who has abused a minor, no matter how long ago, will be permanently removed from ministry regardless of criminal conviction.

How far should the boards push for further investigations and contact with reluctant adults alleging abuse as a minor, who would probably not appreciate priest-investigators or law enforcement showing up at their doorstep, unsolicited letters from the chancery, or their names given to law enforcement to comply with the mandated sexual abuse reporting requirements by clergy? What about tracking down other adults who have been named as potential victims (possibly abused as minors) if they have not voluntarily made complaints themselves? How does the board make recommendations to the bishop with such limited information, honor victim's and their family's rights to privacy, and yet not appear to favor the accused cleric?

Sometimes the only information a review board has is the fact that there is a criminal investigation underway on a priest (without an arrest) and a parallel civil lawsuit. Frequently law enforcement and alleged victims under these circumstances entirely withhold all information from Church authorities. These clergy who are often removed from ministry by responsible bishops or religious superiors can stay in limbo for years pending the criminal investigation outcome and lawsuit litigation during which their ministry and reputations are destroyed.

What about allegations of noncriminal behavior considered "boundary violations" such as a hug, nonsexual touch, or comment that made a child or parent uncomfortable, or an expensive gift given from a clergy member to a teenager? These behaviors may be manifestations of poor judgments, ethnic or racial differences, or insensitivities by the accused clergy, which may be remedied by counseling or training. Or, on the other hand, they may be more serious warning signs of "grooming" behavior in which the clergy member is ingratiating the minor to lower his or her defenses and set the stage for future victimization. Again, psychological assessment may or may not provide useful insights on these types of cases. These are just some of the types of situations presented to review boards for their recommendations on whether or not to remove accused clergy from ministry or to send them for psychological evaluation and treatment.

In addition, removing a priest or deacon from ministry is devastating, not only for the accused cleric, his family and fellow priests, and deacons or religious brothers; the parish or place of ministry is also traumatized. In the past, parishioners were not informed as to the reasons why an accused clergy member was removed or sent to another parish; the cleric often just disappeared. Parishioners and Church staff have the right to be informed that a clergyman is being removed due to allegations of sexual misconduct. This notification may also encourage other victim-survivors to come forward. However, often very little information about the situation can be offered by Church officials due to the legal privacy rights of the accused cleric and/or victim(s). Parishioners are often highly suspicious of the bishop's motives, frequently rallying around the accused cleric and vilifying the victim(s) especially if civil law suits are involved and the victim is an adult. (For a more detailed description of the psychological and spiritual effects of clergy abuse upon congregations, see de Fuentes, 1999.)

RECOMMENDATIONS

Although the basic model of these advisory clergy sexual misconduct oversight review boards is flawed in many aspects, the lay review boards will be around for some time to come. Therefore, I offer the following recommendations for consideration, which are designed to make these oversight boards more effective in dealing with their mandated tasks and challenges.

Investigations

I highly recommend that investigations of all allegations of cleric sexual misconduct on either minor or adult victims only be conducted by lay-individuals with a law enforcement background who are experienced or have training in this area. Priest-investigators, though often well experienced, pastorally oriented, and well intentioned, cannot avoid the appearance of having a conflict of interest nor avoid the taint of the "fox guarding the hen house." I also highly doubt their ability to be totally impartial regarding fellow priests, even when they do not have a personal relationship with the accused clergy. Victim-survivors may also feel less intimidated and be willing to provide valuable information to non-clergy investigators. As already described, some diocesan and religious orders already employ lay law enforcement investigators, and issues regarding canon law and investigations on accused clergy can be resolved. The USCCB should provide more specific protocols for these investigations.

Board Members

To maximize independent and impartial decisions, every effort should be made to make these advisory oversight boards comprise a multidisciplinary team of laypeople that includes

- victim-advocates or healthy victim-survivors or family members,
- legal experts, and law enforcement representatives,
- mental health experts (victim experts and sex offender treatment specialist), and
- leaders of other religious denominations (e.g., rabbis).

The boards should be gender-balanced and reflect the ethnic diversity of the respective diocese/eparch or ministry of the religious order. Board members' identity should be made known to the Church community and, when possible, parish councils and lay Church leadership should provide input into board membership.

Although the norms wisely and courageously mandated membership by an "expert in the treatment of sexual abuse of minors," the participation of victim-survivors and their families is essential to making these oversight boards credible. However, these individuals must be far along in their healing and recovery process and able to deal with the conflicts and challenges board members face. In addition, the person designated to coordinate assistance for the pastoral care of victim-survivors and their families—a person frequently referred to as the "Victim-Assistance Coordinator"—should regularly attend the meetings, even though he or she does not have voting rights. Consideration and care should be provided to prevent burnout and vicarious traumatization among board members and staff. Those emotionally affected should seek professional, confidential consultation.

Board Member Training

All board members should receive specific formal in-depth training on the power dynamics of clergy sexual misconduct. As I previously described, untrained individuals often minimize and excuse cleric sexual misconduct with adults and inadvertently blame the victim(s), or misinterpret serious grooming behavior for "cultural differences" or "poor judgment." The Center for the Prevention of Sexual and Domestic Violence in Seattle, Washington, has an outstanding training program and has conducted hundreds of workshops for religious leaders of varying religious denominations for many years; the Center is an excellent resource to provide review board training.

Sex Offender Treatment Specialists

Board members should be informed on updated research and standard practices on the psychological profiles and assessment/evaluations of sexual offenders. In fact, I strongly suggest that each board make an effort to ensure membership or input by a "sex offender treatment specialist" in addition to the expert on victim issues. It must be noted that expertise and training in these areas varies greatly among mental health experts across disciplines. Possessing a degree or license in the mental health field (e.g., psychiatrist, psychologist, social worker, or marriage and family therapist), does not assure expertise, experience, or even understanding of perpetrator and victim issues.

I also suggest the consideration of the use of a sexual polygraph and the "Abel Assessment for Sexual Interest" (Abel, Jordan, Hand, Holland, & Phipps, 2001) in any forensic psychological evaluation of cleric accused of abusing minors. Although the sex offender polygraph is mainly utilized in the monitoring and behavior containment of convicted adult sex offenders (National Institute of Justice, 2000; O'Connell, 2000), its usefulness in these cases should be explored.

Anonymity and Record Keeping

Identities of accused clergy and alleged victims should be kept confidential and presented to the board in an anonymous fashion when possible.

In high-profile cases, when the identities are unavoidable, board members (especially priests) should excuse themselves from discussions and voting on recommendations. Methods of record keeping should be developed for board members that honor the anonymity requirements, yet provide for ease of tracking cases. All active cases should be reviewed at least twice a year.

Balancing Decision Making

The issue of balancing both the accused cleric's rights and the safety of the community is extremely difficult. Misconduct oversight boards of other professions struggle with this same issue (e.g., psychologists, lawyers, physicians, law enforcement) though they are often mandated to be "consumer" oriented. However, it must be emphasized how difficult and painful it is for victim-survivors to make an abuse disclosure and come forward, even as adults. Frequently they are re-victimized in the process, not only by eager law enforcement, but also by the Church community and even by their own families (de Fuentes, 1999). Lawsuits mainly occur when victims have been ignored by insensitive Church officials, and when financial settlements cannot make up for the trauma caused by clergy sexual abuse. In addition, I have seldom seen a clearly false serious allegation of cleric sexual misconduct in my many years of working in this field. The accused clergy member has many layers of protection with canon law and community support. Therefore, in ambiguous cases as previously described, the boards' emphasis should be on protecting the victim-survivors and the community when evaluating allegations of cleric abuse.

SUMMARY

This chapter has attempted to provide a balanced overview of the new clergy sexual misconduct oversight review boards and to offer recommendations on making them more effective and responsive. These recommendations are not inclusive, but will require a "paradigm shift" and a substantial financial commitment from Church officials for successful implementation. Excuses for lack of funds, especially by the smaller dioceses and impoverished religious orders, though of consideration, must be replaced by creative problem solving and pooling of resources. The review boards can significantly contribute to the prevention and early interventions of clergy sexual abuse, mitigate expensive lawsuits, and help restore faith in the Church leadership.

REFERENCES

Abel, G. G., Jordan, A., Hand, C. G., Holland, L. A., & Phipps, A. (2001). Classification models of child molesters utilizing the Abel Assessment for sexual interest. *Child Abuse and Neglect: The International Journal, 25,* 703–718.

Catholic Diocese of New Ulm. (1994). Responding to sexual misconduct in the Church. New Ulm, MN: Author.

Conference of Major Superiors of Men. (2002). *Improving pastoral care and accountability in response to the tragedy of sexual abuse.* Silver Spring, MD: Author.

de Fuentes, N. (1999). Hear Our Cries: Victim-Survivors of Clergy Sexual Misconduct. In T. G. Plante (Ed.). *Bless me Father for I have Sinned: Perspectives on Sexual Abuse Committed by Roman Catholic Priests* (pp. 135–170). Westport, CT: Greenwood.

Feister, J. B. (2003, April 17). Kathleen McChesney: Helping the bishops get it right. *St. Anthony Messenger,* pp. 1–7.

National Institute of Justice. (2000). *The value of polygraph testing in sex testing in sex offender management: Research report submitted to the National Institute of Justice.* Washington, DC: Colorado Division of Criminal Justice, Office of Research and Statistics.

O'Brien, D. (2003, February 14). How to solve the church crisis. *Commonweal,* 10–15.

O'Connell, M. (2000). Polygraphy: Assessment and community monitoring. In D. R. Laws, S. M. Hudson, & T. Ward (Eds.), *Remaking relapse prevention with sex offenders: A source book* (pp. 285–302). Thousand Oaks, CA: Sage Publications.

U.S. Conference of Catholic Bishops. (1994). *Report on the Ad Hoc Committee on Sexual Abuse.* Washington, DC: Author.

Chapter 6

THE CRISIS OF SEXUAL ABUSE AND THE CELIBATE/SEXUAL AGENDA OF THE CHURCH

A. W. Richard Sipe

"The Church gets involved in politics" Francois Mauriac said, "when she ceases to produce enough saints." The chronicle of the Roman Catholic Church's response to the historic revelations about sexual abuse among its ranks has not yet been recorded. When that story is told, the account will be rife with politics—public relation maneuvers, power plays, legal pressures, and pleadings of astounding logistics. It will record deception. It will reveal a frightening skeleton of raw secular and financial power devoid of any spirituality, but protected under a cloak of genuine religious value and beauty. So far the Church has not produced a saint to be part of the narrative.

I leave that saga for other writers. What I attempt here is to show the connection of clergy sexual abuse of minors with its inevitable destiny— reconsideration of the celibate/sexual agenda facing the Church. That is the real crisis.

THE CRISIS OF AVOIDANCE

Remarkably, Vatican II (1962–1965) in its broad-ranging consideration of the Church in the modern world did not adequately address the practical questions of clerical celibacy or aspects of human sexuality. Replete with genuinely inspiring and idealistic statements about love, both celibate and married, the documents sidestepped the practice of clerical celibacy, including any debate about a married priesthood.

The questions about contraception and "artificial birth control" were addressed in *Humanae Vitae*, the 1968 papal encyclical of Pope Paul VI. In preparing his letter the pope dismissed outright a majority report prepared by a commission of experts he had appointed that recommended approval of contraceptives (the Pill). Repercussions from that document—an openly negative reaction among laypeople and some hierarchy—created a broad and fundamental doubt about the credibility of the Church in matters of human sexuality.

In the 1970 Synod of Bishops held in Rome, the same pope pledged to abide by the vote of the bishops regarding a married priesthood. The vote was only 45 percent in favor. This time he did side with the majority.

Throughout the papacy of John Paul II, bishops have been given personal and explicit directives that they may not discuss issues of contraception, abortion, masturbation, sex prior to marriage or after divorce, homosexuality, a married priesthood, or women's ordination to the priesthood in any terms other than those restating the official teachings of the Church. Inadvertently his sanctions outlined the celibate/sexual agenda fundamental to the current crisis in the Church. Avoidance of open discussion of this agenda creates a pressure cooker atmosphere that will eventually blow up.

THE RHYTHM OF THE CRISIS

The issue of sexual abuse of minors by priests was ushered into public awareness in the United States during the 1984–85 criminal trial of a priest, Father Gilbert Gauthe, in Lafayette, Louisiana. The papal nuncio in Washington, D.C., marked the unique importance of the event by sending an emissary from his office, Father Thomas Doyle, to contain any damaging fallout. It was an impossible task. Father Doyle, Ray Mouton (Gauthe's church-appointed lawyer), and Father Michael Peterson, a board-certified psychiatrist, drew up a confidential report for all bishops and religious superiors to provide information about "a growing problem of sexual abuse of children and adolescents by clerics." Each American bishop received a copy. The year was 1985 (Berry, 1992).

However, as late as November 18, 1992, the president of the National Conference of Catholic Bishops, Archbishop Daniel Pilarczyk, wrote to Doyle, "the fact remains that your report presented no new issue of which the NCCB was unaware or presented information that required some materially different response" (personal letter). This was in the same time frame in which the notorious case of Father James Porter of Fall River,

Massachusetts, was coming to national attention. He admitted to abusing 200 minors during his assignments in five dioceses. He was sentenced to 18 years in a Massachusetts prison. Meanwhile allegations against priest abusers multiplied throughout the country and total financial settlements already mounted beyond 300 million dollars.

A sensationally publicized allegation of sexual abuse by an American cardinal fizzled badly when the accuser withdrew his civil case. The political and public relations efforts to limit investigation turned the event into an effective damper on the witness of other victims' stories of abuse. The incident lent temporary credence to the theory that exposure of clergy abuse was simply overblown hype by the media.

In July 1997, a jury in Dallas deliberating a case against Father Rudy Kos and the Archdiocese delivered a blockbuster judgment of 119.6 million dollars. Clearly the jury perceived the negligence of the bishop and the conspiracy of the diocese to conceal their knowledge of abuse.

After that, aspects of the crisis seemed to cool across the country as the Church became more eager to settle cases silently and seal the documents. Bishops delivered apologies for the harm done, but hoped, "that the victims are willing also to hear our pain." They did all they could to diffuse the focus from clergy and spoke about the "tragedy" of abuse occurring in "all" of society. Their program, Restoring Trust, had slight impact, and was generally unconvincing and ineffectual in stemming the tide of reports of violations and civil cases. The crisis of exposure was brewing but partially contained in 2001.

THE CRISIS OF EXPOSURE

Nothing in the history of the American Catholic Church can compare with the effect of the investigation of clergy abuse by *The Boston Globe*'s Spotlight Team, which published its first of over 1,000 articles on January 6, 2002. The journalists had requested, and received secret Church documents by court order. Those papers revealed beyond any doubt that one archdiocese—Boston—had over 150 priests (diocesan and religious) who had a record of abuse.

Beyond individuals, the investigators traced via the documents the collusion of the chief Church authorities in covering up for abusing priests, and in fact, aiding and abetting their behavior by frequent assignment transfers without warning either priests or people of the potential danger. They did not report crimes of which they were well aware. The same officials intimidated or ignored victims (Investigative Staff of *The Boston Globe*, 2002).

The *Globe* investigation catapulted the crisis to an entirely new level. It unmasked a system that tolerated, excused, covered up, and essentially fostered sexual abuse. Victims came forward in unprecedented numbers in Boston, and across the nation to tell their sad, sordid stories of betrayal and violation. Previously shy and intimidated, they now had a voice and hope of being believed, two things the church had long denied them. Lawyers and victims filing civil cases against priests in widespread jurisdictions began to understand that Boston formed a template of the pattern and process the Church uses in dealing with sex by its members.

Exposure of abuse forced the church to take increasing notice of legal challenges, and the agitation and disgust of people in the pews. The pope called all the American cardinals to Rome. The bishops met to pound out a new policy to deal with offending priests (but not with negligent bishops). Within a year over 400 priests were dismissed from active ministry. Grand Jury investigations were instituted in nine jurisdictions from New Hampshire to California. The Church's most closely guarded secret closet was blasted open. All traditional modes of authoritarian control were failing to stem the tide against a dynamic that could not be reversed.

The *Globe* investigation penetrated the massive, well-defended barricades surrounding the sacred and secret celibate culture. Once the fact of sexual activity by some priests was undeniably established in the popular awareness, where could questions end? Merely with priests who abuse minors? What of the abuse suffered by adult women and men? What is there to know about sexual experimentation by priests and bishops? What of clergy on every level of ministry who maintain long-term consensual sexual relationships of every stripe?

These questions are no longer impertinent or irrelevant to the issue of abuse of minors. Documents and investigations are uncovering proof of sexual activity by cardinals and bishops. Although these activities are not illegal, they provide mounting evidence that such behavior contributes to a web of concealment that tolerates even criminal activity in order to protect major authorities from public exposure and embarrassment.

DEEP ROOTS OF A MODERN CRISIS: CELIBACY AND SEX

Sexual abuse of minors by clergy is not a new problem. But Vatican voices blame the recent culture of sexual awareness and permissiveness that can corrupt even lofty-minded clerics. Moreover, current commentators accuse the press of running wild, chasing sensational bits and pieces of scandal, made all the more juicy because they involve men of the cloth. "Church bashing, priest bashing, Catholic bashing" became the public relations mantra of the American bishops as each new allegation of abuse became public. Other commentators claimed abusers were the subjects of a "witch hunt." Even Church spokesmen who reluctantly acknowledge that clergy abuse is a tragic problem for the Church still minimize it, and its effects on victims and on the culture of celibacy (Jenkins, 1996).

The demographics and epidemiology of sex abuse by Catholic clergy in the United States inevitably will be undertaken. Scientific methods will be used. It is not yet clear how much Church authority will help or hinder such investigations. The bishops have appointed a lay board to monitor bishops' compliance with the norms they set up in 2002 to regulate abusing priests. Hoping that laypeople would be reassured, a former FBI official coordinated the study. But that investigation reviews compliance only since 2002 and is dependent on self-reporting.

Another study that is meant to probe the causes and extent of clergy abuse also is dependent on bishops' reports. The record of bishops concealing documents and their legal maneuvers to keep records from legitimate civil authority does not bode well for a truly transparent accounting. Former Oklahoma Governor Frank Keating, Bishop Gregory's hand-picked chair of the lay board to oversee investigations, resigned his job as chair soon after he said in 2003, "I have seen an underside that I never knew existed. I have not had my faith questioned, but I certainly have concluded that a number of serious officials in my faith have very clay feet. That is disappointing and educational, but it's a fact." In the same interview he likened the behavior of the American hierarchy to "*La Cosa Nostra*" (Stammer, 2003). Perhaps only completely independent reviews, like Grand Jury reports, will be trustworthy.

No matter what studies demonstrate about the current parameters of the problem in the American Church, the long historical account of the sexual problems of Catholic clergy stands firm in the annals of Church history and law. Accounts of those problems consistently include, but are not limited to, sexual activity with minor boys. And the history of clergy sexual malfeasance and abuse is commingled with questions about clerical celibacy.

The earliest written record of any Church council is that of the provincial council of Elvira (Spain, 309). Thirty-eight of the 82 canons deal with sex and celibacy. Bishops, priests, and deacons were forbidden to have sexual relations, even, if married, with their wives. This rigorist stance is one that the Council of Nicea (325) was not willing to take—and one that

Rome was not able to decree until 1139 (Lateran II). Elvira, however, is a clear example of the essential ecclesiastical legalistic reasoning about the connection between priesthood and celibacy.

Asceticism—self-sacrifice for the love of God, the imitation of Christ, and freedom for the service of others—is the most frequently cited reason for the practice of celibacy. And indeed, that rationale is valid and has ancient roots, not primarily in the priesthood, but as a separate vocation of isolation and spiritual concentration. Due to the excellence of spiritual witness exhibited by celibate ascetics, their tradition melded easily with a parallel tradition of celibacy that did exist among some clergy.

But when celibacy came to be legislated, asceticism was not the primary rationale behind codification. In every instance of regulating clerical celibacy by law, three elements echo Elvira's thinking: paternity, property, and power. Bishops and priests should not father children. Generativity should be restricted in the service of social, political, and institutional simplicity. Preservation of Church property for the community and the perpetuation of the local church should remain unquestioned by spouse or children. Control of clergy is assured when dependence, and accountability rests on a relationship with a single superior. The system of power is consolidated by legislated celibacy—a system of checks and balances becomes an elegant bond of rewards purchased by a simple sacrifice of one's sexuality. Power over a person's sexuality confers unprecedented individual and institutional control.

This first council listed a catalogue of sexual violations along with proscriptions for the offending cleric—the heaviest penalties reserved for bishops. Up to 10 years of fasting and even excommunication (with no hope of forgiveness even at the point of death) were the severest, but were not uncommon in cases of abuse of minor boys.

Canon lawyer Thomas Doyle (2003) traces the history of clerical sexual violations from seventh and eighth century Penitential Books (handbooks containing descriptions of particular sins and recommended penances) through the Middle Ages to current Church law. Several advise that clerics who abuse young boys and girls receive up to 12 years of penance; again, abusing bishops receive the harshest punishment.

Saint Peter Damian wrote the *Book of Gomorrah* around 1049—a scathing rebuke of sexually offending clergy. He is particularly hard on superiors who countenance offenders. He recommends that sinning priests be dismissed from the priesthood. He regards contemptuously priests who defile men or boys who come to them for confession or who use the sacrament to absolve their sexual partners.

The author detailed the harm that offending clerics inflict on the Church, and pleaded with the pope to clean house. However, the pope decided to exclude only those (clerics) who had offended repeatedly and over a long period of time. Although Peter Damian had paid significant attention to the impact of the offending clerics on their victims, the pope made no mention of this and focused only on the sinfulness of clerics and their need to repent. That eleventh century scenario sounds an excruciatingly familiar ring to those who have had to play any part in sorting out the current drama.

The *Decretum Gratiani* was published in 1140. It includes specific references "to sexual violation of boys...and offers the opinion that clerics guilty of pederasty should suffer the same penalties as laymen, including the death penalty" (p. 196). The *Corpus Iuris Canonici,* published in 1234, contained all of Gratian's work besides the collection of laws enacted by a wide range of bishops. Those legislative pronouncements comprise the primary source of Church law and accurately reflect the problems of the time.

The history of the Protestant Reformation and the Council of Trent (1545–1563) record the rampant corruption of bishops and priests. It is not hyperbole to speculate that sexually and financially the Church is equally corrupt today. Reform laws then dealt directly with sexually active clerics. Sexual abuse of minors was a major concern for the council bishops who were well aware that even some recent popes had minor protégées. Two of the council canons forbidding sexual contact with minors were the primary source for current canon law. Canon 1395 specifically names sexual contact with a minor by a cleric an ecclesiastical crime.

Doyle summarizes the record:

> The historical development of legislation concerning clergy sexual abuse verifies that it has been a serious problem from the earliest years of the Church. The documentation also shows that the official Church has repeatedly attempted to deal effectively with the problem. Church leaders, especially certain popes, had acknowledged the terrible impact of sexual abuse on children and on Church membership in general. What is remarkable about these attempts is that they were made openly and memorialized in official Church documents. Such official mention of sexual abuse is clearly an indicator of the existence of the problem. There is no sense of the extent of clergy sexual abuse but one can surmise that the official notification betrays a problem of significant proportion. (Doyle, 2003, p. 197)

Church pronouncements from pope and bishops today about clerical sexual abuse ring hollow, self-serving, and frankly deceptive given the explicitness of history and their awareness of the real circumstances proven by documents wrested from secret archives. Every bishop knows sexual involvement by a priest with a minor is criminal activity. Clergy sexual abuse is neither rare nor recent in origin. Most importantly, it is not a phenomenon isolated from celibate culture nor, unfortunately, inimical to it. Celibate culture as it presently exists harbors and fosters abusers. That is why the crisis is epic.

ANOTHER COSMIC CRISIS

Without a doubt, sexual abuse of minors by clergy is an urgent issue, but it is only the symptom of a deeper and more pervasive, fundamental crisis facing the Catholic Church. The theological and scientific basis for its custom and teachings on celibacy and sexuality are inadequate and false. In spite of revised statements since Vatican II, sex remains less perfect, less noble, more tainted, spiritually suspect, and fundamentally sinful in comparison to virginity and sexual abstinence. Sexuality in clerical thought remains intrinsically flawed. Simply note the roster of men and women canonized by the Church.

Clerical celibacy is under attack not because it lacks idealism, but because it lacks sufficient reality to make it convincing. It is stultified by an incomplete recognition of the gospel tradition and retarded because of insufficient consideration of human sexual nature. This does not mean that the requirement of celibacy should be abrogated, but it does mean that it has to be structured so that it becomes a lived reality, not a sham.

There is no theology of sex in the Christian tradition, in spite of manifold moral treatises and the personal attention John Paul II has given the subject (1997). The consistent mistake theological musings persist in making is identical with the flaw in the Copernican crisis—using scripture as a basis for making scientific judgments. Scripture is inspired. It is a perpetual fountain of spiritual insight. It is not a text in biology, endocrinology, sexual or evolutionary psychology, and more. Just as it is not a text in cosmology, astronomy, astrophysics, and more.

Giordano Bruno was burnt at the stake in Rome for heresy in 1600. Prominent among his errors was his assertion that the earth traveled around the sun; he insisted it was neither static nor the center of the universe. The Roman church authorities decreed that anyone who held such a doctrine should be "anathema." In 1633 Galileo was on his knees before a Vatican court on the same charge, pleading for mercy because of his ill health. As Galileo rose—his sentence for heresy being commuted having agreed that he "might have erred" to hold that proposition—tradition has it that he whispered under his breath, *"E pur si muove"* (nevertheless, it does move) (Sobel, 1999).

The condemnation of Galileo remained on the ecclesiastical books until 1992 when Pope John Paul II exonerated Galileo, and made his own the philosophical principle that, "intelligibility, attested to by the marvelous discoveries of science and technology, leads us, in the last analysis to that transcendent and primordial thought imprinted on all things" (Sobel, 1999, p. 374).

Those "marvelous discoveries of science" and reason itself have been ignored when the Church talks about human sexual development in all of its ramifications—sexual identity, premarital and extramarital sex, marriage, and family relationships. The loss of credibility of Church authority in matters sexual is almost irreversible. The revelations surrounding clergy sexual activity is merely the crowning blow that has helped people articulate their conviction, "See, they do not understand. They do not live what they preach. You can't trust them."

The challenge of the abuse crisis cannot be contained as if it were an isolated phenomenon unrelated to the problems of clerical celibacy, and indeed, to questions about the Church's sexual teaching. The teaching in question is the official moral doctrine (against which any dissent is anathema). Namely, sexual behavior outside of marriage is sinful and that marital sexual behavior that is not open to conception is mortally sinful. And in sexual matters there is no poverty of matter.

According to this moral norm, every unmarried person is held to the same level of chaste behavior as a vowed religious or an ordained cleric. When I pointed out in a journal article that the law was "impossible"—it made everyone a sinner—the editor said that he had to "edit out" that statement since it was a "Catholic journal." Here is the hitch in the Church's inability to deal responsibly with sexuality. Chastity is the norm—perfect, but not perpetual for the layperson. Chastity forms the basis of Church teaching about sex. It ignores all that is most obvious about human development. Those who point out the irrationality of the Church teaching on sex are called heretics or worse.

Whatever the Church response to dissent, its teachings about sex remain at a pre-Copernican stage of understanding. Certainly the crisis is dire because the current moral and intellectual challenge matches that of the Reformation and Galileo. It is difficult to buck the Church and say, "You're wrong." But we no longer have to say it on our knees and whisper it under our breath.

THE INEXTRICABLE AGENDA

The Church cannot now avoid the daunting and monumental task to confront sex. Religious leaders when threatened with unsettling questions usually respond with pronouncements. That tactic will not work in the face of the current crisis. Quite simply, the Roman Catholic Church's official teaching on human sexuality in its present state cannot be validated by an act of faith, by human reason and experience, or by the sincere informed conscience of believing Christians. Robert Vitillo, S.J. put it simply, "Theologians have not yet faced the daunting task of elaborating a substantive theology of human sexuality as a creation of God who willed this to be such a strong, dominant, and constitutive element of human nature (1999)." And that theology when it is articulated must be rational, in conformity with nature, straightforward, and credible. It must be a theology that can be lived by clergy and laypeople alike.

Theologian William M. Shea of St. Louis University already in 1986 with eloquence and economy outlined the celibate/sexual agenda of the Church. He called it a tangle of issues that the Roman Catholic leadership has failed to deal with:

> Family life, divorce and remarriage, premarital and extramarital sex, birth control, abortion, homosexuality, masturbation, the role of women in ministry, their ordination to the priesthood, celibacy of the clergy, and the male monopoly of leadership. (Shea, 1986, p. 586)

Shea steered clear of the word crisis, but he was clear that sex (and a related fear and hatred of women) is the issue that "clogs" up the Catholic system.

The confusion surrounding human sexuality will not be clarified by acts of faith in official papal pronouncements. Believing the earth is the center of the universe will never make it so. No amount of emotional and spiritual empathy toward an institution grappling to absorb and incorporate new knowledge can absolve it from its obligation to renew itself and lead credibly. The opposition to Galileo rested more on theological insecurity and political controversy than on science. Changes threaten authority. But no amount of political power can turn back the demand that the celibate/sexual agenda be faced. It is the crisis of our time. Sexual abuse of minors has simply made facing the agenda unavoidable and inevitable.

REFERENCES

Berry, J. (1992). *Lead us not into temptation.* New York: Doubleday.

Damian, P. (1049). *Book of Gomorrah (Liber Gomorrhianus).* Rome: Author.

Doyle, T. P. (2003). Roman Catholic clericalism, religious duress, and clergy abuse. *Pastoral Psychology, 51,* 189–231.

Gratian, D. (1140). *Decretum Gratiani.* Rome: Author.

Investigative Staff of *The Boston Globe.* (2002). *Betrayal: The crisis in the Catholic Church.* Boston: Little, Brown and Company.

Jenkins, P. (1996). *Pedophiles and priests: Anatomy of a contemporary crisis.* Oxford: Oxford University Press.

John Paul II. (1997). *The theology of the body.* Boston: Pauline Books & Media.

Shea, W. M. (1986). The pope our brother. *Commonweal, 7,* 586–590.

Sobel, D. (1999). *Galileo's daughter.* New York: Penguin Books.

Stammer, L. (2003, June 12). Mahony resisted abuse inquiry, panelist says. Cardinal is accused of balking at the church's effort to ascertain the number of accused priests. *The Los Angeles Times.*

Vitillo, R. (1999). National AIDS conference held at Boston College.

Chapter 7

CLERGY SEXUAL ABUSE AND HOMOSEXUALITY

Gerald D. Coleman

In his 1986 landmark book *Sex in the Forbidden Zone,* psychiatrist Peter Rutter revealed a hidden "epidemic" of intimate contact in the forbidden zone. He reports on psychotherapists, physicians, and professors who had sexual involvement with their patients or students and highlights examples where professionals had trouble keeping sex out of relationships where it did not belong.

"Sex in the forbidden zone" is any sexual contact that occurs within professional relationships of trust. When trust is broken, sex becomes exploitation and abuse—literally departing from the purpose (*ab usu*) of the relationship. Rutter warns that no matter how well professionals have prepared themselves through education, training, and experience, when the "sexual magic" exerts its alluring call, one's ability to resist this temptation arises only from a capacity to recognize the harm it causes to a victim and to one's self. This conclusion is alarming when one considers that sexual abusers rarely see any harm in their actions (Connors, 2003; Feierman, 1990). James Newton Poling thus rightly names sexual abuse "evil" (Poling, 1991). It is critical to realize, then, that intellectual training is not sufficient in countering sexual abuse. Personal formation and integration must accompany academic understanding.

As this new millennium dawned, the world became aware that the forbidden zone had been crossed by a number of trusted priests who abused children. As more and more revelations came to light, *U.S. News and World Report* judged this "crossing" as an "unholy crisis" and esoteric concepts such as pedophilia and ephebophilia entered mainstream conversation. At the same time, there was the growing awareness that the majority of priests who entered the forbidden zone did so with adolescent boys, a fact that had been pointed out even before the 2002 crisis. Professor Thomas Plante wrote in 1999 that "Contrary to public perception, the vast majority of priests who sexually abuse children abuse postpubescent adolescent boys..." (p. 2).

In the public mind, clergy sex abuse of adolescent boys soon became synonymous with homosexuality, and the conclusion was reached that the core problem facing the Church was sexual abuse of adolescent boys committed by homosexual priests. As public attention was given to this judgment, many writers offered varying conclusions about the number of priests who have a homosexual orientation. In this context, it is crucial to point out that there are no reliable statistics regarding the number of priests who may identify themselves as homosexual, and estimates in this regard are usually based on anecdote rather than on valid, replicated scientific studies.

The connection between clergy sexual abuse with postpubertal children and homosexuality necessitates clarity of terminology and accuracy of understanding.

Pedophilia refers to any kind of sexual behavior between an adult and a legally underage person—generally 13 years of age and younger (American Psychiatric Association, 2000). Feierman explains that the "scientific definition...is 'sexual attraction to prepubertal children'" (Feierman, 1990, p. 3). The critical point in a pedophile's "sexual map" is the eroticized crossing of sexual boundaries along with the need to have power over another individual. The gender of the victim is normally irrelevant as (a) youth/age and (b) crossing of sexual boundaries (breaking the rules) are the major stimulants. Since the perpetrator is psychosexually immature and desires to relate to a youth as a "psychosexual peer," the gender of the victim is usually nonessential.

A pedophile sustains a psychological disorder characterized by a preference for children as sexual partners. While a fixated pedophile experiences intense and recurrent sexual desires toward children, a regressed pedophile is usually a heterosexual who under extreme stress regresses to a developmentally impaired behavior and engages in sex with children (e.g., a man whose wife is sexually unavailable turns to his daughter for sex).

Clinical and criminal evidence support the data in Philip Jenkins's *Pedophiles and Priests* (Jenkins, 1996) that the sexual abuse of a prepubescent child is "extremely rare" among priests, affecting only 0.3 percent to 1.8 percent of the entire population of Catholic clergy (i.e., only one out of 2,252 priests considered over a 30-year period was afflicted with pedophilia). He concludes that it is a myth that Catholic priests are more likely to abuse children (13 years of age and younger) than other groups of men are.

Ephebophilia refers to sexual attraction to adolescents. Plante and others point out that while sexual involvement with prepubescent children is a psychiatric disorder, sexual involvement with postpubescent adolescents is not currently considered a diagnosable psychiatric disorder (American Psychiatric Association, 2000; Plante, 1999, p. 172). At the same time, however, sexual abuse of any minor is both illegal and a grave offense against the sixth commandment. While a pedophile is an adult who desires to molest a child, an ephebophilia (or at times, hebephile) is an adult who is sexually attracted to adolescents. The terms pedophile and ephebophile must be understood as "diagnostic labels," as not all pedophiles or ephebophiles actually molest children.

There is sufficient data to demonstrate that priests who have abused adolescent boys are likely working out their needs for intimacy by approaching young teenagers with whom they feel comfortable by reason of emotional identification or whom they sensed they could seduce using the respect that belonged to their vocational identity. These priests believed that a peer or someone older could not accept them as a friend. The assertion that this type of "relationship" is an issue of homosexuality has not been substantiated by available research (Connors, 2003). Whatever the psychodynamic reasons may be, some priests who molest postpubescent boys are not, strictly speaking, acting out of a homosexual orientation. Nonetheless, a significant portion, perhaps a disproportionate percentage, of priests who molest postpubescent minors are homosexually oriented. There may well be, then, "stunted homosexuals" who represent a risk factor for acting out with adolescents.

Homosexuality refers to "a predominant, persistent, and exclusive psychosexual attraction toward members of the same sex. A homosexual person is one who feels sexual desire for and a sexual responsiveness to persons of the same sex and who seeks or would like to seek actual sexual fulfillment of this desire by sexual acts with a person of the same sex" (Reich, 1992, p. 671). The *Catechism of the Catholic Church* likewise teaches that "Homosexuality refers to relations between men or between women who experience an exclusive or predominant sexual attraction toward persons of the same sex" (Libreia Editrice Vaticana, 1994, no. 2357).

In the 1994 and 2000 editions of the *Diagnostic and Statistical Manual of Mental Disorders* (DSM-IV), the American Psychiatric Association redefined homosexuality as a "form of sexual behavior" rather than a "psychological disorder" or disposition. In 1986, the Vatican's Congregation for the Doctrine of the Faith (CDF) issued the *Letter to the Bishops of the Catholic Church on the Pastoral Care of Homosexual Persons*. Referring to its 1975 "Declaration on Certain Questions concerning Sexual Ethics," the CDF expressed concern that an "overly benign" interpretation was being given to the homosexual *orientation* (named as a tendency or inclination) and offered this corrective: "Although the particular inclination of the homosexual person is not a sin, it is a more or less strong tendency ordered toward an intrinsic moral evil; and thus the inclination itself must be seen as an objective disorder" (CDF, 1975, no. 3). The homosexual orientation is understood, then, as a "disorientation" that pushes the homosexual person toward homogeneous sex (Keenan, 2003; Rossetti & Coleman, 1997). This teaching of the Church is a philosophical rather than a psychological judgment: meaning, neither the APA nor the Church considers homosexuality a psychological disorder. Rather, the Church teaches that the homosexual orientation "pushes" the homosexual person toward behavior considered immoral (i.e., homogeneous sex). The Church likewise agrees with scientific studies that generally conclude that persons do not choose this orientation (Libreia Editrice Vaticana, 1994, no. 2358).

Dr. Gianfrancesco Zuanazzi, professor of psychology at the Pontifical Lateran University's John Paul II Institute for Studies on Marriage and Family, was reported in *L'Osservatore Romano* on April 23, 1997, to have said, "We state that a deviation (homosexuality) from the sexual norm (heterosexuality) can coexist with perfect mental functioning. In particular, homosexuality should not be regarded as an illness *per se*" (Tettamanzi, 1997). This statement provides a helpful backdrop for understanding homosexuality: while there are a significant number of people who have homosexual inclinations (Libreia Editrice Vaticana, 1994, no. 2358), their psychological functioning is in the normal range. Homosexuality and pedophilia are, then, distinct developmental paths (Tettamanzi, 1997).

Celibacy refers to the obligation placed on clerics to observe "perfect and perpetual continence for the sake of the kingdom of heaven" (Coriden, Green, & Heintschel, 2000, p. 209; John Paul II, 1992, no. 29; John Paul VI, 1967). This obligation requires abstinence from marriage *and* avoidance of all sins against the sixth commandment, *You shall not commit adultery* (Coleman, 2003). Historical perspectives on the interpretation of this commandment provide the framework that has led the Church to prohibit all forms of impurity, immodesty, and seeking venereal pleasure outside marriage. The *Catechism of the Catholic Church* lists these examples: masturbation, pornography, homosexual acts, and conjugal infidelity (Libreia Editrice Vaticana, 1994, nos. 2351–2359). Clerics who sexually abuse, therefore, sin against the sixth commandment and break their promise or vow of celibacy. A predominance of the literature interpreting the recent clergy sexual scandals has missed this point: when a cleric sexually abuses a child, he breaks his promise of celibacy and commits sin.

In his 1995 *Manual,* Dominican priest Thomas P. Doyle points out that for centuries ecclesiastical laws have listed sexual acting out with a minor by a cleric as "particularly heinous." The 1917 *Code* stresses that such an offense is particularly serious if committed by one who has the "care of souls" (Canon Law Society of America, 1983). In other words, clergy sexual abuse of children is considered in Church law to be an especially grave crime (Doyle, 2003) and a sin against celibacy.

In December 2002, the U.S. Conference of Catholic Bishops (USCCB) published *Essential Norms for Diocesan/Eparchial Policies Dealing with Allegations of Sexual Abuse of Minors by Clergy or Other Church Personnel* (USCCB, 2002). This document teaches, "Sexual abuse of a minor includes molestation or sexual exploitation of a minor and other behavior by which an adult uses a minor as an object of sexual gratification..." The judgment is given: "When even a single act of sexual abuse by a priest or deacon is admitted or is established after an appropriate process in accord with canon law, the offending priest or deacon will be removed permanently from ecclesiastical ministry, not excluding dismissal from the clerical state" (USCCB, 2002, no. 8). Compliance with these norms has resulted in the dismissal of hundreds of priests in the United States. While this seminal episcopal document does not deal explicitly with the question of homosexuality, it does lay down a strict standard regarding clergy sexual abuse of any child.

In a symposium on April 2–4, 2003, a panel of eight internationally recognized psychiatric and medical experts met in Rome and told Vatican officials that banning homosexuals from the priesthood is not the answer to the problem of the clergy sexual abuse of children. These experts maintained that although homosexuality may be a "risk factor" in this problem, homosexuality in itself is not the cause of pedophilia. Symposium member Martin P. Kafka, M.D., professor of psychiatry at the Harvard Medical School and president of the Massachusetts chapter of the Association for the Treatment of Sexual Abusers, pointed out that reliable statistics show that the majority of adult men who molest children—boys or girls—are heterosexual, although with the sexual molestation of adolescent boys, the incidence of adult male homosexuality is higher. Kafka concluded that most adult male homosexuals do not molest children or adolescents and that a person should not be banned from the priesthood simply due to a homosexual orientation. Another symposium expert, R. Karl Hanson, senior researcher in the Department of the Solicitor General of Canada, likewise concurred that homosexuality does not significantly increase the risk of sexual molestation of children or adolescents. Kafka concluded, "The great predominance of homosexual males are in no way sexual abusers" (Allen, 2003).

Predating this symposium, some commentators on the question of clergy sexual abuse overemphasized its relationship to homosexuality. In March of 2001, for example, Joaquin Navarro-Valls, M.D., official spokesperson for the Vatican, linked pedophilia and homosexuality and suggested that homosexual men could not be validly ordained. This opinion enflamed the false interpretation that all clergy sexual exploitation of male children amounted to pedophilia committed by homosexual priests. This opinion regarding the validity of the ordination of homosexual men is not seen in other commentators on this subject and is perhaps an example of a psychiatrist making a judgment outside his field of expertise.

A similar but more nuanced judgment is found in Andrew R. Baker's "Ordination and Same Sex Attraction" (Baker, 2002). Basing his argument on St. Paul's admonition: "Do not lay hands too readily on anyone" (1 Timothy 5:22 [Revised Standard Version]) and canons 1030 and 1052:3 (admission to holy orders may not take place if there exists a prudent doubt regarding the candidate's suitability; Canon Law Society of America, 1983), Msgr. Baker, a staff member of the Congregation for Bishops in Rome, concludes that the "scandal of clerical sexual abuse of minors" leads to the judgment that homosexual men (designated as S.S.A., having a same sex attraction) should not be admitted to the priesthood for several reasons: a homosexual priest will struggle with or deny Church teaching about the disordered tendency of homosexuality; he cannot constitutionally renounce marriage due to his "disorientation" which makes him "fundamentally flawed"; he cannot authentically "image God," a judgment which many rightfully consider extremely offensive; he likely manifests other serious problems such as substance abuse and sexual addiction; and he has a tendency to view other men as possible sexual partners. Regarding this latter reason, Baker argues that the all-male environment of the seminary and the priesthood present an ever-present temptation for those with a homosexual disorder. The conclusion is then reached: homosexuals do not make for good priests; and since male children are especially at a risk of being sexually abused by homosexual priests, homosexuals must be barred from the seminary and priesthood.

In a very different vein, Jon Fuller, S.J., M.D. states: "One of the deeply troubling outcomes of the Catholic Church's recent scandals involving sexual abuse...is the call from many quarters to exclude from seminaries men who are gay" (Fuller, 2002). Fuller's opinion matches that of Kafka: the exclusion of homosexuals from the priesthood "...flies in the face of simple logic. Experts have repeatedly pointed out that the sexual abuse in question—pedophilia and ephebophilia—are functions of arrested sexual development, not of a particular sexual orientation" (Fuller, 2002, pp. 7–8). Although "arrested sexual development" has been one model for understanding the etiology of pedophilia, current research suggests that the origins may be organic rather than developmental.

Important Church documents such as *Pastores Dabo Vobis* (John Paul II, 1992) support the conclusion that assiduous discernment is needed before any candidate is admitted to the seminary or priesthood. Referencing homosexuality, the 1975 declaration *Persona humana* from the Congregation for the Doctrine of the Faith mentioned two possible origins of a permanent homosexual orientation, namely, "some kind of innate instinct" or "a pathological constitution judged to be incurable" (CDF, 1975, no. 8). Even though some do not interpret homosexuality as a pathology, they are also willing to admit that it is sometimes associated with pathology and, for this reason, a more careful screening of homosexual applicants is absolutely necessary.

The *Catechism of the Catholic Church* teaches that men and women who have deep-seated homosexual tendencies "must be treated with respect, compassion, and sensitivity" (Libreia Editrice Vaticana, 1994, no. 2358). Whether persons are homosexual by "innate instinct" or "pathological constitution," therefore, every person with a homosexual orientation must be treated with understanding and sustained in the hope of overcoming any possible pathology.

We have already noted that Roman curial member Msgr. Baker maintains that homosexuals should not be admitted to the priesthood. Philadelphia's Cardinal Bevilacqua has likewise noted that "a person who is homosexually oriented is not a suitable candidate for the priesthood even if he had never committed any homosexual act." Archbishop Bertone, the former secretary of the Congregation for the Doctrine of the Faith, similarly states that "persons with a homosexual inclination should not be admitted to the seminary" (Fuller, 2002, p. 8).

In a memorandum to bishops in 1985, Cardinal William Baum, then the Prefect of the Congregation for Catholic Education affirmed, "We prefer to distinguish between practice, orientation, and temptation, the first two being counter-indications of acceptability." In the November/December 2002 publication of its *Notitiae,* the Congregation for Divine Worship and the Discipline of the Sacraments likewise states, "Those affected by the perverse inclination to homosexuality or pederasty should be excluded from religious vows and ordination" because priestly ministry would place such persons in "grave danger" (Congregation for Divine Worship and the Discipline of the Sacraments, 2002). This same point was made in 1961 by the Congregation on Religious: "Advancement to religious vows and ordination should be barred to those who are afflicted with evil tendencies to homosexuality or pederasty, since for them the common life and the priestly ministry would constitute serious dangers" (Congregation of Religious, 1961, no. 30).

We have before us, then, clear statements from Vatican authorities that homosexuals are not acceptable as candidates for the seminary or priesthood. Homosexual "practice" and "orientation" are "counter-indications" to priestly ministry. Father Stephen Rossetti, President of St. Luke's Institute in Maryland, counsels that "extreme" answers to the question of admission of homosexuals to the seminary and priesthood should be avoided: either automatic exclusion or "open inclusion as long as they have the capacity to live a celibate life" (Rossetti, 2002, p. 8). Men with a homosexual orientation, Rossetti maintains, must be "more carefully screened" due to their intrapsychic and interpersonal struggles and challenges. Psychologists Donna Markham, O.P., and Samuel Mikail agree: careful discernment distinguishes between the "secure" and "preoccupied" homosexual and concludes that the question that must be asked is "whether an individual is capable of committing with integrity to a nongenital, nonpossessive, generous life of service in response to the Gospel [punctuation added]" (Markham & Mikail, this volume).

Perhaps one avenue through this very delicate subject might have its start with the acknowledgment in the 1986 *Letter to the Bishops... on the Pastoral Care of Homosexual Persons* that "Today, the Church... refuses to consider the person as a 'heterosexual' or a 'homosexual' and insists that every person has a fundamental identity: the creature of God, and by grace, His child and heir to eternal life" (CDF, 1986, no. 16).

The *Catechism of the Catholic Church* likewise affirms: "These persons are called to fulfill God's will in their lives and, if they are Christian, to unite to the sacrifice of the Lord's Cross the difficulties they may encounter from their condition. Homosexual persons are called to chastity. By the virtues of self-mastery that teach them inner freedom, at times by the support of disinterested friendship, by prayer and sacramental graces, they can and should gradually and resolutely approach Christian perfection" (Libreia Editrice Vaticana, 1994, nos. 2358–2359).

In other words, a man with a homosexual orientation who seeks admission to the seminary or priesthood must be a person whose homosexuality does not consume his whole attention or self-definition; rather he is a man who understands himself as created by God, redeemed by grace, and fully committed to a life of self-mastery lived in chaste celibacy.

While it should be clear at this point that the homosexual orientation must be distinguished from the problem of ephebophilia, one cannot totally divorce homosexuality from this problem, as evidence demonstrates that there is a somewhat higher connection of adult male homosexuality with the abuse of adolescent boys. In addition, there are also other specific psychological and social concerns sometimes generated by or associated with homosexuality, for example, nonacceptance in one's family and culture and malice in speech and action. Consequently, while one does eliminate certain risks by not accepting homosexual candidates as seminarians or priests, this decision does not authentically address the disorder of clergy sexual abuse of children.

The *Code of Canon Law* (Canon Law Society of America [CLSA], 1983) does not cite homosexual orientation as an impediment to ordination; canon 1041:1 does name "psychic illness" as an impediment and some feel that this category matches the "objective disorder" as referenced in the *Letter to the Bishops*. However, this identification rests on faulty grounds since psychologists maintain that homosexuality is not an illness. Canon 1029 provides clear criteria for a candidate's suitability for ordination: integral faith, right intention, requisite knowledge, good reputation, integral morals, proven virtues, and other relevant physical and psychological qualities. A fundamental question remains critical: does the homosexual candidate possess these theological and natural virtues?

Every applicant to the seminary, heterosexual or homosexual, must be carefully scrutinized and evaluated. It would be misleading and harmful to think that all heterosexual candidates for the seminary are "secure" and not "preoccupied" with many factors in their lives, thus mistakenly assuming that heterosexual candidates are flawless and homosexual candidates are precarious. Respecting this point, then, the 1999 affirmation of the

Catholic Bishops of Germany, designed as an internal statement of policy, might serve as a useful tool in discerning whether or not *this* homosexual candidate is a risk:

A. Admission of a homosexual candidate cannot be considered if:

- He shows signs of personality disorders: e.g., pedophilia, obsessive-compulsive behaviors.
- He gives clear evidence that he participates in homosexual practices.
- He possesses an excessive need to speak about his sexual identity and to persuade others to accept this identity.
- He belongs to homosexual groups and speaks publicly about his homosexuality.
- His lifestyle is conspicuous by way of inappropriate friendships, attire, interests, or attachments.
- His sexuality is at the center of his identity and attention.
- He lacks understanding and empathy for those whose viewpoints about homosexuality differ from his own.

B. However, admission of a homosexual candidate might be considered if:

- He is aware of and secure in his sexual orientation.
- He possesses the intra- and inter-psychic stability to handle burdens and temptations.
- He has no need to announce his orientation.
- He can deal well with his needs for intimacy and friendship.
- He is in control of his impulses.
- He is internally and externally accepting of the Church's teaching on homosexuality.
- He evidences a mature relationship with the Church and his bishop.

"Sex in the forbidden zone" unequivocally forbids all sexual abuse and exploitation of children, indeed of any person. Sexual abuse carries a heavier weight when committed by a trusted person in authority. Unfortunately we have witnessed an array of clergy sexual abuse of children and one critical way of addressing this problem is to exclude all persons with the disorder of pedophilia from the seminary and priesthood. This conclusion does not automatically exclude homosexuals from the priesthood, although caution is needed in assessing the candidacy of a homosexual for the seminary and priesthood. John Paul II's instruction is crucial: "...candidates to the priesthood need an affective maturity, which is prudent, able to renounce anything that is a threat to it, vigilant over both body and soul, and capable of esteem and respect in interpersonal relationships between men and women" (1992, no. 44).

REFERENCES

Allen, J.L. (2003, June 6). The word from Rome. *National Catholic Reporter,* 3–4.

American Psychiatric Association. (2000). *Diagnostic and statistical manual of mental disorders* (DSM-IV) (4th ed., text rev.). Washington, DC: Author.

Baker, A.R. (2002). Ordination and same sex attraction. *America, 187,* 7–9.

Canon Law Society of America. (1983). *Code of canon law* (Latin-English ed.). Washington, DC: Author.

Coleman, G.D. (2003). Sexual abuse of a minor: A violation of the sixth commandment. *The Priest, 59,* 42–45.

Congregation for Divine Worship and the Discipline of the Sacraments. (2002). *Notitiae.* Vatican City: Author.

Congregation for the Doctrine of the Faith. (1975). *Declaration on certain questions concerning sexual ethics.* Vatican City: Author.

Congregation of Religious. (1961). *Careful selection and training of candidates for states of perfection and sacred orders.* Vatican City: Author.

Connors, C. (2003). Confronting the reality of sexual abuse. *CMSM Forum, 86,* 5–9.

Coriden, J.A., Green, T. J., & Heintschel, D.E. (Eds.). (2000). *The code of canon law.* Mahwah, NJ: Paulist Press.

Doyle, T. P. (2003). Roman Catholic clericalism, religious duress, and clergy sexual abuse. *Pastoral Psychology, 51,* 189–231.

Feierman, J. R. (Ed.). (1990). *Pedophilia: Biosocial dimensions.* New York: Springer-Verlag.

Fuller, J. (2002). Ordination and same sex attraction. *America, 187,* 11–14.

Jenkins, P. (1996). *Pedophilies and priests: Anatomy of a contemporary crisis.* New York: Oxford.

John Paul II. (1992). *Pastores dabo vobis* [I will give you shepherds]. Washington, DC: National Conference of Catholic Bishops.

John Paul VI. (1967). *Encyclical letter on priestly celibacy.* Washington, DC: National Conference of Catholic Bishops.

Keenan, J. F. (2003). The open debate: Moral theology and the lives of gay and lesbian persons. *Theological Studies, 64,* 127–150.

Libreia Editrice Vaticana. (1994). *Catechism of the Catholic Church.* Vatican City: Author.

Plante, T. G. (Ed.). (1999). *Bless me father for I have sinned: Perspectives on sexual abuse committed by Roman Catholic priests.* Westport, CT: Greenwood.

Poling, J. N. (1991). *The abuse of power.* Nashville, TN: Abington Press.

Reich, W. T. (Ed.). (1992). Homosexuality. *Encyclopedia of Bioethics* (Vol. 2, p. 671). New York: The Free Press.

Rossetti, S. J. (2002). *The Catholic Church and child sexual abuse.* New York: Liturgical Press.

Rossetti, S., & Coleman, G. D. (1997). Psychology and the Church's teaching on homosexuality. *America, 177,* 92–95, 116.

Rutter, P. (1986). *Sex in the forbidden zone.* New York: McMillan.

Tettamanzi, D. (1997). Homosexuality in the context of Christian anthropology. *L'Osservatore Romano, 1482,* 5–6.

United States Conference of Catholic Bishops. (2002). *Essential norms for diocesan/eparchial policies dealing with allegations of sexual abuse of minors by priests or deacons.* Washington, DC: Author.

Chapter 8

WHAT HAVE WE LEARNED? IMPLICATIONS FOR FUTURE RESEARCH AND FORMATION

John Allan Loftus

We have learned much more in the past two decades about the sex lives of some Roman Catholic priests than most of us ever wanted to know. Perhaps I should add immediately that the present tense is really more appropriate here: we are still learning more day-by-day than we ever wanted to know. The education is far from complete. Little is known about sex offending clergy. And interpreting what some of us think we have already learned has become a dangerous ideological sport.

ONE SIDE OF THE DEBATE

On the one side (dare I say the right-hand side), Neuhaus (2003) has emerged as a formidable interpreter. For him, the entire priest sex scandal takes on the aura of a painful but terribly predictable fall from fidelity to the orthodox teachings of the Church. His admitted mantra has become: fidelity, fidelity, fidelity. If everyone, priests and bishops, had simply been faithful to the doctrinally sound and solid Church traditions regarding sexuality, none of this would have happened. What we need are more models of "vibrant orthodoxy" to address the "doctrinal deformations at the source of the scandals" (p. 70). This is a simple, direct, and compelling (to many) critique.

But Neuhaus's broad analysis and critique does not stop here. He also takes on the psychiatric centers that tried to "treat" wayward priests; he refers derisively, for example, to "St. Luke and other centers of putative expertise on sexual pathologies" (p. 70). He also praises those who would simply ban homosexuals from any form of ministry. And, of course, the media take their hit as well: "...they have been vicious, dishonest, and guilty of violating the most elementary rules of journalistic ethics, if indeed one can still speak of journalistic ethics with a straight face" (p. 68). Andrew Greeley (2003), a figure not normally associated with this "camp," seems to agree on at least this point about the print media.

Finally, even the critics of Cardinal Law in Boston receive their chastisement. Neuhaus accosts them in their "high dudgeon" anger over Cardinal Law's letter to a serial perpetrator that the priest's ministry had been "a blessing to many people." Neuhaus reminds the critics that "the repentant priest is still a brother in Christ and ontologically—as in "a priest forever—is still a priest." Neuhaus continues: "The critics would not forgive the Cardinal for not being as mean-spirited as they are" (2003, p. 68).

Neuhaus has scores of vocal supporters and throngs of followers for this analysis. I single him out only because he is articulate and has a broad platform for his ideas. He publishes his own journal and appears regularly on television programs throughout the United States. There is an appeal to his logic; it allows us not to have to ask further or deeper questions about what is transpiring in the Church. The solution to whatever the problem might seem to be is to turn the clock back to a time when everybody just did what they were supposed to do. There, that would solve it! I do not wish to set up a straw man here; there is an obvious appeal to this way of thinking and this is, to many, an obvious and compelling course of action to take in order to stop the hemorrhaging.

An equally articulate spokesman for most of these views is George Weigel. In his recent book *The Courage to be Catholic,* he too states that while the monster of clergy sexual abuse is primarily an issue of homosexual clergy unable to keep their promises, "at its root, however, it is a crisis of fidelity" (2003, p. 22). These are relatively simple and somewhat predictable interpretations of the supposed data on clergy misconduct.

THE OTHER SIDE OF THE DEBATE

There are many voices on the other side (dare I say the left-hand side) of the analysis. And they, too, are for the most part familiar faces on the Catholic left—the "usual suspects," so to speak. Richard McBrian comes to mind as one who has been as vocal and visible in both print and television appearances as anyone.

The argument here falls along equally predictable lines. The priest sex scandal is being caused by the Church's refusal to "update" its theologies and practice around sexuality in general. Included here would be, of course, the long history of misogyny in the churches, the stubborn refusal to reconsider the ground-breaking encyclical *Humane Vitae* banning any artificial forms of birth control, mandatory celibacy for clergy, the patriarchal and thoroughly authoritarian style of governance in the Church, and usually, but not always, the need to revisit the ban on homosexual activity as seriously sinful and disordered. This has been called the "liberal litany," and has an equal number of vociferous adherents.

While not everyone in this group agrees with every one of the "updates" required to move the Church forward into the new century—the issue of gay clergy seems to be particularly neuralgic here—most view the current clergy sex scandal as a wonderful opportunity to force the Church to live up to the vision of the Second Vatican Council, which they see as inviting significant structural and doctrinal change (or at least evolution and development).

The most recently articulated "villain" in this scenario receives almost universal condemnation. It is the patriarchal, misogynist, secretive, clerical "culture" that spawns both the sexual misconduct itself and the cover-ups by authorities. The mantra here might be: reform, reform, reform (Berry, 1992, 2002; Cozzens, 2000; Dinter, 2003; Keenan, 2002).

IS THERE ANY COMMON GROUND?

These "camps" of interpretation have been playing off against each other in countless television, radio, magazine, and newspaper outlets around the world. Both sides offer sometimes plausible explanations for one or another facet of the problem. Both sides always have their own "experts." But when pushed into a corner, there is only one thing I have ever sensed as common to both sides. To be really blunt about it: few really know what they're talking about. They cannot know. The paucity of actual research into the sexual landscape of celibate clergy is staggering.

We can assume—a somewhat dangerous assumption I would argue—that the priest-offenders must be exactly like all the other "offenders" we do know something about. Then we won't have to worry about any significant differences that might actually account for peculiar variations in their behavior. We can assume that we, or "they," (meaning the scientific community), actually do understand a great deal about psychosexual dysfunctions, paraphilias (unusual sexual proclivities), and the like. But we would be greatly exaggerating the fact. The truth is that we do not know much at all about the intricacies of psychosexual development and its variants. And we know even less about how certain persons develop "skewed" maps, as John Money called them. Nor do we know whether, in fact, all the behaviors that manifest themselves as explicitly sexual are, indeed, sexual at all; the "problem" may lie elsewhere on the intra-psychic grid.

Plausible explanations for why priests engage in inappropriate sexual behaviors that are not explicitly psychosexual in their etiology have included gross immaturity, the code of secrecy inherent in priestly "culture," the cognitive dissonance that arises when predominantly gay clergy are forced to preach against their own orientation because of Church teaching on the matter, or the systemic abuse of power throughout Church structures. When it comes to reasons for the priestly "acting-out" problem, there are any number of culprits articulated by a growing number of supposedly "expert" analysts.

Let me be perfectly clear here. Regardless of the confusion regarding etiology, crimes ought to be dealt with as crimes in all circumstances. But if our goal is to enhance understanding, to promote greater protection to the vulnerable, to try to comprehend in order to be able to prevent abuses, then facile extrapolations from meager data and wildly unsubstantiated overgeneralizations will hardly serve anyone.

THE NEED FOR SCIENTIFIC, PEER-REVIEWED RESEARCH

That there is a paucity of empirical research into specifically clerical sexual offenders is hardly a new or particularly insightful observation. Both members of the churches and social scientists have been urging the collection and dissemination of more sophisticated research with the clerical population for years (Berry, 1992; Connors, 1994; Jenkins, 1996; Loftus, 1989, 1990, 1994, 1999; Loftus & Camargo, 1993; McGlone, 2000; Plante, 1999; Plante, Manuel, & Bryant, 1996; Shupe, 1995). Most recently, Laurie Goodstein of *The New York Times* (2003a) marshaled that paper's considerable research capabilities to assess the national dimensions of the clerical misconduct crisis. While providing perhaps the largest strictly numerical assessment of the problem, she, too, admits that there are so many questions that simply cannot be answered "because there are no reliable studies" (2003a, p. 20).

This fact does not stop many serious students of the crisis from offering their opinions on what the problem really might be. Anecdotal evidence abounds; reliable data do not. And as long as no one will take the responsibility to support, fund, and conduct some impartial and scientifically respectable research into priestly sexuality and celibacy, everyone's opinion seems as good as everyone else's. It is a sad state of affairs.

The recently appointed advisory committee to the American bishops on the sexual misconduct of priests has urged precisely such a research priority. But even they are quick to admit that they do not know whether any bishops or priests will cooperate and they have no place, literally, to start (Goodstein, 2003b). Could it be that there are still some people who do not want to really know? I suspect so. As the old saying goes: "There's nothing like a few good facts to ruin a perfectly acceptable theory." As regards the sexual misconduct of priests, we have plenty of theories, lots of anecdotal, therapeutic explanations, but very little fact.

Let me be clear here about the kind of research needed. We probably do know more anecdotally about priests involved in sexual misconduct than just about any other group in society. We have more information about priests, for example, than about other ministers, rabbis, teachers, Scout-leaders, and such (Plante, 1999; Plante & Daniels, in press). We do have some early ethnographic descriptions of priests and sexuality (Sipe, 1990) and a few more empirically designed attempts to gather information (Loftus & Camargo, 1993; Plante, Manuel, & Bryant, 1996). We know that not only priests are involved in age-inappropriate sexual conduct (Francis & Turner, 1995; Gonsiorek, 1995; Isley & Isley, 1990). So there is some information available. What we do not have for priests are empirically grounded, carefully designed, scientifically reliable, peer-reviewed, "hard" data about how they actually live their sexual lives as celibates.

As a result, people in all ideological camps will be able to continue to vent their theoretical explanations and ideological solutions without the burden of evidence needing to cross their minds. Unfortunately, this is as true of social scientists as of media pundits. I, too, am often enough tempted to offer my own clinical experience and supposed expertise with priest-perpetrators as a generalized portrait of priesthood—or at least priests who sexually offend. But my experience offers no generalizable picture of all priests; nor does it even offer a generalizable picture of all priest-offenders. And neither does anyone else's experience. We are all in desperate need of more information and much more carefully designed and executed research studies with priests. This does not make for "good copy," but it is sadly the fact about the state of our understanding of priests involved in sexual misconduct. Yes, we all know now that the scope of the problem is broader than many would have expected; the newspapers tell us that much. But do we understand the phenomenon any better?

We have all seen the compelling press reports about a few priests who do seem to fit the standard pictures of other, non-clergy, sexual offenders. Some of these priests look an awful lot like your average sexual molester about whom we do know a good deal more scientifically; they seem to be either "classic" pedophiles or serial sexual predators. These are, to be sure, a dangerous lot. But among priests, these represent a tiny percentage of an already relatively small percentage of priests implicated in sexual misconduct of one kind or another. They may not be at all representative of priests struggling to contain or express sexual impulses in inappropriate ways. They may be the tip of an iceberg; but they also may be just one relatively small iceberg in a much more troubling sea of freezing swells. We just do not know—yet.

There have been several important and sound research studies on or about priesthood in general or about other specific questions, like whether priests are happy in their vocations, or what makes them leave active ministry. So we know research can be done with this population. A landmark study was conducted in 1972 by Greeley and associates; the report was called *The Catholic Priest in the United States: Sociological Investigations.* This report focused on priestly motivation and resignations. A second study in that same year concluded that priests were "normal" psychologically and not very different from other men surveyed (Kennedy & Heckler, 1972). In 1999 the National Organization for Continuing Education of Roman Catholic Clergy (NOCERCC) commissioned a review of research on newly ordained priests (Hoge, 1999). And there have been several other attempts to gain some baseline information on priests (Hedin, 1995; O'Rourke, 1978).

Hoge's recent study, *The First Five Years of the Priesthood* (2002), draws some interesting conclusions that are germane to the discussion of priests and sexual misconduct. Both resigned and still-active priests made remarkably similar recommendations; Hoge calls their unanimity "an important groundswell" (p. 96). They recommended, first, the need for more openness about sexuality in seminaries: "Seminaries need more open discussion of sexuality in general and of topics such as celibacy and homosexuality in particular" (p. 96). And second, more realistic seminary training is needed.

Hoge concludes his study with a litany of explicitly sexual issues that "[cry] out for more openness and more research" (p. 103). He also suggests that "the situation today is new." With respect to explicitly sexual issues, "either past researchers did not find the same level of concern, or they hesitated to report what they heard" (p. 102).

There is simply too much we do not yet know about this population of priests; there is even less we know about how this population understands and handles issues of sexuality, celibacy, and affectivity in general. And, to repeat, we know practically nothing scientifically about the subset of priests who have become involved in overt sexual misconduct.

The sad conclusion: take with a large grain of salt all of the so-called experts (myself and my colleagues in this volume included) who share their insights—valuable as many of them are—as fact. The reality is that many of us are trying to share experiences, hypotheses, and theories that seem to us to account for some of the behavior we see; no one of us has a large enough or scientifically reliable enough data base on which to actually draw conclusions.

Many people have different theories about the Church, about what should be changed, about what must stay the same, about structure, and so on. It may be that there is no simple right or wrong here (although I, too, have my own opinions). But do not let a personal, theoretical, or theological agenda masquerade as social science fact. The scientific links between our present understanding of the clerical sexual misconduct scandal and the need for whole-scale sociological and ideological change in the Church is tenuous at best. At the same time, the assertion that just leaving everything in the Church the way it was 50 years ago will solve the current crisis has absolutely no social science backing either.

I again urge bishops and priests themselves to cooperate fully with whatever respectable social science research project asks their help. And I urge my colleagues in the social science community to continue to try to design and conduct responsible and careful research into this population. This is the only way we will ever begin to evolve beyond rumor to understanding.

WHAT OF THE NEXT GENERATION OF PRIESTS?

While the social science community has its work cut out for it in detailing the specifics of the crisis (detection, diagnosis, treatment, prevention), the churches cannot avoid their own responsibility—either for the present or the future. One of the most important questions that has been asked in the current climate concerns the next generation of clergy. How will they be better educated and better experientially "formed" than so many of their predecessors? Or, perhaps the real question is, will they be?

There has been a long-standing conviction voiced by many of us who have worked with clergy for decades. Many of these priests and seminarians appeared woefully out of touch with important dimensions of their affective lives, particularly their own sexuality (Connors, 1994; Loftus, 1989, 1990, 1994; Sipe, 1990, 1995). A good number had understandings of their celibate commitment that seemed overly intellectualized at best, and fundamentally flawed at worst. Sipe (1990), Hoge (2002), and Dinter (2003) all point out this potentially very dangerous situation.

Dinter's very recent book, *The Other Side of the Altar: One Man's Life in the Catholic Priesthood,* paints a particularly painful picture of his personal experiences in this regard. He comments of his seminary experience that "in ways I would not understand for years, the whole seminary culture existed on a foundation of prolonged latency" (p. 34). He says further that the problem was "not so much a single-sex environment as a no-sex environment, not anybody's sex, not even ours" (p. 32). In commenting on one recent sexual misconduct case involving a bishop, Dinter is able to say so simply that "in cases like this, the sexual acting out seems to represent the clumsy groping of older men, emotionally and sexually fixated in adolescence, who took advantage of confused and ignorant boys" (p. 71). This description is, again, only anecdotal, one man's experience that can hardly be extrapolated to indict all seminaries of all times, but it does raise frightening questions about what is being done in seminaries to prepare men for their celibate commitment.

Has anything changed since Dinter's days in seminary? Are today's teachings about and understandings of celibacy any more compelling, freeing, energizing? These are terribly important questions that may only be receiving a reluctant and superficial airing in many quarters.

ENDING THE SILENCE

There seems to be a growing consensus that at the very least more open dialogue about sexual issues must be not only allowed but also encouraged in seminary training. The old adage that "what you don't know can't hurt you" seems to have been thoroughly unmasked in the current climate.

Others push the issue further. Psychiatrist and long-time contributor to the Catholic dialogue on sexuality in the English-speaking world, Dr. Jack Dominion, gets more pointed in his call for openness and dialogue. He wants not only more openness in seminary training, he wants a wholesale re-examination of sexual teaching. In his letter to the editor of the *Tablet,* he says that "the crisis over clerical sexual abuse gives us the opportunity to re-examine the theology of sexuality" (2003, p. 19). He continues, "I see a lack of integrity about sex prevalent in the Church. The teaching on contraception, masturbation, and homosexuality is defective, and the whole meaning of sexual intercourse is insufficiently developed" (p. 19).

He is not alone. Theologian Sidney Callahan recently offered much the same viewpoint in the *National Catholic Reporter* (2003). The piece is entitled, "Stunted Teaching on Sex Has Role in Church's Crisis." In it she acknowledges the "traditionalist" approach to turning back the clock as attractive to some, but then dismisses it as a foolhardy attempt to reassert an older fear and disdain for sexuality as a whole. "I see the present teachings on sex and gender as contributing to the current disarray. The last thing we need is a reaffirmation of rigid teachings, which are seriously flawed morally and theologically" (p. 22). And further: "All of these lingering denigrations of sexuality and women have played a part in the sex abuse crisis.... Future priests could hardly be well prepared for the challenges of mature chastity, interpersonal integrity or ministry to the married" (p. 22).

The deafening silence about sexuality in the Church must be broken. It is so clearly no longer enough to reiterate simple moral injunctions; it is so clearly no longer enough to depend on woefully antiquated theories about sexuality; it is so clearly no longer enough to hide behind theologies almost completely divorced from the body. The irony is that there is much positive and healthy that the Church can share about human sexuality. There is a long and honored tradition from which to speak about wholeness and health. "Our religious tradition is both holy and wounded—and some of its wounds are self-inflicted" (Whitehead & Whitehead, 2001).

The self-inflicted nature of some of the recent wounds stems from the inability of the Church to break the silence about sexuality—in all its myriad forms. As the Whiteheads make their case for such an open and fresh exploration of sex in the churches, their starting point is theological. "As the body of Christ, the Christian community carries a shared wisdom about sex and love, a wisdom born of our efforts to have God's word shape our sexuality" (2001, p. 3). There is much positive and hopeful that can be said. But it first has to be spoken aloud. This is particularly true for the experiences of sexuality that actually shape the celibate priesthood.

A PLEA FOR DIALOGUE AND OPENNESS

I often feel as if I have been saying the same things over and over again for the past 15 years. A good friend suggested that is only because it is true.

How can we continue to be so afraid of knowledge, of greater understanding, of openness and truth regarding sexuality in the priesthood? What possible revelations about priests could be worse than what many assume is true already? What possible damage could be caused by open conversation about sexuality that has not already been caused?

Of what are we in the churches so afraid? That we might find out some priests do not observe their public commitments? We already know that. That we might find out some priests molest children? We know that too. That we might find out significant numbers of clergy are gay? Hardly news. We even know that large numbers of laity find the whole Church "thing" on sex almost completely irrelevant to their lives. And we know further that we all live in a culture that is both sexually repressive and sexually obsessed at the same time—that our society is hypocritical, deceitful, and dangerous when it comes to sex. Would it not be nice to know more about all this, and to know it more clearly and objectively? There has never been a better opportunity for dialogue, and both the Church and culture could benefit.

What have we learned from the present crisis? I hope at least one thing we are learning is that there is a clear and pressing need to know more. We must support more research, both inside the Church and within the social science community of scholars. And we must open the doors and windows of church buildings—especially seminaries—to allow unfettered access to the experienced thoughts, feelings, and behaviors surrounding issues of sexuality.

Both the Church and society at large need to learn much more about the etiology, dynamics, and finally the preventive strategies that might work to curtail the tragedy that has become so damaging to so many. But there has often been an overbearing arrogance on the part of both Church authorities and social scientists that has kept both from much mutually enriching dialogue. Neither has benefited. Now more than ever does each need the other. The Church to understand itself and its members better; science to advance into new arenas of understanding in order to improve, and make more safe, life for us all. They can become more interdependent in this search to the benefit of all.

Edith Wharton once observed: "There are two ways of spreading light: to be the candle or the mirror that reflects it" (1902, p. 340). It matters little whether researchers or religionists shine the brightest or shine first; what does matter is that the light grows.

REFERENCES

Berry, J. (1992). *Lead us not into temptation: Catholic priests and the sexual abuse of children.* New York: Doubleday.

Berry, J. (2002, April 3). Secrets, celibacy and the church. *New York Times,* p. 24.

Callahan, S. (2003). Stunted teaching on sex has role in church's crisis. *National Catholic Reporter, 39,* 22.

Connors, C. (1994). Keynote address to the National Catholic Council on Alcoholism. Washington, DC: St. Luke's Institute.

Cozzens, D. (2000). *The changing face of the priesthood.* Collegeville, MN: Liturgical Press.

Dinter, P. (2003). *The other side of the altar: One man's life in the Catholic priesthood.* New York: Farrar, Straus & Giroux.

Dominion, Jack. (2003, March 15). Challenged on sex. *The Tablet,* 19.

Francis, P.C., & Turner, N.R. (1995). Sexual misconduct within the Christian church: Who are the perpetrators and those they victimize? *Counselling & Values, 39,* 218–227.

Gonsiorek, J.C. (Ed.). (1995). *Breach of trust: Sexual exploitation by health care professionals and clergy.* Newbury Park, CA: Sage.

Goodstein, L. (2003a, January 12). Trial of pain in church crisis leads to nearly every diocese. *New York Times,* pp. 1, 21, 22.

Goodstein, L. (2003b, March 12). Catholic group picks academic team to study problem of sexual abuse. *New York Times,* p. 19.

Greeley, A.M. (1972). *The Catholic priest in the United States: Sociological investigations.* Washington, DC: United States Catholic Conference.

Greeley, A.M. (2003, February 10). The times and sexual abuse by priests. *America, 188,* 16–17.

Hedin, R. (1995). *Married to the church.* Bloomington, IN: Indiana University Press.

Hoge, D. (1999). *Expressed needs and attitudes of newly ordained priests.* Chicago: National Organization for Continuing Education of Roman Catholic Clergy.

Hoge, D. (2002). *The first five years of the priesthood: a study of newly ordained catholic priests.* Collegeville, MN: The Liturgical Press.

Isley, P. J., & Isley, P. (1990). The sexual abuse of male children by church personnel: Intervention and prevention. *Pastoral Psychology, 39,* 85–98.

Jenkins, P. (1996). *Pedophiles and priests.* New York: Cambridge University Press.

Keenan, J. (2002, March 30). The purge of Boston. *The Tablet,* 17–19.

Kennedy, E., & Heckler, V. (1972). *The Catholic priest in the United States: Psychological investigations.* Washington, DC: United States Catholic Conference.

Loftus, J. A. (1989). *Sexual abuse in the church: A quest for understanding.* Aurora, ON: Emmanuel Convalescent Foundation.

Loftus, J. A. (1990, December 1). A question of disillusionment: Sexual abuse among the clergy. *America,* 426–429.

Loftus, J. A. (1994). *Sexual misconduct among clergy: A handbook for ministers.* Washington, DC: The Pastoral Press.

Loftus, J. A. (1999). Sexuality in priesthood: noli me tangere. In T. Plante (Ed.), *Bless me father for I have sinned: Perspectives on sexual abuse committted by Roman Catholic priests.* Westport, CT: Praeger/Greenwood.

Loftus, J. A., & Camargo, R. J. (1993). Treating the clergy. *Annals of Sex Research, 6,* 287–303.

McGlone, G. J. (2000). Sexually offending Roman Catholic priests: Characterization and analysis. Unpublished doctoral dissertation, California School of Professional Psychology, San Diego.

Neuhaus, J. N. (2003). The public square: Boston and other bishops. *First Things, 130,* 67–70.

O'Rourke, D. (1978). *The first year of priesthood.* Huntington, IN: Our Sunday Visitor Press.

Paul VI. (1968). *Humane vitae: Encyclical of Pope Paul VI on the regulation of birth.* Vatican City: Author.

Plante, T. G. (Ed.). (1999). *Bless me father for I have sinned: Perspectives on sexual abuse commited by Roman Catholic priests.* Westport, CT: Praeger/Greenwood.

Plante, T. G., & Daniels, C. (in press). The sexual abuse crisis in the Roman Catholic church: What psychologists should know. *Pastoral Psychology.*

Plante, T. G., Manuel, G. M., & Bryant, C. (1996). Personality and cognitive functioning among sexual offending Roman Catholic priests. *Pastoral Psychology, 45,* 129–139.

Shupe, A. (1995). *In the name of all that's holy: A theory of clergy malfeasance.* Westport, CT: Praeger.

Sipe, A. W. R. (1990). *A secret world: Sexuality and the search for celibacy.* New York: Brunner/Mazel.

Sipe, A. W. R. (1995). *Sex, priests, and power: Anatomy of a crisis.* New York: Brunner/Mazel.

Weigel, G. (2003). *The courage to be Catholic: Crisis, reform, and the future of the church.* New York: Basic Books.

Wharton, E. (1902). Vasalius in Zante. *North American Review, 175,* 625–631.

Whitehead, E., & Whitehead, J. (2001). *Wisdom of the body: Making sense of our sexuality.* New York: Crossroads.

Chapter 9

SURVIVORS NETWORK OF THOSE ABUSED BY PRIESTS (SNAP): AN ACTION PLAN

David Clohessy and Michael Wegs

The Survivors Network of those Abused by Priests (SNAP), and similar volunteer self-help organizations, have been established to nurture and revitalize survivors/victims of clergy abuse—countering the unsatisfactory attitude and behavior of the Roman Catholic Church and most specifically, many of the American bishops.

SNAP was established in 1989 by Barbara Blaine of Toledo, Ohio. She reported that she was sexually assaulted in the seventh grade by a priest affiliated with the Oblates of St. Francis de Sales. As an adult, Blaine successfully forced the Diocese of Toledo and the Oblates to settle her case out of court. By happenstance, Blaine's work coincided with the convictions of two notorious priest sex offenders implicated in the scandals of the 1980s and 1990s: Father Gilbert Gauthé, (Lafayette, Louisiana) and Father James R. Porter (Fall River, Massachusetts).

These cases prompted more survivors/victims to share their pain and suffering with therapists, psychiatrists, spouses, partners, parents, siblings, friends, and attorneys. SNAP—and others—also began to realize that Catholic bishops and religious superiors were involved on a massive scale in possible criminal activity such as concealing evidence, witness tampering, and shuffling ordained sexual predators to other churches.

Today the Survivors Network of those Abused by Priests is the nation's largest volunteer, self-help support organization providing comfort to survivors/victims of clergy molestations. SNAP has more than 4,500 members in 55 active chapters in the United States. Each chapter provides a place for healing and solace where survivors/victims may share their stories and begin to recover their souls of lost innocence that, sadly, were often taken from them under the guise of friendship and trust.

SNAP: A CATHOLIC RESPONSE TO AMERICA'S BISHOPS

The current generation of American Roman Catholics has endured the result of more than 100 years of mismanagement by the institutional Church. But they've only discovered the hierarchy's dereliction of duty and their duplicity and mendacity, or plausible deniability, in the last 20 years.

Will the millennial church change course? Or will faithful Catholics continue to challenge this conspiracy of silence and secrecy in order to protect their own children and others from criminal priests? As long as the bishops refuse to deal honestly with the victimization of children that they facilitated, American Catholics can find no peace or consolation.

A SNAP STRATEGIC ACTION PLAN

The Survivors Network of those Abused by Priests strategy for protecting children from predatory priests remains unchanged from the twentieth century to the twenty-first century. A commentary published in the June 13, 2002, edition of *USA Today* addresses this strategic action plan. "Whatever the bishops and the Vatican decide, it must be made clear that they do not have the last word," SNAP policy advisor Michael D. Fleming penned.

"Despite their protestations about clerical privilege, the mandate of canon law, or dual citizenship of prelates, the Church is not on the bench now, it is in the dock. SNAP...encourages the bishops to begin the process of becoming good citizens, but the role of citizens, legislatures, and courts is even more crucial," Fleming continued. "Reform from within the Church is desirable, necessary, and probably inevitable. But if the...bishops...take just one thought away, it must be that, when criminal matters are involved, the Church does not rule; it must obey."

If the millennial Church is to move forward responsibly rather than step back into a scandalous past of child abuse, the hierarchy must begin an honest and respectful collaboration with survivors/victims and the civil authorities. Without this moral covenant with the laity, the hierarchy will never rise above the suffocating mendacity of the last 20 years.

To this end, SNAP believes that the simple action plan is the correct strategy that the bishops of the United States ought to embrace for the safety of children and the protection of the faith.

1. Support the end to statutes of limitations affecting the sexual abuse of children and vulnerable adults, just as it is with murder. As victims have slowly, painfully made the decision to take their cases to court, the Church has used these statutes as a weapon to bar the door to pedophile priests.

2. State legislatures and the federal government must make clergy mandated reporters of child abuse, as are physicians, social workers, even hairdressers in some states. The Church must not be allowed to wave the flag of priest-penitent privilege: the interests of victims outweigh the interest of the Church in laundering its dirty linen in secret. The duty to report crime is incumbent on every citizen, not merely a suggestion that is subject to a bishop's whim or Vatican approval.

3. Hold the bishops accountable. It is now clear that the American hierarchy not only willingly chose to conceal records of abuse from parishioners and the civil authorities, but also engaged in trafficking predators from parish to parish and even from diocese to diocese (Palm Beach, Florida; Phoenix, Arizona; Santa Fe, New Mexico; and Amarillo, Texas, have been identified via media reports and legal actions). As prosecutors file charges, they should consider bishops as co-conspirators, or even principals, based upon their willful involvement in concealing criminal activity.

4. The judiciary and state legislatures should revise employment and criminal statutes that allow the hierarchy to escape punishment.

5. State legislatures must revise charitable-immunity laws, such as Massachusetts', which may make it impossible for any survivor/victim to recover more than $20,000 at the settlement phase of litigation. These laws, enacted to protect the charitable activities of religious organizations, schools, and social-service agencies, have too often created an unbreachable wall behind which the hierarchy continues to hide.

6. Turn over all criminal allegations to the police and prosecutors.

7. Swiftly, severely, and publicly discipline any Church staff member who is discovered to have kept quiet about questionable behavior.

8. Revise privacy laws to exempt pedophile allegations and force the hierarchy to open personnel records to the civil authorities when a crime is reported.

9. Confessed pedophile clergymen must be tried and sentenced in a court of law. The Church must expel priests, deacons, and monks from min-

istry just as teachers, doctors, and lawyers are not permitted to continue their profession when convicted of pedophile crimes.

10. Open financial records dating back to 1960 to independent auditors for a public accounting of expenses paid to resolve sexual crimes.

11. Appoint SNAP members to clergy sexual abuse committees.

12. Attend SNAP meetings on a regular basis to provide pastoral care to survivors/victims.

13. Conduct listening sessions with SNAP members in all parishes where a sexual predator has served. The underlying issue of clergy sex crimes for Catholics, in particular, is that the abuse is also equated with incest. Incest destroys the fidelity of family life: most relatives do not believe the victim; some feel sympathy but are unable to accept the truth; maybe one or two relatives believe. This issue is like lead paint or asbestos. The debris must be removed before the restoration can begin.

14. Review annually with the laity significant information regarding administrative and financial protocol and records. As "shareholders" Roman Catholics deserve a "plain English annual report" that details the financial and business activities of their own diocese. The bishops have demonstrated that they cannot be trusted to protect children; they should not have sole access to the diocesan investment portfolio, which many consider as their own private piggy bank.

15. Publish SNAP meeting schedules in all parish bulletins, diocesan publications, and on Church websites.

16. Designate Abuse Prevention Sunday, in which every priest educates parents about the need to talk with their children about how to protect themselves and what to do if someone tries to molest them.

17. Provide written materials in all churches and schools about "safe touch" and abuse-prevention strategies for parents.

18. Publicly urge victims to report their abuse to civil and criminal authorities (instead of or in addition to Church officials).

19. Encourage and support the publication of survivors' writings, journals, and collected stories, as well as survivor research.

20. Regularly invite local SNAP leaders to make presentations at diocesan training conferences for priests and laity to promote the exchange and collaboration of information and ideas.

21. Regularly invite local SNAP chapters to make presentations to seminarians to support the development and formation of their vocations.

22. Every state Catholic conference of bishops should publish a pastoral letter about the sexual abuse crisis.

Chapter 10

PERPETRATORS OF CLERGY ABUSE OF MINORS: INSIGHTS FROM ATTACHMENT THEORY

Donna J. Markham and Samuel F. Mikail

Sexual abuse of a child by a trusted adult is a horrific and inexcusable act, regardless of the circumstances that may have contributed to the abuser's actions. The impact of such actions on victims most certainly can be tragic and long-lasting. Indeed, there exists a significant body of literature attesting to the noxious impact of sexual abuse on the relational lives of victims (Briere, 1996). Given the gravity of the consequences for victims, Church officials have attempted to make sweeping efforts to remove clergy with any history of sexual involvement with a minor from their ministerial roles. This decision, warranted by the egregious mismanagement by some Church officials, nevertheless makes no room for diagnostic distinctions, the possibility for healing, redemption, or forgiveness; it also disregards the nature of the action, treatment outcome, and prognosis or likelihood of harming anyone again. While the unconditional removal from ministry of clergy with a history of sexual involvement with a minor reflects a pervasive axiom of contemporary behavioral science that stipulates that the best predictor of future behavior is past behavior, our clinical experience has raised questions about this. In the following article, we will attempt to shed some light on this complex situation.

While many theoretical approaches offer assistance in attempting to comprehend the underlying reasons for this tragic situation, we have found insights from research on adult attachment to be particularly beneficial. Prior to examining case material, we would like to elucidate our reasons for making use of this particular theoretical framework. Extensive empirical research has demonstrated that child molesters exhibit a compromised capacity for intimacy and deficits in secure attachment. Seidman, Marshall, Hudson, and Robertson (1994) conducted a series of studies in which they found sex offenders scored lower on measures of intimacy and higher on measures of loneliness than spousal abusers or men in a nonclinical sample. Garlick, Marshall, and Thornton (1996) reported similar findings. Bumby and Hansen (1997) found that child molesters expressed a greater fear of intimacy than any other group of sexual offenders. They also exhibited higher levels of emotional and social loneliness relative to several comparison groups. Interestingly, child molesters were reported to defensively externalize blame in situations of interpersonal conflict or tension (Garlick et al., 1996). In an earlier study Marshall, Barbaree, and Fernandez (1995) reported that child molesters exhibited low self-confidence, social anxiety, and a lack of assertiveness, suggesting significantly compromised social functioning.

Our experience with clergy sex abusers resonates deeply with such findings. The prevalence of loneliness, the lack of rewarding close adult relationships, and the overidentification with the clerical role—thus subordinating a developed positive sense of self—are characteristic of most abusive clergy with whom we have worked. The research by Marshall's group supports our observations that the clergy child abuser exists in a chronic state of anxiety, particularly when relating with adults.

Attachment theory underscores the primacy of emotional attachment in understanding human adaptation and the role of relationship as a source of security in response to experiences of felt anxiety. Attachment behavior has been characterized as a means of establishing a state of security when faced with heightened stress or threat by seeking out supportive others (Johnson & Whiffen, 1999). Our clinical experience has revealed that the child abuser frequently gravitates toward children in an effort to feel a sense of mastery and competence. Such seriously distorted and abusive sexual contact with the child is viewed as a source of affection, affirmation, and security. The abuser perceives the child "partner" as socially and emotionally accepting and nonthreatening.

CLINICAL SETTING

Over the past 36 years, more than 5,000 Church professionals, referred from across the English-speaking world and representing many nationalities and ethnic backgrounds, have been treated at the Southdown Institute, an accredited, residential mental health facility located near Toronto,

Ontario. The inpatient facility at the Institute consists of a 48-bed, not-for-profit, and fee-for-service program that functions independent of any church structure. Services are provided to male and female patients exhibiting a variety of emotional disorders and addictions. The majority present with co-morbid Axis I and Axis II diagnoses as delineated in the *Diagnostic and Statistical Manual of Mental Disorders* (DSM-IV), Fourth Edition (American Psychiatric Association, 2000). Many have not responded adequately to outpatient treatment; some live in parts of the world where there is little or no access to mental health care. Approximately half the cases have been males, 12 percent of who presented with an incident or incidents of sexual abuse of a minor and 3 percent of who met the DSM-IV criteria for a diagnosis of pedophilia.

The residential program is primarily psychodynamically oriented and consists of intensive individual and group psychotherapy conducted predominantly by doctoral-level clinicians. Treatment is multidisciplinary, incorporating biological and interpersonal interventions, along with vocational discernment and pastoral counseling, generally over the course of four to six months. Patients presenting with sexual misconduct issues are placed additionally in a focused, confrontational, cognitive-behavioral group and attend various psycho-educational sessions directed toward heightening their capacity for victim-empathy and toward developing their capacity for establishing adult relationships. In order to facilitate post-discharge planning and the consolidation of treatment gains, regular consultations are conducted, which include the patient, clinical staff, and religious superiors.

In reviewing the cases of clergy who have been removed from ministry during the past year and referred to our facility, we are struck by the fact that the majority of the cases involve incidents that occurred between 20 and 30 years ago when the priest was in his twenties or thirties, and that incidents of abuse have seemingly not recurred in the ensuing decades. As clinicians, we are faced with two histories that are grossly at odds: the time during which the individual was abusive and the long period following when there appears to be no evidence of abuse. In many of these apparently non-repetitive cases, the priest received intensive psychotherapy, participated in 12-Step groups, and regularly sought out spiritual direction. It would appear—and is supported by anecdotal historical accounts—that these priests have achieved a level of healthy relational and emotional integration and spiritual functioning whereby it would be extremely unlikely that they would harm a child or vulnerable adult. On the other hand, we are also tragically aware that there are priests who engaged in predatory, serial abuse of minors. Our data indicate approximately three percent of the men we have treated fall into this category. These individuals must never again have access to minors and should not hold a fiduciary social role. So which historical decade of an offending priest's life should clinicians and/or bishops draw on in their efforts to anticipate future behavior? What are the diagnostic indicators that support "high risk"? It is this dilemma that we hope to address through examining the priest's capacity to form healthy relational attachments.

In working with clergy who have been perpetrators of sexual abuse, it has become clinically evident that there is a wide range of psychodynamic factors that have bearing on treatment outcome and risk of re-offending. While rigorous empirical analysis remains to be undertaken, some elucidation of the dynamics at work within these individuals may serve to shed light on this problem. Three cases will be presented and examined using attachment style as a lens through which to gain insight concerning treatability and risk assessment. Distinctions will also be made based upon considerations of successful achievement of treatment indices.

ATTACHMENT BEHAVIOR, ATTACHMENT STYLES, AND THE PRIEST ABUSER

Bartholomew and Horowitz (1991) distinguished four styles of attachment behavior which they termed "secure," "dismissive," "preoccupied," and "fearful." Their formulation was based on Bowlby's (1973) hypothesis that attachment styles stem from two underlying dimensions: anxiety and avoidance. Anxiety reflects one's sense of self-worth and beliefs about the extent to which the self is accepted or rejected by others, while avoidance refers to one's tolerance of intimacy and interdependence. Bartholomew and Horowitz (1991) suggested that *securely attached* individuals have a positive view of self and their intimate others, and are free of anxiety in their efforts to establish intimacy and interdependence.

Preoccupied individuals possess a negative view of self and a positive view of intimate partners (Griffin & Bartholomew, 1994). They display a high degree of anxiety and low levels of avoidance. Their anxiety is born out of a strong desire for closeness (i.e., low avoidance) coupled with a fear of rejection (i.e., a firm belief that the self is unacceptable). Our clinical experience suggests that priests exhibiting preoccupied attachment tend to be at greater risk for entering relationships in which personal and professional boundaries become blurred. At times of heightened vulnerability these men's need for affirmation, approval, and acceptance can lead them to assume a stance of affable submissiveness that serves to diminish their authority and denies their power. When a priest assumes such a position in a relationship with a vulnerable minor, who may or may not have a compromised attachment history, the possibility of boundary violation, due to the impact of the priest's fiduciary role, increases significantly.

Dismissive individuals have a positive self-image and view others negatively (Griffin & Bartholomew, 1994). Overtly, these individuals display low levels of attachment-related anxiety and tend to avoid intimacy and interdependence. This pattern of avoidance is built on an expectation that others cannot be relied on. Their inflated self-presentation is maintained by viewing others as incapable of responding adequately to expressed needs. The strong conviction that the self is worthy and valuable equips these individuals with the capacity to be aware of their instrumental needs, though perhaps not their emotional needs. Clergy with dismissive attachment are likely to possess a narcissistic personality organization that may include considerable sociopathic features. Their limited capacity to identify emotional needs makes it likely that they will rely on the use of compartmentalization as a primary defense against emotional pain. These individuals are often unable to achieve a healthy integration of their sexuality and spirituality. Sexual needs are likely to be experienced as biological drives devoid of a need for emotional connection or intimacy. Their narcissistic stance propels them to view others as objects or a means to an end, thus heightening the possibility of them engaging in exploitative, abusive behavior toward vulnerable others. It should be noted that consistent with this position is a profoundly diminished capacity for empathy.

Fearful individuals have a negative view of self and intimate others. They exhibit high levels of attachment anxiety and avoidance (Griffin & Bartholomew, 1994). Even though they desire close relationships, their avoidance of intimacy is driven by a fear of rejection and abandonment. Fearful individuals view themselves as unworthy of caring, concern, and believe that they have little intrinsic value to others. Similarly, they perceive others as either disinterested and unavailable or as incapable of offering help. This constellation of beliefs contributes to a chronic state of fear and anxiety. Fearful individuals experience an ongoing devaluing of themselves that results in an inability to identify and recognize basic needs. Thus, in the face of distress, needs are likely to be undefined and experienced as unspecified, generalized anxiety. The expectation that others are unavailable and unresponsive further exacerbates this situation. Thus, they are prone to keep silent about what vague needs they may have. Priests having a fearful attachment style tend to objectify both the self and the other. They view themselves in a mechanistic and somewhat autistic manner. They believe that they are to "do and serve," with little attention directed toward their own emotional and spiritual lives. Their expectation is that others are there to take from them, yet seldom give. Their relational history is often marked by experiences of abuse and neglect and these become the templates from which they engage others, desperately seeking out nurturance from less powerful others who will not hurt them.

ATTACHMENT STYLE AS A BASIS FOR PREDICTING SEXUAL OFFENSES

Hanson and Bussiere (1998) conducted a meta-analysis of 61 studies that examined predictors of recidivism among sexual offenders. The authors identified several variables that predicted relapse in this population. Two demographic variables found to be useful were age (the younger the offender at the time of first offense, the higher the likelihood of recidivism) and marital status (offenders who were single were more likely to re-offend sexually). Within the structure of celibate clerical life, the latter variable would seem to correlate with the presence of stable social and emotional supports, rather than with their "single state." That is, we have found that clergy who were able to establish close adult friendships were far less likely to have become involved in sexual abuse of any sort.

Hanson and Bussiere noted that extra-familial child molesters tend to exhibit limited victim empathy. Within the clinical context, priests diag-nosed as pedophiles often justified their actions by suggesting that they were teaching the victim about sex. Their primary focus was directed toward a gratification of their needs, be they sexual or a need for domi-nance and control, and they demonstrated little, if any, concern about the well-being of the child. We believe these characteristics reflect a dismis-sive attachment style that is likely to become more entrenched over the course of adulthood. Hanson (2001) noted a reduction in recidivism occur-ring around age fifty. He suggested this may be a function of decreased impulsivity and diminished sexual drive consistent with aging.

In contrast, studies of incestuous child molesters (Hanson & Bussiere, 1998) reveal lower rates of relapse. This group of offenders are most likely to act out during early adulthood. This phase of development is marked by a heightened need for non-parental attachment and a desire for greater degrees of sexual expression. It is conceivable that the fear of rejection characteris-tic of individuals exhibiting either a fearful or preoccupied attachment style, coupled with deviant sexual interest, finds expression in incestuous engagements. Once these men are able to establish age-appropriate relationships their level of risk decreases significantly. Our experience has shown that the majority of clergy offenders were more similar to this group. That is, they exhibited psychosexual developmental arrest; they have abused a minor known to them, part of the Church "family."

INDICES OF TREATMENT RESPONSIVENESS AND CASE STUDIES

While the terrible emotional harm done to victims of sexual abuse cannot in anyway be diminished or disputed, clinical evidence suggests that abusers do not reflect a single profile of predatory behavior. The work of Hanson and Brussiere suggests that a number of factors need to be considered when determining the rigidity of the behavior pattern. Of interest is the fact that the majority of sexually abusive male clergy treated at the Institute were psychosexually immature priests in their late twenties and thirties at the time of abuse and were ordained in the 1970s at the height of the sexual revolution. Their victims were typically adolescent males who were known to them and often experienced by the priests as emotional peers.

Typically, when the incident of abuse came to light, the bishop or religious superior referred the priest for a comprehensive assessment and extended residential treatment. At the termination of treatment, a discharge plan was formulated that included, among other things, a summary of the following indices of treatment responsiveness:

- the extent to which he was forthcoming about his abusive behavior, that is, did not deny his behavior
- his awareness of the seriousness of the violation of his fiduciary role
- the extent to which the priest exhibited remorse and victim-empathy
- his capacity to engage affectively with peers
- his willingness to adhere to strict ministerial supervision
- his commitment to ongoing outpatient psychotherapy and spiritual direction

The clinical team's assessment of the priest's demonstrated resolution of and acceptance of these factors comprise the basis for determining potential for re-offending.

A Case of Dismissive Attachment

Father A, a 57-year-old priest, was referred following being reported to his superiors for having allegedly fondled two prepubescent boys over the course of several years. The events were purportedly to have occurred approximately 18 years ago when the priest was in his late thirties. He presented as superficially cooperative, articulate, bright, and clearly minimizing the seriousness of the allegations. Of interest was his style of staring fixedly into the eyes of each clinician who evaluated him, an attempt to assert his dominance and control. He repeatedly and vehemently denied he had behaved in a sexually exploitative manner, continually stating that his behavior had been "misinterpreted" by the boys and exaggerated by the parents.

Although his superiors had already made the decision to remove him from any future ministry, they felt it was in Father A's interest to assist him in addressing the dynamics that led to his abusive behavior and in developing strategies to contain his behavior, thus increasing safety to the community at-large.

Results of psychological testing supported diagnoses of Narcissistic Personality Disorder with antisocial traits and Pedophilia. Test data indicated that at the time of the evaluation, despite the seriousness of the allegations, he was experiencing no acute distress. His difficulties appeared rooted in significant deficits in self-esteem and fears about being caught and consequently shamed. That is, fear of punishment outweighed any apparent moral incongruity with his behavior. In an effort to deal with this internal state, test results further suggested that he would likely employ a variety of narcissistic and manic defenses. This was borne out in the clinical setting. For example, in the context of his therapeutic program, he tended to relate to others in an overly dramatic manner calling for attention, adulation, and special treatment. When his efforts proved unsuccessful, he resorted to conflictual interchanges permeated with devaluation and open disdain for those whom he perceived he could not readily manipulate. This included most of the therapists who worked with him. Treatment consisted of four months of daily psychodynamically oriented group therapy, individual psychotherapy, participation in a cognitive behavioral groups focusing on sexual acting-out behavior, individual spiritual direction, and a variety of psychoeducational groups.

His initial attitude toward the treatment team was overtly compliant. As the intensity of treatment sharpened, however, and he was faced with challenges to his relational style and confronted with the contradiction between his behavior and his public position as a trusted cleric, he became increasingly defiant, argumentative, and devaluing. He was able, nonethe-less, to contain any direct expression of rage toward other patients or toward staff members, however, preferring to attempt to manipulate others in order to obtain a positive "report" to his superiors.

As it became quite evident to the clinical staff that Father A was not likely to benefit to any significant extent from further residential treat-ment, he was discharged with the recommendation that he be prevented from any unsupervised contact with minors. Father A was infuriated at the discharge summary and appended a five-page handwritten letter to the discharge report in which he refuted the treatment team's recommenda-tions and sarcastically commented on the ineptness of the therapists. Some months later, he attempted to devalue the clinicians and treatment facility as he responded to media requests for interviews concerning his allegations.

Understood from the perspective of attachment style, it is obvious that Father A employed a dismissive, avoidant relational style. The extent of his seething rage toward others combined with a need to exert absolute control over those whom he perceived to be inferior to him. Such a long-standing toxic pattern of manipulation and exploitation underlay his abil-ity to present himself to others as quite competent and affable. Thus he was able to engage vulnerable others in a seductive ploy, enticing them to become entangled in a chokehold of sadistic charm. He exhibited an entrenched pattern of denial concerning his sexual exploitation and no vic-tim empathy. He saw no need for further therapy and discredited the pos-sibility of spiritual direction.

Clinically deemed a treatment failure, based upon his failure to meet indices of treatment responsiveness, Father A remained at high risk for continuing his exploitative, abusive behavior. He became engaged with the criminal justice system and was charged with and sentenced for abuse of minors.

A Case of Preoccupied Attachment

Father B is a 60-year-old who turned himself in to the civil authorities 35 years ago after he fondled a teenaged boy while under the influence of alcohol. He was convicted and sentenced to prison. During the time of his two-year incarceration, he became involved in Alcoholics Anonymous (AA) and in a sex-offender treatment program. Following his release, he continued in AA, weekly psychotherapy, and monthly spiritual direction. After a period of several years, during which time he had no relapses in drinking or in sexual acting out, he was assigned to supervised ministry.

His superiors were aware of his history, and were in contact with his therapist. His immediate supervisor in his ministerial setting was also apprised of Father B's history. For 25 years, Father B served as a well-liked, effective priest whom people felt was approachable, level-headed, and kind. Throughout that time, he continued in AA and met regularly with a psychologist and spiritual director as "insurance" for his continued healthy and honest functioning as a priest. In the throes of the U.S. bishops' "zero-tolerance" document, however, Father B was removed from ministry. He became distraught, reported suicidal ideation, and referred himself for a psychological evaluation and possible residential treatment.

Test results supported a diagnosis of Adjustment Disorder with Mixed Anxiety and Depressed Mood. There was no diagnosis on Axis II. Results of the Abel Assessment of Sexual Interest did not support pedophilic interests. Father B's testing evinced an expressive, affectively available, psychologically minded man who currently was plagued by shame, loneliness, self-blame, and profound sadness. Intrapsychically, he presented as highly self-critical, prone to ruminate on aspects of himself that he finds reprehensible. In contrast to the way he feels about himself, others are likely to experience him as a kind, mature, even-tempered, and flexible person to whom they feel drawn. Given other circumstances, Father B would likely not have met admissions criteria for residential treatment. However, given the circumstances he was facing and the extent of his depression, it was felt that he would benefit from a supportive inpatient setting as he tried to come to terms with the apparent loss of his ministry. Throughout the course of his three months in residential treatment he maintained a transparent, forthcoming relationship with his therapists and with those in his psychotherapy groups. He felt drawn to prayer and was highly regarded by the other residents as a peer leader in the community of faith, a man who was able to face his sinfulness and failure without losing his relationship with God, a person who sought forgiveness, and who was able to forgive.

Father B exhibits a preoccupied attachment style, self-denigrating but drawn positively toward others. His warmth was engaging and disarming and he manifested little need to exert control over others. He presented as more passive in his relational style, although a man with significant cognitive and interpersonal strengths. His care for others and his capacity for veracity suggested that his track record of over 30 years of fidelity to his priestly vocation was not likely to be tarnished. He demonstrated significant remorse; was forthright with his superiors, therapists and appropriate peers about his history; and he was willing to adhere to ministerial supervision. Consequently, the clinical team did not deem him to be at risk for exploitation of minors or of anyone else.

A Case of Fearful Attachment

Father C, a 42-year-old recently ordained priest was referred for assessment following a complaint of boundary violations that allegedly occurred 17 years ago. The incident took place while Father C was an adult volunteer leader in a youth program. Father C was accused of having invited a youth to his office where he showed him pornographic materials. Other complaints were received in which it was noted that during the same time period Father C tried to push youths into friendship, and in one instance wrote several letters to one of the boys that had the tone of love letters. Father C denied the allegations and stated that they were motivated by anger.

When Father C was a child, both parents physically abused him. His father was a violent man who beat him frequently while intoxicated. His mother disciplined him by locking him in a closet. Father C also reported that an older brother abused him sexually. He described his childhood as bereft of affection or signs of caring. He and his siblings were fearful of the parents and distant from each other.

Prior to ordination, Father C's work history was highly varied. His adulthood was characterized by a pattern of wandering from place to place in search of a home and a source of approval. Eventually, he applied to the seminary and was admitted.

Father C exhibited marked disdain for himself and a fear of others. He typically approached relationships anticipating rejection or abuse. Yet, he always held out the hope of being loved and embraced. The slightest sign of disapproval evoked a self-protective stance that was characterized by the axiom "might makes right." When feeling threatened, he displayed an interpersonal brutality that bordered on cruelty. In more hopeful moments, he assumed a stance of dependent self-absorption. His early life experience was characterized by a persistent invalidation of his needs and emotions, particularly his feelings of fear and terror. These experiences led Father C to mistrust his appraisal of his emotions.

His attraction to adolescent boys and young men was understood as being rooted in a desire for affection and admiration within the context of relationships in which he was unlikely to be viciously dominated as he had been by members of his family. Father C exhibited a fearful attachment style.

When the allegation came to light nine years ago, Father C was referred for intensive psychotherapeutic residential treatment extending for six months. Throughout that time Father C struggled in his efforts to regulate his experience of others and self. During the initial weeks of treatment, he fluctuated between intimate engagement, sullen withdrawal, hostility, and a desire to keep others at a distance. His self-perception vacillated between apparent competence and hopelessness. Stress often paralyzed him. For a period of time, Father C assumed a stance of extreme dependence, demanding that others give him direction and assurance as to how to live and behave. During this phase of treatment, he vacillated between narrow self-focus and reckless self-neglect. These patterns were confronted repeatedly using empathic reflection and resulted in an expanded capacity for self-soothing and a heightened sense of self-worth. Gradually, as Father C became more self-aware, he recognized his interpersonal impact and the ways in which it recapitulated early experiences of abuse and neglect. Father C did not satisfy diagnostic criteria for pedophilia. His attraction to adolescent males had been motivated by a deep need for affection and affirmation superimposed on a profound fear of abuse and humiliation.

While Father C demonstrated remorse for the adolescents he abused, a profound awareness of the breach of his fiduciary role as a priest, and did not withhold the extent of his acting-out behavior from the clinical staff, he nonetheless was deemed to be at moderate risk for relapse. This determination was based upon the fact that his capacity for healthy peer attachment remained fragile and his self-esteem, while significantly improved, was still compromised. It was recommended that he continue in ongoing therapy and that any ministry be circumscribed and directly supervised. Father C was assigned as a chaplain in a prison under the mentorship of a senior priest and was not permitted any ministerial activity in the presence of minors. When Father C was removed from ministry as a result of the American bishops' zero-tolerance policy he had completed eight years of chaplaincy without any evidence of relapse.

CONCLUSION

Our experience makes it clear that clergy sex offenders are not a homogeneous group. While the result of the abusive behavior is the same for the victim, the path that led a priest to engage in this criminal activity varies considerably depending on attachment history and personality organization. This suggests the need for careful consideration regarding the potential for rehabilitation and subsequent risk to the community. In instances of clergy with a dismissive attachment style and narcissistic or sociopathic personality organization, it is clear that there should be no opportunity for ministry. Given these situations, no role of power should be considered. An attachment style characterized by the capacity for mature peer-relationships, however, affords greater latitude. Risk of relapse is significantly diminished when there has been a fundamental shift in the priest's sense of self. That is, he demonstrates responsiveness to therapy evidenced by a shift from self-loathing and devaluation to heightened self-esteem accompanied by a trust of and empathy toward others. In such cases, it may be possible for the priest to serve in supervised ministry successfully and without risk to the community.

It should be noted that these reflections are based upon a growing body of research from the public forensic population (see Anderson, 2002 for an overview), as well as on our clinical experience with hundreds of clergy who have had an incident of abuse of a minor. There is a compelling need for comprehensive longitudinal research that focuses specifically on this population in order to refine these indices of treatment responsiveness. Until such work is completed there remains the sad reality of applying the same consequences to each person who has engaged in exploitative or abusive behavior, regardless of the nature of the behavior, regardless of remorse and the desire for reconciliation, and regardless of the achievement of significant resolution to the intrapsychic conflicts that led to the abusive behavior.

NOTE

This chapter appeared as an article by the same title in *Studies in Gender and Sexuality,* 5(2), 197–212. Published by The Analytic Press.

REFERENCES

American Psychiatric Association. (2000). *Diagnostic and statistical manual of mental disorders* (DSM-IV) (4th ed.). Washington, DC: Author.

Anderson, D. (2002). *The utility of interpersonal circumplex theory in research and treatment of sex offenders.* Unpublished dissertation, Queen's University, Kingston, ON.

Bartholomew, K., & Horowitz, L. M. (1991). Attachment styles among young adults: A test of a four-category model. *Journal of Personality and Social Psychology, 61,* 226–244.

Bowlby, J. (1973). *A secure base: Parent-child attachment and healthy human development.* New York: Basic Books.

Briere, J. (1996). *Therapy for adults molested as children* (2nd ed.). New York: Springer Publishing Company.

Bumby, K. M., & Hansen, D. J. (1997). Intimacy deficits, fear of intimacy, and loneliness among sexual offenders. *Criminal Justice and Behavior, 24,* 315–331.

Garlick, Y., Marshall, W. L., & Thornton, D. (1996). Intimacy deficits and attribution of blame among sexual offenders. *Legal and Criminological Psychology, 1,* 251–258.

Griffin, D. W., & Bartholomew, K. (1994). Models of the self and other: Fundamental dimensions underlying measures of adult attachment. *Journal of Personality and Social Psychology, 67,* 430–445.

Hanson, R. K. (2001). Age and sexual recidivism: A comparison of rapists and child molesters. *Public Works and Government Services Canada.* Catalogue Number JS42–96/2001. Ottawa, Ontario, Canada.

Hanson, R. K., & Bussiere, M. T. (1998). Predicting relapse: A meta-analysis of sexual offender recidivism studies. *Journal of Consulting and Clinical Psychology, 66,* 348–362.

Johnson, S. M., & Whiffen, V. E. (1999). Made to measure: Adapting emotionally focused couples therapy to partners' attachment styles. *Clinical Psychology: Science and Practice, 64,* 366–381.

Marshall, W. L., Barbaree, H. E., & Fernandez, Y. M. (1995). Some aspects of social competence in sexual offenders. *Sexual Abuse: A Journal of Research and Treatment, 7,* 113–127.

Seidman, B. T., Marshall, W. L., Hudson, S. M., & Robertson, P. J. (1994). An examination of intimacy and loneliness in sex offenders. *Journal of Interpersonal Violence, 9,* 518–534.

Chapter 11

COLLABORATION BETWEEN THE CATHOLIC CHURCH, THE MENTAL HEALTH, AND THE CRIMINAL JUSTICE SYSTEMS REGARDING CLERGY SEX OFFENDERS

Curtis C. Bryant

The purpose of this chapter is to argue that the Catholic Church, the criminal justice system, and the mental health system can find common course and collaboration in the goal of protecting the vulnerable from clergy sexual abuse. The Church in particular needs to bring about reconciliation and healing at a level that the criminal justice and mental health systems cannot.

This essay follows an earlier article I wrote, which had as part of its conclusion: "Treating priest sexual offenders means coming to terms with the fact that the problem is complex and tenacious and that promises of rapid solutions are not likely to be fulfilled. Treatment and rehabilitation are ambitious undertakings requiring constancy of purpose and sustained mobilization of social resources. The required degree of cooperation between the criminal justice and mental health systems has rarely been achieved. To send people who seek treatment for their sexual disorders to the criminal justice system is ineffective and inhumane" (Bryant, 1999, p. 106–107).

In the ensuing four years, much has happened on the clergy sex offenders' front. The Catholic Church and the mental health system have lost even more credibility. What are the implications for this development? Neither institution is trusted to ameliorate this lamentable situation. The Church is largely perceived as dealing with the situation of clergy sexual abuse with more care for the Church's and priests' reputation than for its suffering children.

(i) lack of
      screening

...d as having made claims about the
...s that it could not back up. The sys-
...could be successfully treated and
...ies have used the outcome of men-
tal health prognoses as a reason for returning priests to ministry only to
find out that they have subsequently re-offended.

Therefore it was left to the criminal justice system to address this
calamity through "law and order": to bring priest perpetrators to justice
and to expose and prosecute, when appropriate, Church authorities who
frustrated due process.

What does the criminal justice system do well? Law enforcement is critical in gathering and interpreting evidence. Prosecutors make charging
decisions and can refuse to accept pleas that downgrade charges to nonsexual assault cases. Judges are empowered to order offenders to receive
the supervision and treatment that is paramount to reducing recidivism
risk and enhancing public safety. Defense attorneys counsel offenders on
probation and parole, explaining the expectations of the court (e.g., that
their compliance with community supervision restrictions may reduce
their risk of recidivism and incarceration). Criminal justice officials oversee registration and community notification of sex offenders, and work
with victim advocates educating residents about convicted offenders living in their neighborhoods and about preventing future victimization.

What does the criminal justice system not do well? While there are
undeniable criminal elements involved in most clergy sexual abuse, one
cannot deny that the origin of this misconduct lies in one or more of a variety of psychopathologies. In simply taking a punitive approach to clergy
sexual offenders, the object being incarceration, and ignoring the pathological origins of their maladaptive behavior, with a therapeutic objective,
the criminal justice system fails to address the cause of behavior that will
in many cases recur when an opportunity presents itself outside the criminal scrutiny. Moreover, in exposing those offenders who are "nonviolent"
to long-term incarceration with the general prison population, with the
likelihood of violence directed against them, the criminal justice system
may even be guilty of imposing "cruel and unusual punishment" pro-
scribed by the Constitution.

The above approach of many criminal justice professionals is often a
response to the fears of society about all sexual offenders, especially the
clergy. While prudence dictates that law enforcement take all reasonable
efforts to protect citizens, especially the most vulnerable, the approach
must take into account the long-term solutions that will most likely affect

the general well-being and avoid a knee-jerk reaction that will likely generate not only recidivism, but attitudes of vindictiveness and crimes of revenge by the convict, by his fellow inmates, and by members of the community into which he returns upon parole (vigilantism).

Public fear about clergy sex offenders presents a unique challenge to those working to improve policies related to supervising and treating sex offenders in the community. Public sentiment that the criminal justice system should do more to safeguard the community from sex offenders in general has led to the enactment of a host of measures in recent years, such as sex offender registration, community notification, and involuntary civil commitment for some sex offenders. Numerous statutes have also been passed that reflect the public's belief that violent criminals, including sex offenders, should be incarcerated for longer periods of time. Despite such laws, however, most convicted sex offenders will be released into the community at some point—whether directly following sentencing, or after a term of incarceration in jail or prison. The criminal justice system has the responsibility to manage these offenders without unduly risking victim and public safety or undercutting the offender's rehabilitation or successful reintegration into society.

Another misdirected approach is suggested, namely, the tendency to equate all sex offenders and all sex crimes. While it is true that some are perhaps so ill as to be a perennial threat to society and thus require permanent isolation, there is a wisdom in admitting degrees of offenses and of the pathology of the offender, with consequent differences in treatment, rehabilitation, and incarceration policies.

Those who serve time in jail or prison face a high chance of re-offending since quality sex education and related services are not offered though the present day criminal justice system. The lack of mental health professionals and sex therapists with expertise in this area, a lack of accurate diagnosis, and a lack of police understanding and intervention remain a problem.

What does the mental health system do well in the clergy sexual abuse story? There has been an attempt to do research that might guide treatment. Based on surveys from the general population, the sex offender is known to the victim or family in 80 to 95 percent of the cases. The offenders who are not family members are less than 50 percent of all occurrences and are identified as acquaintances (neighbors, coaches, teachers, religious leaders) in the remaining cases. Clergy represent a not-significant proportion of the offenders, however painful their activity in this regard may be.

Sex offenders differ greatly in terms of their level of impulsiveness, persistence, the risks they pose to the public, and their desire to change their behavior. Effective public policy needs to be cognizant of the differences among offenders rather than applying a "one size fits all" program.

Historically, some priests are what could be described as "transient pedophiles," because their attraction to children was temporary and dissipated as they matured and/or received treatment. Why is this so? A significant number of clergy abusers had their adolescence and sexual development delayed by entering celibate religious order or seminary life as teenagers. Sexually inexperienced when they entered, they generally were given little or no opportunity to discuss their sexuality, much less integrate it. For example, a 70-year-old priest who entered the seminary when he was 13 and who had a brief relationship with a teenager 40 years ago and went into treatment poses little risk of being a sex offender victimizing minors today. Yet, human behavior being what it is, it is impossible to predict with certainty whether this clergy sex offender or any other will commit another act of abuse.

What kind of treatment is effective with clergy sex offenders? In another chapter in the book, *Bless me Father for I Have Sinned: Perspectives on Sexual Abuse Committed by Roman Catholic Priests* (1999), edited by Thomas Plante, I have reviewed the literature and identified the most robust means of doing therapy. For the purposes of this essay, treatment issues will be greatly abbreviated.

Treatment for sex offending is still a developing field because sex offenses have been hidden for so many years and there was little research on the topic other than prison population studies until recently. Those studies were very pessimistic in their treatment outcomes. However, this population represented a relatively small percentage of the entire offenders' group. The research treating the clergy in particular did not receive priority attention until the 1980s. Since then, sufficient progress has been made allowing for the identification of strong indicators about the treatment approaches most likely to be successful.

The core approach used in many programs is "cognitive-behavioral," which utilizes a relapse prevention model. The goal of this approach is to enable the offenders to understand and take responsibility for the behavior. It also increases motivation to change harmful behavior and learn the skills necessary to control their impulses. The precise sequence of the relapse process will be different for each offender. Among some offenders, exposure to a particular situation may trigger the sequence of events leading to an offense. In others, it may be a negative emotional state or a specific event, such as being reprimanded for a poor sermon.

With training in relapse-prevention techniques, clergy sex offenders learn to identify the chain of thoughts and behaviors that, if uninterrupted, could culminate in the commission of a sex offense. In addition to learning to identify the chain, the offender masters alternative non-harmful techniques to intervene and stop the progression of behaviors.

Is treatment sufficient to reduce a sex offender's risk to the community? Because sex offenders, including clergy sex offenders, represent a heterogeneous group, some will respond well to treatment intervention and others will not take advantage of the treatment modalities provided. A formal risk assessment conducted by a qualified professional offers the best method of estimating the risk posed by a particular sex offender. An appropriate assessment incorporates a review of the offender's history, clinical impressions, as well as risk prediction utilizing tests that have research validity.

Conducting longitudinal studies of clergy sex offenders and identifying their rates of re-offending can objectively measure risk reduction. An effective treatment program should be able to reduce the recidivism of its participants, compared to similar offenders who did not receive treatment.

Early intervention and preventive measures are essential to protect possible future victims and in helping clergy sexual offenders learn healthy and appropriate ways to express their sexuality. Community agencies commonly used the following interventions when addressing sexually offensive behavior: increased supervision, behavioral intervention, mental health services, environmental modifications, sex education, and legal sanctions.

Should clergy and other sex offenders be held accountable for their actions? Absolutely. Diversion programs may be the only opportunity sex offenders, including clergy, will have to learn about appropriate sexual behavior. Creative sentencing options can be used to encourage actual behavior change and relapse prevention, which is preferable in some cases to a jail or prison sentence.

However, the mental health system may be more optimistic than the data allow about its ability to effect change. As a mental health professional, I will confess that my hopes for individual clergy not to relapse have been disappointed.

What does the Church do well? Historically, seminary training precluded much in the way of sexual education. Therefore, a good deal of ignorance about sexual matters was part of many priests' lives, especially if they were part of the minor seminary structure. What that meant was that seminary candidates began their training at age 14 or earlier. Until 1980 or perhaps later, seminaries did not offer much in the way of sexual education. Therefore, ignorance of what is considered appropriate, inadequate social education about boundary- and limit-setting, and poorly developed or absent self-control was not addressed. Other factors with the seminarian at an earlier age included:

- lack of information about or opportunities for legitimate expressions of intimacy;
- lack of social skills and training or appropriate behavior and boundaries with others;
- lack of appropriate relationships, particularly with adult women;
- a history of sexual or physical abuse which went undisclosed and undetected;
- exposure to pornography in private settings that was difficult to discern;
- pervasive use of restriction in daily life;
- difficulty predicting consequences of behavior;
- difficulty recognizing and expressing emotions;
- authority, community, or others denying that the behavior was happening.

This was largely the picture of seminary training before 1985 and the first media attention given to the problem. Most of the clergy sex offenders were trained in the seminary prior to reforms enacted before 1985. In this situation, the Church has been most responsive. Those who enter the seminary now do so when they are older and therefore experience much more maturity. Seminarians take classes during their years of training that deal with sexuality, celibacy, intimacy, boundaries, and ethics.

The Church has not done well in being accountable to the people. It is considered too secretive in its process of handling offending priests. The so-called "zero tolerance" was reactive, indiscriminate, and, finally, something Rome corrected.

In conclusion, developing a collaborative approach to clergy sex offender management is a daunting but essential undertaking. Building relationships among individuals representing different agencies and interests—many of whom have traditionally played adversarial roles—is a key challenge. However, agencies charged with the management of sex offenders are compelled today more than ever to cross traditional lines in their work toward a common mission—to end further sexual victimization.

While the sex offender management field is fairly well united in the belief that the responsible management of sex offenders includes rigorous community supervision and sex offender-specific treatment, public opinion can influence whether such initiatives will be supported or accepted in a jurisdiction. The Church must be willing to stay involved in helping priests after they have left ministry or returned from incarceration.

Conventional wisdom holds that when it comes to criminal justice, "the boundaries of political permission" established by public opinion are narrow and circumscribed, and that the public just wants to "lock offenders up and throw away the key." However, numerous studies have shown that this is a serious misreading of the public's perspective. Most people are open to innovative ideas, especially if they have the opportunity to consider and have input into the issue.

In a democratic society, leadership is ultimately accountable to the will of the people. Regardless of the subject, leaders who make policy outside of these "boundaries of permission" may see the public repudiate that policy, and advocate to replace it with a radically different approach. The bishops have not seen themselves as accountable to the people in many ways. They are starting to learn the consequences of not being accountable to the people. Over the past few years, our society has faced political, business, and religious scandals. The resolution of these problems has been driven by public opinion. Citizens and leaders may be more willing to support community supervision and treatment initiatives for convicted sex offenders when:

- they understand that it is not feasible to incarcerate all sex offenders indefinitely;
- misconceptions they may hold about sex crimes and offenders are replaced with facts;
- they are given an opportunity to learn more about how supervision and treatment can foster successful and safe reintegration of sex offenders into society and prevent future sexual victimization; and
- they are offered qualitative and quantitative data that help demonstrate how supervision and treatment programs are effective in protecting the community from convicted sex offenders.

For at least the last 15 years, the topic of clergy sex offenders has been a topic full of pain and anger. The pain and anger is multifaceted: Victims are angry with priest perpetrators. Priests are angry with the two to six per cent of their brother priests who have seriously compromised their reputations and ministry. Priests are also angry with the episcopacy, many are angry with the media, and many faithful Catholics are angry at all the above.

The Church must take the lead in teaching gospel compassion, which must, first of all, go out to the victim. This crisis, asks us, furthermore, to take compassion on the priest perpetrator who is ill. Can there also be compassion for the bishops who have blundered?

REFERENCES

Bryant, C. (1999). Psychological treatment of priest sex offenders. In T. G. Plante (Ed.), *Bless me father for I have sinned: Perspectives on sexual abuse committed by Roman Catholic priests* (pp. 88–110). Westport, CT: Greenwood.

Plante, T. G. (Ed.). (1999). *Bless me father for I have sinned: Perspectives on sexual abuse committed by Roman Catholic priests*. Westport, CT: Greenwood.

Chapter 12

THE RELATIONSHIP BETWEEN THE TREATMENT FACILITIES AND THE CHURCH HIERARCHY: FORENSIC ISSUES AND FUTURE CONSIDERATIONS

Leslie M. Lothstein

During the last three decades an estimated 2–6 percent of the Roman Catholic priesthood was accused of sexually abusing minors (Berry, 1992; Burkett & Bruni, 1993; Jenkins, 1996; Lothstein, 1990, 1991; Lothstein & Rossetti, 1990; Sipe, 1995). Faced with serious moral, spiritual, political, and financial crises, the Church hierarchy[1] initially referred errant clergy to a number of clinics, residential centers, hospitals (both Church- and non-Church-affiliated), and other entities (such as guest houses, that is, small monastic retreats). It was hoped that clergy with alcohol abuse, substance abuse, angry and disruptive behaviors, or sexually errant behavior problems could be evaluated, treated, and returned to ministry. These Church-treatment institutional relationships are the focus of this chapter.

Where a scandal was anticipated some sexually errant clergy were sent to non-therapeutic monastic enclosures where they were secluded from the press and irate parishioners. Others were relocated to distant dioceses where they could not be identified by their victims. As a result of these practices some critics have suggested a possible conspiracy among the bishops to cover up the clergy abuse of minors (*Boston Globe* Staff, 2002). Indeed, a series of almost 900 articles in the *Boston Globe* revealed a pattern of practice among the bishops that led to the convening of grand juries throughout the country to investigate whether Catholic bishops conspired to protect priests while engaging in racketeering and criminal activity.

During the first phase of Church-treatment/institution relationships the Church hierarchy related differently to the secular institutions over which they had little control. At the very least they insisted that secular treatment facilities provide a spiritual component along with psychiatric care. The bishops and superiors knew little about the science of sexuality that led to specialized treatment techniques for sex-offending clergy (Schwartz, 1999, 2002; Schwartz & Cellini, 1995, 1997). Their primary aim was to prevent scandal while obtaining therapy for the errant priests/religious. The Church hierarchy knew about 12-step models of treatment and approved of them because of the spiritual component. In addition to sexual disorders, many sex-offending priests also suffered from serious medical illnesses, alcohol and drug addictions, and other mental disorders that could not be treated at a monastic enclosure (Harrington and Lothstein, under review; Lothstein, 1999, 2000; Lothstein & LaFleur-Bach, 2002). During the second phase of Church-treatment/institution relationships (post the 2002 meeting of the bishops in Dallas and the publicity of Cardinal Law's deceits) errant priests were rarely sent to treatment as they were publicly identified and defrocked.

As the number of priests accused of sexually abusing minors increased, the Church hierarchy raised several questions to the secular and religious treatment centers: (1) How could seminarian candidates who were likely to be homosexual or molest children be identified? (2) How could one determine which priests/clergy would be sexually abusive towards minors? (3) How could one identify homosexual clergy, many of whom the Church hierarchy believed were responsible for the sexual abuse of minors? (4) How could one determine whether clergy who sexually abused minors could be returned to any form of ministry?

The issue of having mental health professionals identify homosexual clergy was, at best, a moral dilemma for many secular practitioners. Indeed, the American Psychological and Psychiatric Associations do not view homosexuality as a mental disorder and do not discriminate against homosexuality. I have always refused to perform such assessments.

The issue of homosexual priests has been responsibly addressed by Sipe (1990) and Cozzens (2000) and, more creatively, by Jordan (2000). The research is clear in that there is no scientific basis to conclude that homosexuality is a cause of child sexual abuse (although it may be a risk factor for some errant priests who molest male children). And given estimates that more than 40 percent of Catholic priests are homosexual (Cozzens, 2000), and the vast majority of them do not abuse anyone, the request to evaluate priests or priest applicants to diagnose homosexuality seems odd.

All of the treatment facilities (religious and secular) engaged in specific fiduciary and professional relationships with the Church hierarchy in which possible ethical conflicts existed that could influence the outcome of the evaluation and treatment of clergy. There were Church-owned and operated institutions (St. Luke's Institute, Servants of the Paracletes, St. John Vianney) that directly reported to the Church hierarchy and whose existence depended on Church monies and whose medical records were sometimes shared with the referring bishop or superior. All of these religious institutions were in competition with each other for the same patients. Referrals were only made to secular institutions where a relationship was formed with a program.

The Church-institutional relationships have been the subject of intense scrutiny regarding possible dual agency and conflict of interest. There were secular institutions (the Institute of Living, Johns Hopkins University, the Isaac Ray Center) that treated clergy where no apparent overt conflict of interest or dual agency existed as with the religious institutions. However, whenever fiduciary and power relationships with the Church hierarchy exist, the potential for ethical lapses and unprofessional behavior are always possible.

Dual agency is a particular problem for Church-sponsored treatment centers. Dual agency exists when a person has obligations to two parties that may interfere with one's ethics, objectivity, and professionalism. All Church-sponsored treatment centers have potential dual relationships and problems with dual agency when they act as treaters but have priest-therapists as staff. A priest makes a vow of theological obedience to his bishop, who is also his employer. In the secular world no such employer-employee relationships exists (even loyalty to the organization does not come close to the Catholic priest's vow of obedience to his bishop), and the employer has no legal right to obtain information about the treatment of his employee.

Bishops often act under the rule of *parens patriae* with their priests. There is a tendency to infantilize the priest, which may encourage social and sexual immaturity in the priest and may lead to a dependent relationship between the priest and his bishop, a relationship that may interfere with the priest's autonomy in decision making and eventually in understanding why the bishop becomes his adversary once allegations are made. Many bishops expect the doctors and clinicians treating their clergy (even secular treatment centers) to report to them directly about the priest's treatment. At Church-owned treatment facilities, the bishops or superiors (or their representatives) may oversee the facility and have access to the medical records of their priests. They may also control all funding to the facility. When clergy are treated at secular treatment centers, issues of patient confidentiality and privacy are the norm and while bishops wield little influence there they may stir up intense counter-transference issues especially among Catholic staff. Once bishops began to use third-party insurance carriers, managed care, and federally funded Medicare and Medicaid programs to pay for a priest's treatment, the bishops' access to a priest's medical data was limited, and the power of money to corrupt the system diminished.

In Church-sponsored treatment facilities, the potential ethical, professional, and legal conflicts that arise around issues of privacy, confidentiality, and limits of self disclosure are compelling. Whatever a priest tells his bishop is not subject to the same privacy and confidentiality statutes as those in the secular world. Bishops expect that their priests (and those treating them at religious treatment centers) will discuss the details of their sexual misbehavior with their superiors. Some bishops, sensing the danger of such disclosure, may choose to consider the priest's communication as occurring under the seal of confession and therefore not discoverable. However, using the confessional to protect disclosure of child sex abuse has been questioned by the courts.

Once a diocese is sued because of a priest's errant sexual behavior, the priest and the bishop become adversaries, and the attorney for the diocese cannot represent the priest's interests. Most priests are not aware of this potential area of conflict with their bishops. The accused priest has to hire his own attorney to protect his legal rights. Because priestly salaries are so low, most priests do not have the funds necessary to defend themselves. In cases involving the sexual abuse of minors, it is not uncommon for the bishop to suspend the priest's faculties, limit his freedom, and restrict his vocation, issues that can adversely affect treatment. Clergy being treated in secular treatment facilities are probably more aware of their legal rights and the consequences of disclosing crimes to their bishops.

The Church hierarchy has a history of being dismissive of civil law and hiding behind the cloak of canon law. One bishop, while trying to protect his church's assets, went a step further, and argued in court that priests in his diocese who abused minors were really independent contractors and that the Church hierarchy was not responsible for their actions. In effect he opened the door to a breach in the priest-bishop relationship. Some priests were angered by the bishop's stance, believing that the precious priest-bishop relationship was no longer a sacred trust. While the bishop's legal arguments were not accepted by the court and viewed as a poor rationalization for his own negligent hiring, supervision, and retention of problem priests, the end result was a breach of trust between the bishop and his priests and the establishment of an adversarial relationship between the diocese and at least one treatment facility.

Another area of potential ethical conflict between bishops/religious superiors and the treatment centers is the confusion that exists about what is expected from the treatment centers in terms of their evaluations and recommendations. What may start out as a request for a traditional psychiatric evaluation may turn into a request for a risk assessment and fitness-for-duty evaluation. The bishop/religious superior may assume that the treatment center will agree with his decision to return sexually errant priests to some form of ministry (even those that abuse children).

It has been argued that in all cases the risk factors would be too great to return a priest who had sexually abused prepubescent children to pastoral ministry (Lothstein, 1991). Typically the Church hierarchy placed these sexually errant priests in a hospital chaplaincy, nursing home, or convent (to administer Mass): that is, places where the Church hierarchy believed that they would not have access to vulnerable populations. However, this line of reasoning was quite naïve. Children are also patients in hospitals and often visit grandparents in nursing homes. Indeed, one priest who worked in a hospital chaplaincy program in a pediatric hospital and dressed as a clown to entertain children was arrested and is now serving jail time for molesting children who were patients in the hospital. Where treatment facility recommendations failed, it may have been the result of not fully understanding the various routes of access that clergy child sexual predators had to youth.

Prior to the resignation of Cardinal Law, as lawsuits escalated, there was an increasingly hostile environment between many bishops and treatment centers. There was some difference between the religious superiors and also regional differences in the Church's response to the treatment centers. In recent cases some bishops have deflected blame onto the treatment centers. The *Boston Globe* staff (2002) reported that members of the Church hierarchy appeared to be putting pressure on some individual treaters or treatment facilities to return sexually offending priests to ministry, even if their risk to sexually re-offend children was high.

What may have begun as a cooperative relationship between a bishop and a treatment facility not infrequently often turned into a combative one (especially with regard to the secular facilities), as the Church hierarchy tried to transfer their liability (blame) onto the treatment centers. As lawsuits increased and fiduciary responsibilities became more important, one of the most unusual lawsuits to date was filed, when the Diocese of San Bernardino sued the Boston Archdiocese in 2003 for "damages resulting from its failure to disclose a priest's prior history of sexual abuse," as the priest later abused minors in a new diocese (*New York Times*, 2003). The shift from blaming the treatment centers to blaming the referring diocese was a low point in Church politics.

In another example of poor Church leadership, a bishop was quoted in his deposition as saying that he withheld important information from a secular treatment center about prior allegations of sexual misconduct by one of his priests, because he did not want to spoil the reputation of the priest. Such arrogant leadership ignored the victim's rights and placed vulnerable populations at further risk for a priest's sexual misconduct.

In one case I was involved in, a bishop referred a priest to our treatment center and never mentioned that the priest was accused of sexual misconduct and that criminal proceedings were underway. The priest was referred for depression and workaholism (with no mention that he was alleged to have raped a minor). In the first interview, the priest disclosed the molestation and said that he was sent cross-country to protect his diocese from scandal. When he was told that it was his bishop's duty to report his sexual activity with a minor to the police, he said that he had already shared this information with the bishop and was assured that the information would be kept confidential. A call to the bishop led to the bishop's admission that he knew of the allegations but had not made a report and had withheld them from the treatment center. Under pressure from the treatment facility, he filed a police report. However, when an arrest warrant was eventually issued for the priest, this time the bishop failed to inform the treatment center or the priest about the warrant. Subsequently, the priest was dramatically arrested at the hotel residence affiliated with the hospital in front of patients and their families and a front-page news story intimated that the treatment center was knowingly housing a fugitive. That was the last priest we accepted for treatment without requiring that all bishops and superiors had to sign a letter stating that they would agree to full disclosure of their priest's personnel file and background.

Psychiatric treatment centers need to know about a priest's criminal history, especially if children are being treated at that hospital. Psychiatric treatment centers need to determine whether a priest meets the requirement of medical necessity in order to be evaluated for a mental disorder or dual diagnosis (alcohol or substance disorder). The bishop's need, however, may be to avoid scandal and to have a place he can put the priest until the furor settles down.

Some priests who presented for treatment were emotionally vulnerable or had severe personality disorders. When these priests drank or used drugs they were at high risk for re-offending. Some of these men needed a forensic risk assessment for dangerousness to self and others. A risk assessment for sexual dangerousness may also be part of a violence risk assessment. Most bishops were less interested in a risk assessment than a fitness-for-duty assessment. However, it is not the role of a residential and day program or inpatient treatment facility to perform a fitness-for-duty assessment, though recommendations may be made on when an individual is stable enough to return to work. Nothing in a psychiatric assessment implies that the employer must take a patient back to work. A fitness-for-duty assessment needs to be done on an outpatient basis by a third party, independent of the treatment team. Only the bishop can make the ultimate decision on whether a priest is fit to return to work. This was highlighted in one evaluation in which a bishop, in response to suggestions by the treatment team that the priest not return to public ministry because of his imminent sexual violence risk toward children, (involving a long history of impulsivity and disinhibition, the use of alcohol and other disinhibiting substances, and a diagnosis of psychopathology), replied "I make the decisions, not you, so don't tell me what to do." In effect, he was right. It was his job to make the final decision regarding whether a priest returned to ministry. It was not the job of the treatment center.

The potential for the blurring of boundaries when the Church hierarchy and the treatment centers perceive their roles differently needs to be addressed at the outset. For example, some bishops wanted the treatment centers to prove or disprove the allegations of sexual misconduct based on a psychological examination. Such a request can only be addressed by the police or other investigative agencies. The treatment centers can be expected to perform an independent psychiatric examination in order to assess and diagnose any mental disorders or dual diagnoses that may be contributing to the priest/religious' sexual misconduct. But a treatment center cannot perform police functions.

If a treatment facility did a risk assessment and concluded that the priest was "at low risk" for imminent sexual re-offense based on actuarial and clinical prediction tools, a bishop reading the report might conclude incorrectly that the priest could resume his ministry because he was at low risk. However, low risk is still risk, especially when the risk is to sexually offend against a child.

In summary, some of the major forensic issues facing the Church hierarchy and the treatment facilities involved the following potentially tricky issues: (1) the different ways confidentiality and privacy issues are handled by Church-sponsored versus secular treatment facilities; (2) how dual

agency and conflict of interest affect fiduciary and professional relationships and can buy influence and power when priests are sent for treatment;
(3) how the type of evaluation provided (psychiatric evaluation versus risk
assessment or fitness-for-duty) may be driven by nonprofessional issues;
and (4) how the various goals delineated by the bishop/religious superiors
and the treatment facilities may be at odds with one another.

THE FINDINGS OF FACT AND THE CHURCH
HIERARCHY'S COVER-UP

The tensions between the treatment facilities and the Church hierarchy
reached an apex, according to the *Boston Globe*, when one treatment facility, The Institute of Living (where I am employed), had to confront the dis-
tortions of the bishop in his deposition regarding information he received
from the treatment center regarding some of the sexually errant priests.
This area of conflict focused on the management of the information flow
from the diocese (bishop) to the treatment facilities. In a deposition, the
bishop said he relied on the advice of treatment centers regarding his
placement of sexually abusive priests.

Deflecting liability has become the Church's main defense. In one case,
a bishop stated (in what he thought was a sealed deposition) that a treatment facility gave him the green light to place a sexually errant priest back
to work in his diocese. The *Hartford Courant* got a copy of the sealed deposition and compared the bishop's testimony to the actual clinical findings
in the case. The journalist concluded that the bishop was not entirely
telling the truth and was attempting to transfer liability and blame from
himself to the treatment center. Members of our management team agreed
to meet with two *Hartford Courant* staff members, and eventually a
lengthy newspaper article appeared on Easter Sunday 2002 with the following headline "They Lied to Us." The *Boston Globe* in their book
Betrayal quoted me as saying of the Church hierarchy that "I found that
they (one diocese) rarely followed our recommendations. They would put
(priests) back into work where they still had access to vulnerable populations." The authors concluded, "Lothstein's comments marked a new
chapter—and a clear break—in the relationship between the Church and
psychiatrists." A more sobering view would be that it was a new chapter
for some bishops who were abusing their authority. It was the opinion of
our management staff that the bishop had been realistically apprised of the
imminent risks some priests posed to the safety of the children in his diocese. He chose to ignore those warnings. That was his prerogative as
bishop.

Psychologist Gary Schoener (2002) suggested that blame be shared by the treatment centers. He noted that in some cases the centers had to be faulted "for accepting the Church's investigations at face value." He assumed that the Church actually did an "investigation." Schoener went on to say, "they (the centers) failed to contact victims. They left responsibility for follow-up to the priests' dioceses. In short, the psychiatrists saw the Church as their boss." Aside from the counter-transference issues of idealizing the authority of the Catholic Church, there is only merit to Schoener's argument if one accepts that it is the duty of the treatment centers to act as detectives and ferret out legal issues. However, mental health professionals are not detectives and are not trained, credentialed, or certified to do police work.

I disagree with Schoener's idea that the treatment centers should have interviewed the victims of clergy abuse. It is not up to the mental health professionals to take on such an investigatory role and potentially violate the confidentiality of victims who may not want to come forward. In many cases no legal actions were pending. One may argue that it would be a violation of confidentiality for an evaluator to contact "victims" to verify their stories. Lawyers would never approve of such a meeting since it could have an adverse effect on future legal issues while also intimidating "victims." While I, however, may disagree with some of Schoener's arguments, there is no doubt that in some cases the treatment centers did contribute to bad decision making and that public safety should be a high priority for all of us, especially when vulnerable populations such as children are at risk.

In the early spring of 2003, the Boston Archdiocese threatened to subpoena the records of therapists treating claimants who were suing the Church. They hoped that these threats would end the lawsuits. Many therapists were outraged. They believed that such a process might re-traumatize their patients and force them to give up their lawsuits. These were the very same patients whose therapy the archdiocese had agreed to pay for. While the Church has the right to utilize the adversarial process in American civil law, it is ironic that this was one of the few times they sought its protection.

When a priest discloses ongoing abuse of a minor to a treatment team, that information is not privileged and must be reported to the appropriate state authorities. Any parishioner who reports ongoing sexual abuse of a minor in confession should be advised to seek professional help and report his crimes before he can truly take accountability for his actions and receive penance. Unfortunately, at times the confessional has been used for purposes other than penance (Valenti & diMeglio, 1974).

A good-faith contract is expected to exist between the Church and the treatment centers. Because of the dual agency of Church-sponsored treatment centers, it may have been more difficult for them to confront their bishops. By withholding information, the Church authorities opened the doors to accusations of a cover-up. Aside from the fact that they were violating civil law, once they chose not to disclose information of child abuse they put their credibility and their parishioners' lives at stake.

STANDARDS OF HIRING, SUPERVISION, AND RETENTION

Secular treatment centers may be unaware of the theological and legal issues governing the employment status of their clergy patients. They may find it hard to imagine that the institution of the Roman Catholic Church has little, if any, accountability to provide the kinds of safeguards, supervision, and disciplinary practices for its employees that are standard in most workplaces. In some areas of employment law, religious institutions may be exempt from fair employment standards and can potentially discriminate against any group with immunity. These issues need to be understood as part of the evaluation/treatment process.

Typically, most employers are required by law to meet a certain threshold of responsibility to the people they employ. It is expected that anyone hired for a job is qualified for that job, and applicants are screened if they are to work with children. Once hired, individuals are supervised and provided ongoing performance evaluations of their work. When an individual's behavioral performance is substandard or violates ethical and professional guidelines, it is expected that she or he will be dismissed. Failure to ensure that the people hired are competent for the job and appropriately supervised in their job may lead to lawsuits focusing on negligence. That is exactly what happened to the Catholic Church to the tune of suits totaling over one billion dollars. These lawsuits have forced the Church to adopt safety policies for working with vulnerable populations; secular institutions have had these policies in place for years.

Most priests and clergy who are assigned to youth ministries have little or no training in this specialty. Teenagers, who are bristling with sexual energy, may pose a specific challenge to a priest who never experienced his adolescence in terms of dating, intimacy, or sexual awakening. Many naïve and socially immature priests may be vulnerable to the opportunities to become sexually involved with youth. Some priests who have a history of pedophilia (sexual interest in prepubescent children) or ephebophilia (sexual interest in teenagers) prior to entering ministry may cross sexual boundaries with young parishioners (Gabbard & Lester, 1995) and become sexual predators in their roles as youth ministers. In Texas, a man with a prior history of sexual perpetration against children was accepted into the seminary and later ordained a priest. The issue of negligent hiring was part of a related lawsuit. During his priesthood, he went on to sexually abuse many children. Most organizations would not have hired him on the basis of his past history.

Through the 1990s the Catholic hierarchy had no universal policies, training manuals, or seminars geared toward helping supervisors identify clergy at risk for abusing minors or educating clergy on how to maintain boundaries when working with youth. Moreover, there were no policies on how to deal with accusations of sexual involvement with minors against priests/clergy, and there was little or no supervision of a priest/cleric's behavior towards children. Until recently, when clergy were accused of being sexually involved with minors, their cases were swept under the rug. These decisions often led to continued sexual predation of minors that was supported by the Church hierarchy's decisions as evidenced by Cardinal Law's arrogant management of the priest sex abuse cases in his administration.

In the case of the Servants of the Paracletes in Jemez Springs, New Mexico, a Church-sponsored treatment facility, working with a diocese, used poor judgment by allowing errant sexual priests under their care to continue to minister to vulnerable populations of children whom they eventually sexually exploited. The Jemez Springs case led to the ouster of the bishop, who was also accused of sexual misconduct. Eventually, the treatment facility for priests in Jemez Springs, New Mexico, closed and moved to Saint Louis, Missouri.

While the Church hierarchy lacked any standard protocols for managing the priest sex abuse crisis, they could not plead ignorance regarding the burgeoning literature on specialized sex offender treatments and competencies for therapists who treated sex offenders (Schwartz & Cellini, 1995).

THE RESEARCH PROJECT

There are many voices calling for research into the pedophile-priest issue. However, the debate has been going on for a decade. Around 1990, I was part of a research team that made a petition to the National Council of Catholic Bishops (NCCB) to fund a national research study of priest pedophiles by a consortium of treatment facilities (The Institute of Living,

St. Luke's Institute, and the Servants of the Paracletes, Southdown, and later, St. John Vianney). This research study was meant to address most of the core issues posed above (except the homosexuality issue). There was a lot of enthusiasm about the study, and a research protocol was developed and consultation arranged with senior researchers, including experts from National Institute of Mental Health. The study was designed to address the reasons for the "epidemic" in the clergy of the sexual abuse of minors. However, at the last minute the study was quashed as the NCCB withdrew support. The bishops feared that any findings of the study were potentially discoverable in court and could be used in lawsuits against the Church. An independent lay commission was set up in 2003 to explore the very issues our original research project intended to address. It is my opinion that, given the secrecy and politics of the Roman Catholic Church, such a study will never be completed.

FUTURE ISSUES

Treatment centers must be very specific about what they can and cannot do during the evaluation and treatment of sexually errant priests. Issues of spirituality and psychotherapy need to be clearly differentiated (Braceland, 1972; Farnsworth & Braceland, 1969).

Unless a bishop agrees to sign a statement that he is disclosing all records pertaining to the priest's sexually offending behavior, all complaints against the clergyman over the course of his career, and all files pertaining to allegations of sexual misconduct, the evaluation should not be undertaken. Unless a cleric has an identified psychiatric disorder she or he should not be evaluated in a psychiatric treatment center. No inpatient, intensive outpatient, or day-treatment program should perform a *fitness-for-duty* evaluation. However, as part of a sexual violence risk assessment, a trained professional may comment on how the priest/cleric may put specific, vulnerable populations, during a certain time frame, at risk for future sexual abuse.

The Church hierarchy needs to reconsider some of the premises underlying their secrecy and moral teachings on sex. This will enable both clergy and parishioners to develop a mature integration of their intimacy needs and psychosexual development in order to further protect vulnerable populations from being sexually exploited.

It is encouraged that the Church promote open discussions of sexuality, including previously forbidden topics such as masturbation, contraception, homosexuality, married priests, and having sex with a minor. While

Catholic clergy are expected to be celibate, they are not prepared for the lifelong consequences of celibacy. The lack of healthy sexual narratives has left many priests and clergy isolated, lonely, and needy, with no social support to discuss their sexual isolation. One result has been that some priests tend to sexually act out secretively and destructively (Sipe, 1990, 1995).

Recent scandals suggest that the Church hierarchy seems to be more interested in protecting the Church from scandal and preserving their financial resources than protecting minors from abuse. If one doubts this after the resignation of Cardinal Law, just consider the way the group Voices of the Faithful is being treated by many bishops, who won't even allow them to meet on Church property, much less donate any funds to the Church. The role of the laity must expand if the Church is to become a safe place for youth.

Burkett and Bruni (1993) argued, "confronted with a choice between justice for the victims and benevolence towards abusive priests, Church leaders have consistently opted for the latter. Pray, they told the offending priests. Repent. And when priests did, they were transferred to new parishes where they were free to molest and molest again." This process has to change.

Perhaps it is a healthy outcome that the treatment centers and the Church hierarchy are at loggerheads. It is only through healthy conflict that new paradigms may arise that will allow a more ethical and professional relationship to develop between these two groups.

NOTE

1. By Church hierarchy I mean the bishop, his representative, the Cardinal, any superior of a religious order, lawyers for the Church or any official representatives of a diocese or religious order or their national organization that are able to speak for the Church's policies or religious order's rules and are given decision-making authority to represent the Church or the religious order.

REFERENCES

Berry, J. (1992). *Lead us not into temptation: Catholic priests and the sexual abuse of children.* New York: Doubleday.

Boston Globe Staff. (2002). *Betrayal: The crisis in the catholic church.* New York: Little Brown.

Braceland, F. (1972). *The institute of living, 1822–1972.* Hartford, CT: Institute of Living.

Burkett, E., & Bruni, F. (1993). *A gospel of shame: Children sexual abuse, and the Catholic church.* New York: Viking.

Cozzens, D. (2000). *The changing face of the priesthood.* Collegeville, MN: Liturgical Press.

Farnsworth, D., & Braceland, F. (Eds.). (1969). *Psychiatry, the clergy, and pastoral counseling.* Collegeville, MN: St. John's University Press.

Gabbard, G., and Lester, E. (1995). *Boundaries and boundary violations in psychoanalysis.* New York: Basic Books.

Harrington, C., & Lothstein, L. Sexual misconduct and neuropsychiatric disorders in Roman Catholic clergy. Under editorial review.

Jenkins, P. (1996). *Pedophiles and priests: Anatomy of a contemporary crisis.* New York: Oxford University Press.

Jordan, M. (2000). *The silence of sodom: Homosexuality in modern Catholicism.* Chicago: University of Chicago Press.

Lothstein, L. (1990). Etiology and psychological theories of pedophilia and ephebophilia. In S. Rossetti (Ed.), *Slayer of the soul.* Madison, CT: Twenty-Third Publications.

Lothstein, L. (1991). Can a sexually addicted priest return to ministry after treatment? Psychological issues and possible forensic solutions. *Catholic Lawyer, 1,* 89–113.

Lothstein, L. (1999). Neuropsychological sequelae of priests who have sexually abused. In T.G. Plante (Ed.), *Bless me father for I have sinned: Perspectives on sexual abuse committed by Roman Catholic priests.* Westport, CT: Greenwood/Prager.

Lothstein, L. (2000, October 22). *Recommendations to the Governor's Commission on credentialing for sex offender treaters.* State of Connecticut Documents. Hartford, CT: Author.

Lothstein, L., & LeFleur-Bach, R. (2002). Group therapy treatment of sex offenders: A hybrid psychodynamic approach. In J. Magnavita (Ed.), *Comprehensive handbook of psychotherapy.* New York: John Wiley & Sons.

Lothstein, L., & Rossetti, S. (1990). Myths of the child molester. In S. Rossetti (Ed.), *Slayer of the soul.* Mystic, CT: Twenty-Third Publications.

Schoener, G. (2002). *Betrayal: The crisis in the Catholic church.* New York: Little Brown.

Schwartz, B. (1999). *The sex offender: Theoretical advances, treating special populations and legal developments* (Vol. 3). Kingston, NJ: Civic Research Institute.

Schwartz, B. (2002). *The sex offender: Current treatment modalities and systems issues* (Vol. 4). Kingston, NJ: Civic Research Institute.

Schwartz, B., & Cellini, H. (1995). *The sex offender, corrections: Treatment and legal practice* (Vol. 1). Kingston, NJ: Civic Research Institute.

Schwartz, B., & Cellini, H. (1997). *The sex offender: New insights, treatment innovations and legal developments* (Vol. 2). Kingston, NJ: Civic Research Institute.

Sipe, R. (1990). *Sexuality and the search for celibacy.* New York: Brunner/Mazel.

Sipe, R. (1995). *Sex priests and power: Anatomy of a crisis.* New York: Brunner/Mazel.

Valenti, N., & diMeglio, C. (1974). *Sex and the confessional.* New York: Stein and Day.

Chapter 13

BARRIERS TO RESPONDING TO THE CLERGY SEXUAL ABUSE CRISIS WITHIN THE ROMAN CATHOLIC CHURCH

John C. Gonsiorek

As I finalize this chapter, the media have focused in the past week on for-mer Oklahoma Governor Frank Keating's resignation as Chair of the National Review Board to oversee the Catholic Church's response to the sexual abuse crisis in the Catholic Church in the United States. His open and sharp criticism of Los Angeles Cardinal Roger Mahony and others for refusing to fully cooperate with the Board was considered sufficiently egregious that it rendered his leadership untenable.

The other story of note this week was the arrest of Bishop Thomas O'Brien of Phoenix, Arizona, for his fatal hit-and-run of a pedestrian, then followed by his resignation. Recently, Bishop O'Brien had entered into a highly unusual agreement with local prosecutors in which he surrendered some of his administrative authority in exchange for avoiding criminal prosecution for his role in knowingly transferring priests with a history of sexual abuse, without informing their receiving parishes or supervisors. This last apparently did not warrant his resignation.

I will return to these twin events at the end of this chapter, as they rep-resent dramatic, but unfortunately not uncommon examples of institu-tional barriers to responding to the clergy sexual abuse crisis within the Roman Catholic Church. While these specific stories will soon become old news, I suspect they will be replaced with comparable accounts.

I approach this topic from a series of experiences that have shaped my perspective. In the late 1970s, fresh out of graduate school, I worked at an agency that tried to respond to the problem of sexual exploitation by psychotherapists by providing services for victims, consultation for professions and agencies, and eventually evaluations for professionals engaged in sexual exploitation. After leaving that agency, I continued to work independently in that area, especially with the last component, eventually developing with colleagues an evaluation model for sexually exploitative mental health professionals (Gonsiorek, 1995a; Gonsiorek & Schoener, 1987; Schoener & Gonsiorek, 1988), and then expanding the model to health care professionals in general, clergy, teachers, and other helping professions. In addition to rendering such evaluations, I also provided training and education, and expert witness testimony in these and related issues. I worked for many years with the Episcopal Insurance Trust, providing for them and various Episcopal dioceses evaluations of impaired clergy; but I have also evaluated clergy from most major denominations. Throughout this, I also provided psychotherapy for both victims and perpetrators of professional exploitation. Finally, I also developed an entirely different area of expertise and practice in the area of sexual orientation and identity. As these latter issues sometimes became confounded with sexual exploitation issues, a perspective from sexual identity was often a useful adjunct to understand sexual exploitation. These perspectives and experiences, like any others, are accompanied by particular lacunae, but I believe I have a reasonably well-rounded take on sexual abuse by clergy.

Throughout all this, I have developed a hypothesis that there truly is something different in the Roman Catholic Church about the problem of sexual exploitation, different from its manifestations in health care professions, and even different (for the most part) from its manifestations in most other religious denominations. I do not believe the differences lie in the usually named suspects of the left and right: celibacy; anti-Catholicism; the Church's views of women, homosexuality, or sexuality in general; the purported corruption of North American society; greedy attorneys and litigious clients; and others. These all do add to the brew, although perhaps not in ways their advocates purport.

Rather, I believe what is distinctive about the manifestation of this general problem in the Roman Catholic Church in particular has most to do with idiosyncrasies of Church structure, especially its leadership structure. Simply stated, sexual exploitation in its varying forms occurs in most environments where there is opportunity. Whether it is managed, or whether it spreads and becomes institutionalized, is a function primarily of the response to it. When there is a consistent clustering of exploitation, and when it remains unamenable to amelioration over time: then that is a very different problem, namely a pervasive failure and dysfunction of leadership.

I will review a number of barriers that I believe are common to all entities responding to sexual exploitation, with special emphasis on their
application to the Catholic Church. I will then describe barriers I believe
are more or less distinctive to the Catholic Church, and will discuss implications and possible remedies.

TYPICAL BARRIERS IN RESPONDING TO SEXUAL ABUSE

Insensitivity/Denial/Lack of Awareness

Every helping profession/institution that has addressed the problem of
sexual exploitation would like to believe that it did so voluntarily, driven
by its own sense of ethics. This is an illusion. In fact, the profession/
institution responded because it had to, not because it chose to. In every
case, the initial responses were denial, blaming the messenger, and insen-
sitivity. Malpractice or other civil action, adverse publicity, public outcry
and resulting pressure from policy makers, and the like necessitated
change. In most cases, change was driven by relentless attorneys, unyield-
ing media, a few courageous victims, and even fewer courageous insiders
within the profession/institution. Once change occurs, this history is con-
veniently forgotten (see Gonsiorek, 1995b; Schoener, 1995).

I do not mean this in a cynical way: it is the nature of power and human
failing. The Roman Catholic Church is no better or worse in this regard, in
terms of the degree of its initial maladaptive response. What does appear
to be emerging as distinctive, however, is its seeming intransigence in
responding to the forces of change, even to the point of operating against
its own self-interest. I speculate about this below.

Difficulties with the Investigatory Process

Once actually responding to sexual abuse became a goal of professions/
institutions, how to investigate such complaints in a legally effective manner emerged as a challenge to law enforcement and regulatory agencies,
such as health care licensing boards. After a few decades of trial and error,
and much borrowing of ideas and methodologies from law enforcement,
such agencies have generally evolved protocols and procedures. These are
imperfect, they continue to be revised, they may be inconsistently applied,
but they are a reliable start. In many jurisdictions, complaints will generally be processed in a consistent manner that often passes legal scrutiny,

and is congruent with the technologies and methodologies available. Further, there is often receptivity to altering and improving procedures as experience and case law dictate.

The situation has been more difficult for religious institutions, as they typically do not have available the legal mandates, clear jurisdiction, and internal expertise to easily render such investigatory processes. But, this gap can be bridged, often by adapting relevant aspects of investigatory processes from non-religious professions/institutions.

The Episcopal Church is a case in point. For each diocese to independently develop such structures was daunting, especially so for smaller, less wealthy dioceses. The Episcopal Insurance Trust, which offers malpractice and other coverage to dioceses, also offers investigatory consultation, referrals to approved evaluators, training to the entire Church leadership, and similar services. Following Insurance Trust protocols is required for those dioceses insured with them, although Episcopal dioceses are not required to be insured through them. However, by creating a methodology and a standard, the Trust has effectively shaped and moved forward the responses to sexual abuse of an entire denomination. The dioceses retain the degree of autonomy that is part of the Episcopal tradition; yet, a more or less organized, coherent, and effective mechanism for responding to sexual abuse in that denomination has emerged. Many questions remain, such as whether the Episcopal Church as a Church should require a uniform response to sexual abuse from all dioceses. Nevertheless, the Episcopal Church has developed an organized mechanism for responding to sexual abuse while it considers the implications of further responses.

My impression of the Roman Catholic Church in this regard is one of positive movement, but with noteworthy elements of variability and fragility. Some Catholic dioceses have adopted investigatory mechanisms as sophisticated as any that currently exist (for example, see Maris & McDonough, 1995), others are essentially random or chaotic in their investigatory responses, and every variation along that continuum also exists. Any given diocesan response style often seems dependent on the skill and/or commitment of particular bishops, vicars general, or other staff. A shift in local policy is vulnerable to a change in personnel. As the Roman Catholic Church in the United States considers the pros and cons of various response mechanisms, it would do well to look to other denominations for creative, albeit imperfect, models for striking a balance between an organized Church-wide response and traditions of local authority. In reality, all responses at this point in time are imperfect; moving ahead with a "good-enough" more-or-less consistent process, may be as good as it gets.

This issue is especially salient because more so than in most mental health evaluations, an accurate behavioral history of an alleged offender is central to an effective evaluation. (See Gonsiorek, 1995a, pp. 155–159.) Sexual abuse behaviors are noteworthy for the degree to which other markers of mental health or behavioral problems are generally minimal or absent. It is only a slight exaggeration to state that the behavioral history is the diagnosis. If an accurate behavioral history is lacking, an evaluation will be hampered. Mental health evaluators have serious ethical constraints in performing investigatory functions on those whom they are evaluating. More germane, they also generally lack skill and training in such investigation, which is more properly a law enforcement function. A private investigator or retired police detective may have much more to offer in this regard than a psychologist.

Problems with the Evaluation Process

In recent decades, methodologies have developed for estimating whether and under what circumstances an impaired professional might return to practice. These methodologies have been applied to a variety of health care and other helping professionals and clergy, and a variety of models have been put forth. (Bryant, 1999; Gabbard, 1989, 1995; Gonsiorek, 1995a, 1999; Irons, 1995; see also Bryant, Lothstein, and Markham & Mikail, this volume).

All existing methodologies at this point in time are tentative and works in progress. As noted above, all are dependent on accurate and complete information about the alleged impaired professional's behavioral history from investigatory sources outside the evaluation process. All are weakened when referring institutions otherwise attempt to shape the process.

The question of whether mental health evaluators led the Church astray regarding sexual predators has recently emerged as a heated topic. Over the years, I have certainly read enough reports from other mental health evaluators to attest that there has been no shortage of such evaluators who are ill trained in their methodologies, reckless in their recommendations, and grandiose in their ability to predict. At the same time, the rough and tumble of scientific inquiry and debate and the distinct interest taken by state licensing boards in these matters, has resulted in a system in which there is evolution of ideas, critical feedback, and some degree of accountability.

This issue is multisided. Many dioceses have heavily utilized Church-sponsored or Church-affiliated institutions for such evaluations. As Leslie Lothstein describes in this volume, Church leaders have often not been shy in attempting to shape evaluation outcomes even in non-Church-affiliated institutions; the pressures on Church-affiliated institutions can only be assumed to be more intense.

Ultimately, the power to refer or not in itself provides great clout. Institutions and individual practitioners who provide such evaluations are highly specialized, and there are a finite number of referral sources. Institutions are especially vulnerable: an individual provider can more easily practice in other areas than an institution can develop new programs, when referral sources dry up. Church institutions have been very particular in their selection of evaluators, and have been inconsistent in whether they select primarily on the basis of quality and independence, versus responsivity to needs of the referral source. I have sometimes pondered while reading a poorly rendered evaluation of an impaired priest, "Where do they find these evaluators?" I do not exactly know, but they do find them.

Lack of a Sound Database

As John Loftus has detailed in this volume, our areas of ignorance exceed our areas of knowledge in the domain of clergy sexual abuse. This is not unique. There is a similar dearth of information on outcomes in the rehabilitation of impaired health professionals, and similar resistance in the health care professions to remedying the situation.

Such research is expensive, funding is difficult to come by, and proper methodology for the research is a significant challenge; the usual litany of impediments exists, and these are as genuine as they are potentially manageable. But more centrally, there is also a lack of will and commitment. No state/provincial licensing board or professional ethics committee unambivalently welcomes longitudinal research that will elucidate these issues and, simultaneously, adumbrate their failures and inconsistencies. I know of no state/provincial licensing board or professional ethics committee that requires those under its jurisdiction who have been disciplined to submit to longitudinal research as part of their requirements for professional reinstatement. I have approached three boards with this suggestion, without success; and the idea is not original to me. The boards do have the ability to stipulate this. Some are beginning to require impaired licensees to document follow-through with rehabilitative plans via monitoring programs, and this is a start. The central issue, however, remains whether such professionals will avoid re-offense until death or retirement, and that is a much taller order than compliance with a time-limited stipulation.

Again, in this regard, the religious denominations and the Roman Catholic Church in particular, are no better or worse than the health care professions. There is another avenue for data collection which is available to the health care professions, and is beginning to be utilized by some religious denominations: claims data from malpractice carriers. For example, as a psychologist with malpractice insurance through the American Psychological Association Insurance Trust (APAIT), I can inquire of them what are the riskiest areas of professional practice in my state, what are typical settlements for certain malpractice actions, and so on. They track and dispense such information. It is admittedly incomplete, and it reflects the recent past, not the present; but it is helpful. They also develop risk management workshops for psychologists based on the trends they have observed in malpractice actions. They provide consultation to insureds to help manage potentially litigious situations as they emerge. This is beyond the scope of a traditional malpractice carrier that merely defends the insured when sued, but it is increasingly emerging as part of the risk management package provided to insureds. The Episcopal Insurance Trust provides comparable services to its insured dioceses.

This expanded role of the malpractice carrier can only develop out of an objective, thoughtful, and most importantly, transparent appraisal of claims data. Again, claims data are an imprecise and incomplete reflection of the problem of sexual abuse, but they are a start, and one with pragmatic and helpful applications. The Roman Catholic Church would do well to emulate such examples.

The Current State of Typical Barriers

It is generally forgotten that some infectious diseases that plagued humankind were managed before the advent of antibiotics and other specific therapies. Tuberculosis is a case in point: public health measures, modern sanitation, and isolation of the infected drastically reduced prevalence of the disease decades before actual specific treatments were discovered.

I believe we are at a similar point with professional exploitation. We lack important data; we have what I am certain will eventually be considered rudimentary methodologies of investigation and evaluation; and we are essentially experimenting with a range of remedies in criminal, civil, and administrative law. It is insufficient, yet it has been "good enough" to initiate and, so far, sustain a process of change. Professions that once treated sexual exploitation with a wink and a nod have moved to consistent condemnation and accountability. Mechanisms of justice are being attempted and refined. Some data collection is occurring, albeit often through a risk-management motivation. Practice patterns have evidenced some shifts to less risky alternatives.

Change, imperfect but nonetheless real, has occurred. Why then, does the Roman Catholic Church seem like an outlier in this change process? I have no final answer to whether the Roman Catholic Church is in fact an outlier or not. However, to ascribe to the media and legal professions the role of unjust and biased persecutor of the Roman Catholic Church has always seemed a bit facile to me. My observation is more that they are equal opportunity, not affirmative action, in their selection of targets; they tend to go where the action is, indiscriminately. As some of the journalists in this volume have detailed, at least some Roman Catholic dioceses have consistently operated in ways to warrant the legal and media attentions they have earned.

I will operate on the assumption, not the certainty, that there is something different about the Roman Catholic Church in this regard, and speculate about what these features might be.

BARRIERS IN RESPONDING TO SEXUAL ABUSE DISTINCTIVE OF THE ROMAN CATHOLIC CHURCH

I speculate that the factors below are not unique to the Roman Catholic Church, but that they are more or less distinctive about its response to the clergy abuse crisis, and likely beyond.

Leadership as Aristocracy

For many years, I puzzled over the seemingly wild variations in personnel practice sometimes exercised by the Roman Catholic Church. Most institutions handling sexual abuse matters displayed greater than typical variability, and struggled to find workable responses. But the Catholic Church seemed more so, acting at times against its own self-interest, even to being frankly self-defeating. A number of denominations allow bishops the degree of local control the Catholic Church does; many institutions experience episodic shifts between local and central control. These did not seem like adequate explanations.

It has occurred to me that the Roman Catholic leadership functions as a true aristocracy, in that it operates on an assumption that those outside leadership have lesser worth, and exist in large part to service leadership. Clergy are above laity; high-ranking clergy count more than priests; laity with means have more worth than those without. From this perspective, the point of reference is always above: the crucial factors in decision making are the needs of the layer above. The different layers can have different needs, and as difficult situations rise to the attentions increasingly higher in the hierarchy, the operative needs change, and the Church's responses seem contradictory. The immediate impression is one of chaos, but the underlying principle is that the operative needs of the next level up will govern decision making. Consistency is not especially salient.

This operating principle runs contrary to the expressed moral values of the Church, which means it is unarticulated, officially denied, and often suppressed internally even by those who operate on its basis. This hypothesis cannot be proved in any formal sense, but it can be useful in understanding the fluctuations in Church response to many of the challenges of sexual abuse. Priests who should not be reinstated, are; while those who should, languish without positions. Promotion seems more loyalty- than competence-driven. The bishops will determine one course of action and the Vatican another. Apply it to situations where you have enough specific information to test it; I believe you will find it often has explanatory utility.

The drift into a sense of aristocracy may well be a risk to all holders of power. The Roman Catholic Church seems unusual in the degree to which this predicts their behavior, and it is literally the social structure from which Church leadership evolved historically. I believe it is fair to describe it as characteristic of them.

Priesthood as Ontological Transformation

Many faith traditions conceptualize the role of priest as involving a transformation of the person. The sacramental view of priesthood in the Roman Catholic tradition involves a view of a profound ontological transformation in the person who is made priest.

This essentially theological perspective becomes relevant in the clergy abuse crisis because it poses a significant barrier to recognizing and accepting that some priests may be too flawed to function as priests in the world. Rather, the implicit assumption in the Roman Catholic tradition is that the flawed priest should be able to return to priestly functioning once he has fully re-engaged his priestly role. This re-engagement is spiritual.

Unfortunately, none of the available literature predicting recidivism outcomes in sexually offending persons suggests that such a variable is relevant as a predictor. As a result, there is a chronic and pervasive tendency in the Roman Catholic Church to confound forgiveness and reconciliation in a spiritual sense, with rehabilitation in a psychological sense. What I am suggesting is that these are orthogonal to each other; they are apples and oranges, one does not reliably predict the other. What might be helpful to the Roman Catholic Church is to develop a theologically understandable status for those individuals who may meet spiritual criteria for re-engagement as clergy, but who do not meet mental health criteria for rehabilitation to the point where they are estimated to be able to practice safely.

As a psychologist, not a theologian, I do not have any ideas on how to accomplish this. However, I have followed with interest the efforts of St. John's Benedictine Abbey in Collegeville, Minnesota, which has in its community a number of clergy who have sexually offended. They are working out a mechanism to retain such members in the community, while simultaneously removing them from contact that might pose a risk.

Unusually Adversarial Relationship with Behavioral/Social/Medical Sciences

These sciences and many religious denominations have a turf battle: both attempt to understand and effect positive change in the human condition. The conflict with these sciences is especially pointed, because there is a very close match with the missions of both, but a wide disparity in ways of understanding, methodologies, and traditions. The conflict is much less so than with the physical sciences, although this was not always the case. The Church once claimed these, too, as their province, and only slowly relinquished these.

As these sciences increasingly have substantive benefits to offer society, the adversarial relationship has worsened. Perhaps I am being partisan, but my perspective is that until recently, the attitude from the sciences was one of indifference to religion, and the attitude of religion was one of active distrust. As the status of these sciences has risen, some denominations have actively developed parallel science to provide a more credible vehicle for their perspective, resulting in "creationism science," private foundation-created "research," and aggressive disinformation campaigns, this last most typically to provide "scientific" justifications for certain theological positions about sexuality. As a result of these attempts to co-opt science, mutual active distrust is increasingly common.

I suggest that the greater loser in this will be religion. Scientists have a long tradition of challenge, confrontation, and discarding theories that do not make the grade empirically. We may resent it when others masquerade as scientists, but ultimately all the players in scientific debates will be subjected to the same scrutiny and leveling process, and if an outsider has a better idea (as they sometimes do), we will shamelessly and gladly incorporate it as our own.

But when some religious denominations believe their own press, and become confused (as some seem to be) about what is disinformation they have sponsored versus what is scientific discourse, they lose a source of information that can serve as a wellspring to challenge and invigorate theological discourse. At one time, the Church could find no way to incorporate the notion of the earth as round. Some denominations have found that evolutionary biology poses no real threat and offers some catalytic ideas. Emerging scientific understandings of human nature and human sexuality in particular can, I believe, be a positive source of theological development if scientists do science well and creatively and theologians do theology well and creatively.

In this characteristic, the Roman Catholic Church is clearly in company of a number of conservative Protestant denominations.

Theologically Rationalized Abnegation of the Human Body/Sexuality

The faith traditions in the Judeo-Christian lineage vary considerably in their views of sexuality. Within that lineage, the Roman Catholic tradition is among the group most ill at ease with sexuality and the body; no other tradition in that lineage idealizes celibacy to the extent the Roman Catholic tradition does (see Richard Sipe, this volume).

If one is of the belief that the solution to the clergy sexual abuse crisis will entail a re-examination of many aspects of sexuality, it seems likely that the Roman Catholic Church, as it currently conceptualizes the body and sexuality, is particularly handicapped in this task. If one perceives sexual expression as illegitimate, except for the purpose of procreation, and elevates celibacy even above that, it is difficult to appreciate the reality of sexual abuse on a fundamental level. The essential spoiling of sexuality that typically accompanies sexual abuse cannot be comprehended if sexuality is not seen as valuable in its own right, and on its own terms, without necessary reference to a procreative purpose. I believe this is one of the reasons the celibate, aspirationally if not behaviorally, Church hierarchy has such a difficult time coming to terms with the meaning of sexual abuse of minors, who have no legitimized procreative function.

Another impediment exists in the Church's pervasive sexism, which becomes framed predominantly as a question about the ordination of women. The theological ramifications of this issue are best left for theologians, who have offered a variety of opinions within the Christian traditions. On a pragmatic level, there is a high price to pay in not having individuals socialized to take care of children (i.e., women) in substantive roles in the Church power structure. When this issue becomes predominantly focused on women as clergy, other options are neglected. If lay leadership were to have a substantive role as Bill Spohn suggests in this volume, opportunities would exist for serious female leadership. Even more to the point, a pool of potential female leadership whose loyalty, energy, and commitment are proven, already exists: female religious. Literal priesthood is not the only vehicle for meaningful power, as the experiences of other Christian denominations indicate. Simply stated, if the leadership of the Roman Catholic Church is serious about treating women as full and legitimate members of a faith community, let it create vehicles for women in the Church to have roles of power, and not hide behind the women-as-clergy issue.

I say this not to be argumentative, but in recognition of the sea change that has occurred in the area of sexual abuse in those denominations that have genuinely embraced women in positions of power. This alone does not solve the sexual abuse problem—there is no magic bullet—but the shift in denominations such as the Episcopal Church has been palpable, surprisingly rapid, and less contentious than feared. With the existence of female religious traditions in the Roman Catholic Church, as developed and venerable as those of male religious, the lack of serious efforts to engage women as substantive leaders is difficult to comprehend except as sexism plain and simple.

The final example of this characteristic discussed here is homosexuality, although the potential examples are legion. The persistent efforts of the Church hierarchy to blame pedophilia on homosexuality are without foundation from a behavioral sciences perspective (articles by Cantor, 2002; Ream, 2002; and Stevenson, 2002, provide a solid introduction to this issue). Similarly, the persistent efforts of the Church hierarchy to appropriate scientific credibility by couching theological arguments against homosexuality in the language and terminology of science (e.g., labeling homosexuality as intrinsically disordered) are arrogant and fraudulent. This is not a useful or credible stance for an arbiter of morality.

Even in attempts to be accepting, the Church has trouble with this issue. In Coleman's contribution in this volume, he describes the German bishops criteria for possible admission of a homosexual candidate. They seek men who are secure in sexual orientation, possessing of psychic stability, with no need to announce sexual orientation, who deal well with intimacy, and who are internally and externally accepting of the Church's teaching on homosexuality; among other factors.

Such a person is simply unlikely to exist. The existing research that addresses factors predicting sound psychological adjustment in homosexual individuals consistently cites self-acceptance, a support system of other homosexuals, comfort with reasonable disclosure, and similar factors as predictive (see Savin-Williams & Cohen, 1996, for an introduction to this literature, especially chapters 5, 8, and 20). It is difficult to understand or even take seriously a position that asserts that truly accepting oneself as intrinsically disordered and avoiding disclosure can correlate with stability, security about orientation, and the ability to sustain intimacy.

In summary, institutional Church teaching on human sexuality and the body has developed in such an abnegating manner that it lacks credibility, even to most identified Catholics. The only way it seems to make sense is as an enhancement and justification of the status of an aspirationally celibate aristocratic hierarchy.

Siege Mentality as Characteristic Response to Criticism

This characteristic can perhaps best be seen as an outcome of aristocratic leadership. The first response to criticism of the Church often seems to be outrage. Voicing criticism in itself makes one suspect, and unless it is quickly mollified and repudiated, the usual reaction is to neutralize the critic at all costs regardless of the merits of the criticism, the stature of the critic, or the cost in credibility to the institutional Church. Witness Frank Keating, who merely uttered what many viewed as self-evident, and what some in Church leadership themselves had in effect stated.

The operating principle seems to be that those lower are always out of line if they criticize those higher, because their lowered status gives them no right to do so, and in fact, it is unnatural to the order of things if they do so. This characteristic interacts with the adversarial relationship to science described above. While no scientist likely enjoys criticism, most operate on the principle that criticism is the engine that keeps science moving along. The disrespect of criticism by Church hierarchy engenders disrespect of the Church hierarchy by scientists. Finally, this characteristic may provide additional assistance in understanding the communication and understanding problems between the Vatican and the American Church, which John Allen describes in this volume. Americans have long had a deep distrust of aristocracies; aristocracies find subversive those who do not acknowledge their prerogatives.

FINAL THOUGHTS

I have outlined some barriers to responding to sexual abuse faced by all professions/institutions, and suggested some ways in which the Roman Catholic Church can learn from these efforts.

Some of the features I have hypothesized as barriers characteristic of the Roman Catholic Church require theological solutions, for which I have little to contribute. I can, and hope I have, directed attention to areas that might be productive to consider. My experience with the Roman Catholic Church in recent decades has been akin to watching a person fall down the same flight of stairs over and over again. I do not believe I can necessarily instruct the person on how to walk differently, but I feel I can say with some certainty that that is the task before them.

My instinct is that the characteristic barriers will likely be manageable, if the Church hierarchy can disabuse itself of its heritage of leadership as aristocracy. Bill Spohn in this volume has more specific suggestions along those lines. From where I stand today, however, it is difficult to find cause for optimism on that issue. The Keating affair was demoralizing enough; turning the page and reading about Bishop O'Brien was more so. It has been this way for months, and there is no end in sight. These particular events will fade from memory, as have the specifics of the myriad missteps of the Roman Catholic leadership in recent years. Unfortunately, I suspect they will be replaced with new outrages. The laity and frontline priests have generally shown the patience of saints and the persistence of martyrs, and have little but hierarchical scorn to show for it.

In the end, all I can offer is the observation that the vast majority of non-sexually offending priests, who work very hard on the front lines, and the laity who have by and large remained faithful and hopeful, deserve a great deal better than the inept and profoundly disappointing leadership they have so far endured. I do not think they will wait forever.

REFERENCES

Bryant, C. (1999). Psychological treatment of priest sex offenders. In T. G. Plante (Ed.), *Bless me father for I have sinned: Perspectives on sexual abuse committed by Roman Catholic priests* (pp. 87–110). Westport, CT: Praeger.

Cantor, J. M. (2002). Male homosexuality and pedophilia. *American Psychological Association Division 44 Newsletter, 18* (3), 5–8.

Gabbard, G. O. (1995). Psychotherapists who transgress sexual boundaries with patients. In J. C. Gonsiorek (Ed.), *Breach of trust: Sexual exploitation by health care professionals and clergy* (pp. 133–144). Newbury Park, CA: Sage Publications.

Gabbard, G. O. (Ed.). (1989). *Sexual exploitation in professional relationships.* Washington, DC: American Psychiatric Press.

Gonsiorek, J. C. (1995a). Assessment for rehabilitation of exploitative health care professionals and clergy. In J. C. Gonsiorek (Ed.), *Breach of trust: Sexual exploitation by health care professionals and clergy* (pp. 145–162). Newbury Park, CA: Sage Publications.

Gonsiorek, J. C. (1995b). Epilogue. In J. C. Gonsiorek (Ed.), *Breach of trust: Sexual exploitation by health care professionals and clergy* (pp. 392–396). Newbury Park, CA: Sage Publications.

Gonsiorek, J. C. (1999). Forensic psychological examinations in clergy abuse. In T. G. Plante (Ed.), *Bless me father for I have sinned: Perspectives on sexual abuse committed by Roman Catholic priests* (pp. 27–57). Westport, CT: Praeger.

Gonsiorek, J. C., & Schoener, G. R. (1987). Assessment and evaluation of therapists who sexually exploit clients. *Professional Practice of Psychology, 8,* 79–93.

Irons, R. R. (1995). Inpatient assessment of the sexually exploitative professional. In J. C. Gonsiorek (Ed.), *Breach of trust: Sexual exploitation by health care professionals and clergy* (pp. 163–175). Newbury Park, CA: Sage Publications.

Maris, M. E., & McDonough, K. M. (1995). How churches respond to victims and offenders of clergy sexual misconduct. In J. C. Gonsiorek (Ed.), *Breach of trust: Sexual exploitation by health care professionals and clergy* (pp. 348–367). Newbury Park, CA: Sage Publications.

Ream, G. L. (2002). Fundamentalist attribution error. *American Psychological Association Division 44 Newsletter, 18* (3), 13.

Savin-Williams, R. C., & Cohen, K. M. (Eds.). (1995). *The lives of lesbians, gays and bisexuals: Children to adults.* Fort Worth, TX: Harcourt Brace.

Schoener, G. R. (1995). Historical overview. In J. C. Gonsiorek (Ed.), *Breach of trust: Sexual exploitation by health care professionals and clergy* (pp. 3–17). Newbury Park, CA: Sage Publications.

Schoener, G. R., & Gonsiorek, J. C. (1988). Assessment and development of rehabilitation plans for counselors who have sexually exploited their clients. *Journal of Counseling and Development, 67,* 227–232.

Stevenson, M. R. (2002). Understanding child sexual abuse and the Catholic Church: Gay priests are not the problem. *American Psychological Association Division 44 Newsletter, 18,* 9–11.

Chapter 14

EPISCOPAL RESPONSIBILITY FOR THE SEXUAL ABUSE CRISIS

William C. Spohn

At their meeting in November 2002, the American Catholic bishops issued an important document on the morality of the proposed invasion of Iraq. As the Bush administration was trying to build a coalition in the United Nations Security Council, the bishops raised serious questions about the morality of the newly declared American strategic policy of preventive war. A few weeks before, Bishop Wilton Gregory, the president of the conference of bishops, had warned that preemptive action against Iraq failed to meet the Just War criterion because the threat from Iraq to the United States was neither clear, grave, nor imminent. Although the November meeting had concentrated on the Vatican response to the Charter for Victims of Sexual Abuse, the conference strongly affirmed Bishop Gregory's criticisms of the proposed invasion.

The document was presented to the press by Cardinal Bernard Law of Boston, who was the chair of the committee that produced it and also the central figure in the scandal over clerical sexual abuse and official cover-up. The irony may have been lost on the bishops, but not on the public. The document had no discernible effect on U.S. Catholic support for the invasion and quickly sank from public view. Within weeks, Cardinal Law was beset by new revelations about his reassignment of habitual offenders to parishes where they continued to abuse young people, and under growing pressure from laity and clergy in Boston, he resigned his post.

This incident was not only an astonishing failure of public relations, but also a symptom of a deeper crisis in the episcopacy. Apparently no bishop had the courage to point out that the cardinal's lack of moral credibility would thoroughly obstruct the message. It was like having Enron's Chairman Kenneth Lay giving a lecture on business ethics. More importantly, the incident signaled a disturbing institutional change in the American Catholic Church: the sexual abuse crisis had turned into a crisis of leadership and severely compromised the bishops' moral authority.

This erosion of authority is especially troubling to moral theologians like the author, who cannot effectively serve the Church unless the bishops fulfill their role as moral teachers. Moral theologians are not merely agents of the hierarchy. They bring insights of contemporary culture and scholarship into the discussion, bishops contribute the wisdom of the tradition and perspectives of the global communion of churches, and the laity provide their own expertise and experience. Bishops, moral theologians, biblical scholars, social scientists, policy makers, and ordinary citizens worked together to produce the 1983 document on nuclear deterrence, the most effective intervention in the history of the Catholic Church in America (Greeley, 1985, p. 226). If today's bishops tried to exercise similar leadership, would anyone pay attention?

Many observers fear that the bishops have lost their moral voice in American society because of the actions of some of their number in the sexual abuse crisis. As a Catholic moral theologian, I fear the loss is real and hope that it is only temporary. American culture needs the moral witness of bishops like John Hughes, John Ireland, Raymond Hunthausen, and Joseph Bernardin. So long as the bishops appear to be more committed to protecting the institution than to protecting children and adolescents from predatory clerics, they will forfeit any claim to moral leadership. As moral theologian Lisa Sowle Cahill of Boston College wrote:

> The church and its leaders want to provide moral leadership for Catholics and non-Catholics alike, not only on issues like abortion but also on capital punishment, health care, welfare reform, and foreign policy. Their traditional commitment has been to stand up for the rights of society's vulnerable. But revelations that the church has allowed some members of the clergy known to be pedophiles to remain in the ministry may call into doubt the sincerity of this commitment.

Cahill calls for extensive lay involvement to make lasting changes in "a closed society largely insulated from the realities and values of ordinary people and in denial of many aspects of human sexuality" (Cahill, 2002, p. 25).

In this essay I want to address briefly the moral responsibility of bishops for the crises of sexual abuse and official cover-up and then propose two specific measures for repairing the damage done to the Church's ministry. The first recommendation is the removal from office of every bishop who knowingly reassigned clerical abusers who subsequently victimized more young people. The second recommendation is for systemic reform of the way in which bishops are chosen. The historically recent centralization of episcopal appointment into the hands of the Vatican violates Catholic tradition and has made many bishops less accountable to the people of the local churches they are ordained to serve. Apologies and expressions of regret will not resolve the crisis of leadership in the American Church. Structural reform is needed to address the fundamental problem because the current process of selection too often produces bishops whose primary loyalty is to their patrons in Rome rather than to the people of God.

EPISCOPAL RESPONSIBILITY

This essay is not the place to assess the religious or legal responsibility of specific bishops for the current crisis. Matters of conscience are between the individual and God; legal liabilities must be worked out in the courts and lawsuit settlement conferences. What must be judged is the level of public moral accountability. With the exception of two who have resigned, American bishops have not been directly involved in sexual abuse of minors. The question is what *indirect* responsibility ecclesiastical leaders incurred by dismissing reports of abuse, shielding offenders from prosecution, reassigning them to positions where they could abuse again, covering up ecclesiastical records, and resisting just claims of the victims? The traditional moral theology aptly described this situation:

> The guilt of *indirect or negative co-operation in injustice* is incurred by any one who permits injury to be done to others, either by omitting to restrain the criminal by words (*mutus*), or in deed (*non obstans*), or by neglecting to report his conduct to the proper authorities (*non manifestans*). (Koch and Preuss, 1924, p. 401)

Restitution to those damaged is obliged only when "the negative cooperators" were bound to prevent the injustice by their office or by contract.

The concept of indirect responsibility is common in legal systems. Military officers are indirectly responsible for their subordinates' war crimes when they fail to restrain them in combat or when they cover up crimes later. The analogy is clear: when bishops contribute to the abuse of minors by failing to restrain offenders or covering up for them, they bear indirect responsibility for the crimes. Even though the evil of abuse was not directly caused by shielding and reassigning offenders, those actions were the necessary, though not the sufficient, conditions for the subsequent abuse of minors. The evil would not have continued if the appropriate superiors had exercised the "due diligence" required of their office.

Sexual abuse of minors is, sadly, not uncommon in American society. As Thomas Plante argues in this volume, the rate of abusers in the priesthood is estimated to be lower than among teachers, coaches, and other occupations that have contact with youth. Although there is a higher proportion of sexual offenders in these other occupations, the most notorious clerical offenders had a surprisingly high number of victims. Instead of being reported, fired, and criminally charged, priests were often shielded from such consequences by their superiors. Some bishops and superiors of religious orders reassigned offenders to parishes and schools without notifying pastors or parishioner of their history. One of the Archdiocese of Boston's worst offenders, Rev. Paul Stanley, was recommended for incardination into the Diocese of San Bernardino without any mention of his long and sordid record. The bishop of San Bernardino subsequently filed a lawsuit against the Archdiocese of Boston, an extremely rare occurrence in the Church. This pattern of secrecy and institutional protection enabled the offenders to victimize many more young people. The crisis of sexual abuse by priests raised serious questions about their selection and seminary training. It was, however, the unfolding revelations of episcopal complicity in protecting abusive priests that exposed the crisis of abuse as an historic failure of leadership on the part of the hierarchy. This leads to the first recommendation:

> Any bishop who reassigned a known clerical abuser after 1992 to a situation where subsequent acts of sexual abuse of minors occurred should be removed from office. This recommendation also applies to present bishops who, before they became bishops, as diocesan officials participated centrally in the reassignment of such clerical abusers.

The problem of indirect responsibility for the actions of subordinates was at the core of the Congressional investigations in the Watergate scandal. Senator Howard Baker repeatedly asked the relevant questions about the accused, including President Nixon: "What did he know and when did he know it?" Since the accused officials were not forthcoming, the investigators had to establish the probable knowledge of the accused from the testimony of others. Prosecutors could not enter the psychological history of the defendants, but they could judge what any reasonable person would have concluded from the evidence that the defendants had available to them.

What did the relevant bishops know about sexual abuse and when did they know it? Most informed observers admit that psychological understanding of pedophilia and ephebophilia changed significantly from the 1960s to the 1980s. Many professionals originally believed that these conditions could be treated and the offenders rehabilitated. This medical optimism reinforced the tendency of Churchmen to look on sexual abuse as a moral problem that could be remedied by repentance and conversion. Over time, the recidivism rate of abusers and their resistance to treatment led professionals to conclude that the condition was a deeply rooted pathological disorder. As the 1980s went on, their risk assessments about reassigning offenders became progressively more cautious.

At what point should Church leaders have known that their earlier approaches were futile? By the middle of the 1980s, social workers and many psychologists were changing their standard treatment for sexual abusers. At the same time many religious orders were changing their policies in light of the revised understanding of this disorder. In 1985 a report commissioned by the bishops and circulated among them strongly recommended against reassignment of clerical offenders. The National Conference of Catholic Bishops did not officially endorse that report and did not issue directives until 1992, a delay motivated in part by confusion over whether the national conference had canonical authority to impose policies on local ordinaries, who are answerable only to Rome according to canon law. While determining the exact year when bishops should have adjusted their policies to the developing standard of treatment is debatable, sufficient evidence had accumulated by 1992 to indicate that reassigning offenders to parishes or schools would put children and adolescents at considerable risk for being abused.

While several dioceses like Oakland in California instituted programs to contact victims and assist in their healing and reconciliation to the Church, others simply ignored the 1992 directives. Those bishops who did so bear indirect responsibility for the subsequent abuse of minors. In some cases, this responsibility is shared by those mental health professionals who offered overly optimistic assessments of abusers they had treated. However, as Leslie Lothstein explains in this volume, some Church leaders withheld information about the sexual history of offenders from treatment centers, pressured the professionals to produce positive reports on offenders, or ignored the negative assessments they received and reassigned the offenders to pastoral situations where they would be in regular contact with minors. Still other bishops agreed to provide specific forms of support and monitoring recommended by treatment centers as a condition for abusers to return to priestly ministry but then failed to put these supports in place, leading to new cases of abuse.

Decisions to protect abusive priests were made not only by bishops, archbishops, and cardinals, but also by officials in their chancery offices. Chancellors of dioceses, directors of priest personnel, and other mid-level clerics were usually part of the process. Since the present system of episcopal selection allows powerful bishops to have their subordinates ordained as bishops, a number of mid-level diocesan officials who participated in decisions about abusive priests are now themselves bishops. For instance, six of Cardinal Law's former officials are now respondents in lawsuits being brought by victims of abuse from Boston. Given the usual path of advancement in the hierarchy, it is not unlikely that many of the present U.S. bishops made decisions that indirectly led to subsequent abuse of minors after the standard of diagnosis and treatment had clearly changed. These officials, who are now bishops, should resign if they were central in reassignment of abusive priests.

I am not proposing a mechanism by which bishops who knowingly made these decisions should resign. One would hope that they would voluntarily step aside or that their episcopal confreres would encourage them to do so, even though only the pope can command a bishop to resign. Any episcopal resignation has to be accepted by the pope, and some American bishops may have already requested the Vatican to allow them to resign. As John Allen explains in this volume, there is a different attitude in the Vatican about Church leaders resigning because of malfeasance. In American culture, civic and business leaders who have discredited their institutions are expected to resign or be removed from office by vote of the board of directors or impeachment. Their forced retirement is not a reward for service but an admission of public failure and the sign that the institution intends to reform itself. Thus, the resignation of Richard Nixon and the impeachment of Bill Clinton strengthened the American Presidency by demonstrating that no person is above the law. Retaining a discredited leader sends the signal to the American public that the institution minimizes the offense and has no intention to reform.

It is unclear how many bishops would have to resign if the policy I am recommending were adopted. While this would be a high price to pay for taking a chance on their confreres' rehabilitation, it must be admitted that the lives of victims have been permanently scarred by the decisions of these officials. They cannot provide the "restitution" that the traditional moral theology required for those who indirectly cooperated in damage done to others. Although they are unable to make restitution to the victims, the restitution they can make is to resign in order to restore the good name of the Church in the United States. As long as the American hierarchy contains bishops who were complicit in the cover-up of sexual abuse of minors, it will not regain its moral authority, nor should it. Those bishops may retain the power of office without moral credibility, but they will have forfeited the authority of the Gospel.

However the issue of accountability is resolved, the question that lingers in the minds of many American Catholics is how some bishops could have had greater loyalty to the institution than they did to the young of their flocks. The answer in large part lies in the current process by which bishops are selected. This leads to my second recommendation:

> The present system of Vatican selection of bishops must be decentralized so that the local church is restored to a central role.

The current selection of bishops by the Vatican (a) contravenes the ancient tradition of the Church, (b) distorts the theological meaning of the episcopacy, and (c) produces a false understanding of accountability in the minds of many bishops themselves. The first two charges have been substantiated in recent theological investigation; the third charge is an inference based on the conduct of some members of the hierarchy.

The current process of episcopal selection creates the impression that bishops are the pope's representatives in the diocese, his legates for carrying out the universal policies of the papacy and Roman curia. Bishops often act as though they saw themselves as branch managers of a multinational corporation in which fidelity to headquarters is the path to professional advancement. Those who have been chosen because of their connections to well-placed members of the hierarchy will naturally see themselves as primarily accountable to their patrons rather than to the people of their local churches. Structurally, the Church has a surprisingly "flat" structure since bishops are directly responsible to the pope, not to the pope's representative in their country. They are not obliged to be transparent in their financial dealings or to be accountable to any ecclesiastical equivalent of a board of directors. The next promotion to a larger, more prestigious, post depends on how the Vatican views their performance, not on how the people of a diocese assess a bishop's service.

First, let us look at the Church's tradition on the selection of bishops. Currently, Rome appoints almost all the bishops in the world. When an opening occurs, bishops of the region are encouraged to make suggestions about candidates, although bishops not deemed ideologically safe are often left out of the consultation. Confidential questionnaires are sent to bishops on the candidates' suitability. The consultation process is widely viewed as a mere formality. One bishop said that he usually receives four to five such questionnaires a year. However, in 15 years of being a bishop, none of his suggestions has ever been acted upon. Names are forwarded to the *apostolic nuncio,* the Vatican ambassador to the country. He composes his own list, often including names recommended by powerful prelates and ignoring the original list of candidates drawn up by the regional bishops. Cardinals and archbishops in favor with the Vatican routinely manage to promote their subordinate officials. Though these may be worthy candidates, their path to preferment is political.

Former Archbishop John R. Quinn writes, "So far as I can determine, no one, not even the president of the episcopal conference ever knows what names are on the list that the papal representative finally sends to Rome" (1999, p. 129). The *nuncio*'s recommendations are usually accepted by Vatican secretariats and affirmed by the pope, who retains the prerogative to select someone not mentioned on any list. The local diocesan clergy, religious orders, and laity usually play no role in this process. Frequently they have never heard of the man appointed by Rome to be their ordinary for the next 20 or 30 years and the appointee know little about the diocese. Ignoring the centuries-old prerogatives of certain European dioceses to have a voice in selecting their bishops, the Vatican has unilaterally appointed men more qualified by their ideology than by any pastoral experience.

By contrast, in the first millennium the local clergy and people played a central role in electing bishops. "By the third century, the selection of bishops was shared in a vital and significant way by three parties: the laity of the local church, the clergy of the local church, and the bishops of the region" (Buckley, 1998, p. 86). St. Augustine was chosen bishop of Hippo by acclamation of the congregation, as St. Ambrose had been chosen to head the Church at Milan. A vestige of this ancient form of ratification occurs in episcopal ordination today when the congregation is asked to affirm the candidate by their applause. At times there was direct election of bishops, at others the consensus of local synods of bishops was determinative, or that of cathedral chapters of clergy (Fitzgerald, 1998).

For most of the history of the Western Church the selection of local bishops was never seen as a necessary component of the papal ministry (Henn, 1997, p. 226). In the three centuries following the Council of Trent, the pope appointed only a few bishops outside the Papal States. In 1829, 555 of the 646 diocesan bishops were appointed by civil governments, 67 by cathedral chapters, and the pope appointed 24 bishops outside the Papal States. With the collapse of the old monarchies in Europe and the emergence of secular states hostile to the papacy, more and more appointments were made directly by the Pope. In the last 150 years direct selection of bishops by the pope has become the norm. In 1975, of over 2,000 residential bishops in the Latin Church, the state appointed fewer than 200 and cathedral chapters elected only 18. Over 90 percent of the bishops today are directly appointed by Rome (Quinn, 1999, p. 122). A method of selection that arose as an historical accident is now widely seen as an essential function of the papacy.

Roman selection combined with the highly centralized governance of the current Vatican curia reinforces the impression that bishops are primarily Rome's local representatives. Theologically and historically, this is an aberration. Even the traditionalist Pope Pius IX insisted in 1875 that bishops are not the pope's legates, "mere papal functionaries with no personal responsibility" (Quinn, 1999, pp. 80–81). Bishops are ordained into the college of bishops, which collectively is the successor to the first group of apostles. They are ordained into the college of bishops when they receive the fullness of priestly ordination at the hands of at least three bishops, not by powers conferred by delegation from the papacy. As Vatican II teaches, they are the vicars of Christ, not of the pope: "The pastoral charge, that is, the permanent and daily care of their sheep, is entrusted to them fully; nor are they to be regarded as vicars of the Roman pontiff; for they exercise the power which they possess in their own right and are called in the true sense prelates of the people they govern" (Pottmeyer, 1998; Second Vatican Council, 1964, par. 27). From the New Testament on, the primary role of bishops is one of service to the local church. Vatican II clearly affirmed this priority, and John Paul II has repeatedly confirmed this position that the ministry of bishops is to foster the unity and communion in faith of the local church by teaching, leading, and sanctifying. They are to support it as part of the communion of churches that is the Church universal.

A strong theological case can be made that both the papal primacy and episcopal collegiality are ministries the success of which is to be measured by how well they fulfill this service of the people of God. "The primacy is to serve collegiality, just as collegiality is to serve the Church" (Buckley, 1998, p. 78). The referent for "Church" is the people of God joined in Christ, not the institution that is meant to support the communities of faith. The purpose of the college of bishops is to maintain and strengthen the communion of all the churches. Following the example of Jesus who came "not to be served but to serve" (Mark 10:45 [Revised Standard Version]), both the pope and the bishops are ordained for a ministry of service. The bishops serve the local church by building up the communion of faith and the pope serves them by confirming them in the unity of faith, hence the papal title of "servant of the servants of God." The "Petrine ministry" of the papacy is derived from the charge given to Peter by Jesus to strengthen his brothers in faith (Luke 22:31 [Revised Standard Version]). The papacy exists to support the college of bishops, of which the bishop of Rome is a member, not a separate entity (Rahner & Ratzinger, 1962, pp. 79–80).

According to Pope John Paul II, the "first part of the Acts of the Apostles presents Peter as the one who speaks in the name of the apostolic group and who serves the unity of the community..." (Pope John Paul II, 1995, par. 97). Christ is the head of his Body, the Church, while Peter leads as "*primus inter pares,*" the first among equals in the group of the apostles. The pope is "the first among the bishops precisely because he is the servant of the local church, which is the guardian of the supreme confession of the apostolic faith. And this faith is the ultimate ground of Christian *koinonia*" [communion] (Tillard, 1987, p. 137).

The primary focus, therefore, of every bishop ought to be the local church. While maintaining bonds of unity with the worldwide college of bishops and the papacy that is part of that college, the bishop serves the people of God in a particular locale. The same person who teaches the apostolic faith also coordinates the various charisms and gifts of the people in all their diversity to build up their faith and common life. Contrary to the popular belief of many Catholics, the primary embodiment of the Church is not the institution headquartered in Rome but the living communion of the faithful in the local church gathered around the table of the Eucharist. The local community of faith is not a pale shadow of an institution that exists in its fullness at headquarters. Vatican II restored the patristic understanding of the importance of the local church: each community authentically celebrating the Eucharist is the actualization of the Catholic Church. The universal Church is the communion of all these local churches (Kasper, 2001; Komonchak, 1995; Ratzinger, 2001; Second Vatican Council, 1965, par. 26). "It is because of this presence of the one and indivisible church of God (the apostolic and catholic church) in each local church that the bishops together form an indivisible group, a college. The college is for the maintaining and strengthening of the *koinonia* of the churches" (Tillard, 1987, p. 136).

This fine theology of service, however, is subverted by the actual practice of a monarchical, highly centralized papacy. When power, truth, and grace are seen to trickle down from the top of the institutional pyramid, it is no wonder that mid-level officials pay more attention to headquarters than to the local church they were ordained to serve. Bishops are too often chosen for their loyalty to headquarters and connection to a powerful patron rather than for their ability to teach, sanctify, and lead the people of God. The lack of leadership shown by the American bishops in responding to the sexual abuse crisis is not primarily an indictment of the bishops themselves but of the system that produced them. Rome has gotten the sort of men that it wanted: managers rather than prophets, cautious bureaucrats whose first instinct is to look first to headquarters. When faced with clerical abusers, their first reaction was not surprising: protect the institution, ward off the scandal. No doubt they were also concerned about the violation of children, but it did not appear to be their primary concern. When they finally responded to public pressure to act directly on the crisis, they focused all the responsibility on the priests and ignored the tragic misconduct of their fellow bishops.

If bishops were selected through close consultation with the local diocesan clergy, religious communities, and laity, there would be a different kind of leadership in the American church. There is no historical or doctrinal necessity for the Vatican to select all the bishops in the world. Doctrinally, bishops must be approved by the pope but they do not have to be directly chosen by him. There is ample precedent in the first millennium of the Church for laity, local clergy, and regional bishops to take primary responsibility for selecting bishops. They should have "a significant and truly substantive role in the appointment of bishops" (Quinn, 1996, p. 124). Systems of selection might well be different in various cultures and political traditions. No method of selection would be flawless, but a system that is transparent in its processes, contains adequate checks and balances, and engages the whole local and regional Church would be far preferable to the present system. While conservatives are fond of reminding us that "the Church is not a democracy," that is not true for the election of the pope, arguably a crucial process for the life of the Church. Although there can be no guarantee that a more democratic selection of bishops would produce pastoral leaders of holiness and courage, it would have the singular advantage of turning the focus of bishops to the people they serve. Since bishops are likely to be accountable to those who chose them, having the local church fully involved in their selection will locate episcopal accountability in the right place.

A second practice of the first millennium would further cement this relationship to the local church. Bishops remained in the same diocese for life.

Since their bond to its people was likened to the marital bond, their permanent commitment was seen as a sacred obligation. Any ambition for appointment to a more prestigious diocese was condemned as adultery. It was not until 882 that someone was elected bishop of Rome who had served in another diocese (Quinn, 1999, pp. 135–136). By removing the temptation to ambition after a more prestigious appointment, bishops would concentrate their energy and loyalties on the people of their diocese. Some of the few prophetic members of the American hierarchy cheerfully admit that their ecclesiastical careers are going nowhere.

In 1982, Karl Rahner advocated that representatives of the diocese should "participate fully in the process of the episcopal search. This is not only consonant with today's democratic processes, but this would also offer the bishop the greatest measure of trust, willingness to cooperate, and so on, from the diocese in order to be successful" (Rahner, 1986, p. 322). Two decades later, we are no closer to realizing this reform; but the need for it has been amply demonstrated by the lack of responsibility exercised by many bishops when faced with the greatest scandal in the history of the Catholic Church in America. Unless the American episcopacy is reformed by resignation of those responsible and reform in its method of selection, it is unlikely to regain its moral voice in this culture for a long time to come.

REFERENCES

Buckley, M. (1998). *The primacy and the episcopate: Towards a relational understanding.* New York: Crossroad.

Cahill, L. (2002, March 6). Crisis of clergy, not of faith. *New York Times.*

Fitzgerald, P. (1998). A model for dialogue: Cyprian of Carthage on ecclesiastical discernment. *Theological Studies, 59,* 236–253.

Greeley, A. (1985). *American Catholics since the council.* Chicago: Thomas More.

Henn, W. (1997, December). Historical-theological synthesis of the relation between the primacy and episcopacy during the second millennium. *Il primato del successore de Pietro: Atti del simposio teologico.* Vatican City: Libreria Editrice Vaticana.

John Paul II. (1995). Ut unum sint. *Acta Apostolica Sedis, 97,* 978–979.

Kasper, W. (2001, April 23). On the church: A friendly reply to Cardinal Ratzinger. *America, 184* (14), 8–14.

Koch, A., & Preuss, A. (1924). *A handbook of moral theology.* St. Louis, MO: B. Herder Book.

Komonchak, J. (1995). The theology of the local church: State of the question. In W. Cenkner (Ed.), *The multicultural church: A new landscape in U.S. theologies* (pp. 35–49). New York: Paulist.

Pottmeyer, H. (1998). Towards a papacy in communion: Perspectives from Vatican Councils I & II. New York: Crossroad.

Quinn, J. (1996, July 18). The claims of the primacy and the costly call to unity. *Origins, 26* (8).

Quinn, J. (1999). *The reform of the papacy: The costly call to Christian unity.* New York: Crossroad.

Rahner, K. (1986). *Karl Rahner in dialogue: Conversations and interviews, 1965–1982* (P. Imhof & H. Biallowons, Eds.). New York: Crossroad.

Rahner, K., & Ratzinger, J. (1962). *The episcopacy and the primacy.* New York: Herder and Herder.

Ratzinger, J. (2001). The local church and the universal church: A response to Walter Kasper. *America, 185* (16), 7–11.

Second Vatican Council. (1964). *Lumen Gentium: Dogmatic Constitution of the Church.* Vatican City: Libreria Editrice Vaticana.

Tillard, J. (1987). Bishop. *The new dictionary of theology* (J. Komonchak, M. Collins, & D. Lane, Eds.). Collegeville, MN: Liturgical Press.

Chapter 15

WHAT THE BISHOPS FAILED TO LEARN FROM CORPORATE ETHICS DISASTERS

Kirk O. Hanson

A *National Catholic Reporter* editorial in the August 1, 2003, issue was headlined: "Time for some more bishops to resign" (*National Catholic Reporter,* 2003). While some American Catholics might dismiss the call as the rant of a liberal publication, the same sentiment has been on the minds of vast numbers of Catholics, liberal and conservative. How did we come to this point?

The simple answer is that the American Catholic bishops ignored—or were ignorant of—standards of compassion, communication, and timely response absolutely essential in times of crisis. Such standards, far from being just contemporary "conventions," embody core ethical concerns and principles repeatedly violated by some American bishops. An examination of these standards can highlight both what went wrong and how Church officials should handle future crises.

Ironically, American business has led the way in recent years in identifying standards of good crisis management. A succession of corporate scandals and crises in the 1980s and 1990s has led corporate executives, consultants, and management theorists to codify standards of good crisis management (Blythe, 2002; Fink, 2000; Institute for Crisis Management, 2003; Mitrof, Pearson, & Harrington, 1996). While many business leaders still fail to follow these norms at moments of crisis, the American public has come to expect these standards as responsible behavior. This article identifies 12 principles of good crisis management violated repeatedly by

American bishops as they responded to the priest sex abuse crisis that began early in 2002 in Boston.

At the core of these principles is the ethical belief that institutional leaders in America, even leaders of church institutions, are stewards and servants of the interests of the organization's members and of others they lead. The concept of stakeholders and stakeholder management, which is rapidly becoming the conceptual framework for examining an institution's proper role in society, holds that the institution and its leaders have ethical responsibilities to a set of stakeholders affected by that institution's behavior and very existence (Phillips & Freeman, 2003; Scharioth & Huber, 2003; Svendsen, 1998).

The American Catholic Church clearly has a vast set of stakeholders, including all American Catholics, but also those of other religions affected by the behavior and status of the Catholic Church, and the American public, which is affected by the Church's moral influence and its public policy interventions. In the case of sexual abuse by priests, specific stakeholders include, first, the victims and their families, but also the priest abusers, all clerics whose reputation and effectiveness is reduced, the institutional Church, and all lay Catholics.

The following principles address the legitimate interests and welfare of these stakeholders.

PRINCIPLE #1—TAKE CARE OF THE VICTIMS

In any crisis situation, the first ethical obligation is to provide immediate care for the victims and to remove them from harm's way. The initial ethical test of any leader is whether he or she is concerned more about the impact of the crisis on the institution—or on the victims.

Sadly, institutional concerns too often dominated bishops' responses to the sexual abuse crisis. Concerns for the scandal to the Church and for the impact on the morale and reputation of the clergy frequently overshadowed concern for the victims. Some bishops undoubtedly found the charges so shocking that they concluded those reporting abuse were mistaken. Others likely convinced themselves that the incidents must be isolated and only aberrations in the behavior of otherwise good priests. Still others may have concluded the charges being brought were false and evidence only of attempts to extort money from the Church.

Another likely explanation for the priority given to institutional concerns is that the bishops lacked direct experience with the victims of abuse. Many, and perhaps most, could not understand the lifelong impact such abuse could have on children and adolescents. Their lack of experience raising children and dealing with the impact of life's events on children of their own may have made them less empathetic, and thus less compassionate.

The extraordinary session at the June 2002 National Bishops Meeting in which all bishops attending sat and listened to victims for several hours may help those bishops focus first on the victims. One can hope that all bishops will now consider the suffering of victims their first priority.

PRINCIPLE #2—PREVENT FURTHER DAMAGE AND VICTIMIZATION

The second principle of crisis management is to prevent any further damage or abuse of additional victims. When an unexplained military air crash occurs, standard military procedure is to order a "stand-down" until the cause of the crash is clarified lest there be additional crashes due to the same unknown cause.

This is the principle that led Johnson & Johnson to recall all Tylenol from the shelves of American stories in 1990 after a customer was poisoned. The company's leaders concluded that its responsibility was to prevent additional deaths, though the recall cost the company more than $100 million (Murray & Shohen, 1992). Undoubtedly, concern for a company's reputation enters into such a decision. Would anyone forgive Johnson & Johnson if another death occurred and it could have prevented it? The company's decision was partially validated when Tylenol regained 94 percent of its market share when reintroduced several weeks later.

This second principle was repeatedly violated whenever a priest was reassigned to another parish or ministry after an incident of abuse. While the understanding of abusers was very incomplete decades ago, there was a point at which a responsible bishop or other official (school principal, camp director, etc.) had access to enough medical knowledge to conclude there was great risk in reassigning an abusing official. It is clear that bishops continued to reassign priests far beyond this point.

The debate in ethics, liability, and public policy over when officials should know risks demanded prudent action to prevent further damage has led the European Union to embody in law what is known as the "Precautionary Principle." While it applies only to environmental damage, it is based on sound ethical thinking. The principle holds that one acts and protects against further damage even if the science is still uncertain.

PRINCIPLE #3—EXPRESS PUBLIC APOLOGY QUICKLY AND OFTEN

Once an incident or crisis has engulfed an organization, it is critical that the organization express sincere regret for the damage done to individuals, to property, and to the environment. Such heartfelt apologies must be expressed early—and often.

American officials have been among the least of the world's managers willing to apologize. In other cultures, particularly Japan, leaders are expected to immediately apologize, even before blame is determined. Facing a difficult liability system, American CEOs, encouraged by their lawyers, have hesitated to speak anything like an apology, for fear it will be taken later as an admission of guilt. Advised by their lawyers and their insurance company's lawyers, many bishops adopted a head-in-sand approach and refused to comment or admit any fault. Some even refused to meet with victims due to legal considerations. The unfortunate side effect of this strategy of silence is that it prevents a leader, particularly a bishop as a pastoral leader, from adequately expressing his sorrow and regret that the events occurred.

Fortunately, in the corporate arena, more top executives are telling their lawyers that they will apologize and express regret anyway. Faced with this, lawyers are getting better at helping top executives write apologies that express genuine regret for the damage done, a determination to get to the bottom of the problem, and a firm resolve to do whatever to change policies or personnel so it does not happen again—without taking full blame. Some observers suggest that quick expressions of apology and regret may have the instrumental effect of reducing plaintiffs' demands in liability suits.

PRINCIPLE # 4—MEET WITH YOUR CRITICS

Whenever a crisis strikes an organization, it usually becomes the "cause" of one or more interest groups. Often, the impact of the crisis itself creates the interest group, as with the Survivors Network for those Abused by Priests (SNAP). While the inclination of most leaders is to avoid contact with those seeking redress or changes in the organization's behavior, there is usually no more important time to meet with critics.

Dialogue with critics can accomplish several important goals. The institutional leader can be seen as concerned about the issue and compassionate toward the victims. The leader can hear in a different way the concerns of the interest groups. The leader can explain legitimate institutional concerns face-to-face. Sometimes the concerns of the interest group can be addressed in ways that are not that disruptive or costly to the organization. Sometimes the victim interest groups simply want to be heard by their bishop-pastor.

Those who have studied such meetings with critics and activists suggest they have predictable phases. Leaders should expect to let the individuals or group vent, often in strong language, at any initial meeting. The role of the leader in these initial sessions is to listen and empathize, communicating verbally and nonverbally that he or she knows the individual or group is hurting and is concerned about something real. Real dialogue can take place once the venting has occurred.

Some bishops have failed to meet with victim groups, or have resisted meeting with victims represented by national groups such as SNAP. Other bishops have resisted meeting with lay groups such as Voice of the Faithful. Some bishops are now resisting meeting even with representatives of the National Bishops Conference assigned to do audits and evaluations. Such resistance is self-defeating if these bishops hope ever to put this issue aside and restore confidence in their leadership.

PRINCIPLE #5—LEARN EVERYTHING ABOUT THE INCIDENT; KNOW MORE THAN ANYONE ELSE

One of the most damaging aspects of most crises is the tortuous step-by-step revelation of the dimensions of the problem or of the culpability of major figures. Crisis managers have long understood that the institution facing a crisis must dominate the availability of information about that crisis. The damage to the institution is always greater if the information leaks out bit by bit, and is always more damaging if others uncover information the institution should have known. Companies and other institutions facing crises are encouraged to launch an immediate and thorough investigation into the incident or crisis.

In the case of the Boston archdiocese, the role of Cardinal Law and his auxiliary bishops in the reassignment of abusive priests to new parishes was uncovered almost entirely by aggressive reporting by *The Boston Globe*. The number of abusive Boston priests grew month by month in a kind of water torture. The story was tragic, but the Boston archdiocese would have retained some credibility if it had been the one to identify and release the damaging information.

Unfortunately, the priest sex abuse scandal unfolded at different rates in different dioceses, and bishops reacted with different levels of commitment to get the facts quickly. Many, if not most, times, the press uncovered new allegations of abuse or patterns of priest assignment before a diocese did. With each revelation uncovered by an outside party, the diocese lost credibility.

PRINCIPLE #6—KEEP HEADQUARTERS AND OTHER UNITS INFORMED

In the study of crisis management, there are many examples of different levels and units of the same company working at cross purposes in the management of an issue. The most important lesson drawn is that an issue must be managed by a single person or level, which in turn stays in constant communication with all levels and units of the organization that are affected.

Shell Oil in the United Kingdom was unsympathetic to environmental concerns over the disposal of an oil-drilling rig at sea despite the fact that a surprisingly effective consumer boycott was underway against Shell Germany over the disposal. Shell UK felt it was doing the right thing because it met the standards of one British regulator, ignoring the reality that the issue was much broader and would be addressed by environmental regulators at the European Union and global levels. This lack of awareness and failure to communicate among organizational units led to widespread criticism of the company (Baron, 2000).

The challenge for bishops managing the sex abuse crisis has been that no one individual or level can guide what is done in more than 200 American dioceses. Each bishop retains a substantial canonical independence from the National Bishops Conference and even from the Vatican. Bishop Wilton Gregory may be the elected representative of the American Catholic Bishops, but neither he nor the Conference can compel every bishop to cooperate in a collective effort to address priest sex abuse.

What the National Bishops Conference can do is to keep all bishops informed about developments in the crisis—both new accusations and new ways of managing the response at the diocesan level. The national conference can also set standards, establish the auditing process it has adopted, and use every form of moral suasion to compel bishops to cooperate. The National Bishops Conference must also keep the Vatican informed and coordinate its responses with the appropriate curial agencies. This compounds the crisis management task. At minimum, intensive communication between the Vatican and the American bishops and between the National Bishops Conference and every American diocese is essential.

PRINCIPLE #7—TELL WHAT YOU KNOW AND DON'T KNOW—OPENLY AND HONESTLY

Disclosure has become one of the cardinal principles of crisis management. In times of crisis, where some individuals may be exposed to risk, and where the public has a stake in knowing that an issue is being handled, it is critical that the organization keep the public informed, usually through the media, but also directly.

Once an issue has been revealed and has attracted widespread attention all information will be disclosed—by others if not by the institution itself. Therefore, it becomes important that the organization disclose information first, particularly unfavorable information. While this is necessary for defensive purposes, doing so also gives confidence that the institution is serious about dealing with the issue and is willing to do so in an open manner.

The bishops' response to the sex abuse scandal has unfortunately often been less than candid. In some cases, lawyers and public relations advisors seem to have convinced bishops that they should not be open lest any admissions hurt them later in lawsuits. Just the opposite probably occurred. The reluctance of some bishops to talk openly about the crisis led some prosecutors and many members of the public to conclude that a cover-up was indeed in process, and that the bishops could not be trusted to deal with the scandals.

Other bishops were undoubtedly well intentioned in their silence, seeking to protect some victims from identification and some of the accused priests from false accusations. But when the faithful and public have begun to lose faith in the Church leadership, it is even more critical to be transparent in attempts to address the problem. In mid-2003, many dioceses were grappling with the decision whether to name all accused priests. Crisis management principles would suggest that full disclosure is the best path and gives a bishop the chance to highlight cases, like those of Cardinal Bernardin several years ago, which are based on little evidence or testimony. A well-functioning diocesan review board can also deal with cases rapidly to limit the damage to a priest's reputation.

One public relations technique that has grown out of crisis management is to release some solid piece of news every day during a crisis so that the press's continued coverage focuses on news you choose rather than new dimensions of the scandal they uncover or create themselves. If a story is big, a reporter will be responsible for filing a follow-up story each and every day. After a poisoning incident involving one of their all-natural

fruit juices, Odwalla, Inc. held a press conference each morning and delib-
erately released some substantive piece of news about what it had learned,
how it was investigating, or how it was managing the continued produc-
tion of other juices (Hanson, 1998; Martinelli & Briggs, 1998). Most news
stories used this daily piece of information provided by the company. In
the absence of such a news lead, reporters assigned to a continuing story
have had to find some other feature—another accusation of abuse, a member of the laity horrified by their bishop's behavior, or other profile of a
victim.

PRINCIPLE #8—SEARCH FOR THE CAUSES OF THE CRISIS

Immediately after an incident occurs, it is critical that the institution be
seen as deeply concerned with the causes of the incident, and about how it
might be prevented in the future. Johnson & Johnson determined, with the
help of the FBI, that the poisonings were the work of a single deranged
individual. Odwalla determined that the poisonings could be traced to a
single batch of apple juice and that the equipment was disinfected immediately after that batch. Odwalla's daily news briefings traced their search
for the cause, finally settling on the most likely explanation, that a worker
had picked up apples off the ground that were contaminated by animal
droppings (an action clearly prohibited by company policy).

The American bishops have been less successful in communicating their
own search for causes for the hundreds of cases of sexual abuse by priests.
They were too often seen as defending individual priests for their "aberra-
tional behavior" and defending the vast majority of priests against "a few
bad apples." Because the bishops did not effectively engage the public in
a search for true causes, simplistic answers popped up in the press—it is
all due to celibacy; it is all due to gay priests; it is due to the repressive
behavior of bishops. The reality was that the behavior of even a few priests
who violated their positions of trust was a crisis. And the vast number of
priest abusers, particularly in Boston, suggested the problem was more
systematic.

PRINCIPLE #9—REPORT ON THE CAUSES AND SOLUTIONS

A major crisis of the proportion of the sex abuse crisis will not leave the
front pages and the evening news broadcasts until the cause is known and

a program is in place to make a recurrence extremely unlikely. A "final report" must be released. To accomplish this, only the National Bishops Conference, through thorough investigation and national standards for managing cases of priest sex abuse, can take effective action.

Odwalla succeeded in getting its poisonings off the front page by issuing a report that the cause was contamination of fruit that had fallen on the ground, and by admitting candidly they could not guarantee that this would not occur again in the future. The company announced all apple juice would be treated by "flash pasteurization" or sterilization of the juice. While this made the juice less "natural," the company had concluded that was the only way to assure another poisoning would not occur.

Johnson & Johnson got its Tylenol poisoning off the front pages by announcing that they and the FBI had concluded the poisoning was the work of one person and that the company would adopt tamper-proof packaging to make another incident much less likely. Diagnosis and credible action were key to moving the crisis to the back pages or out of the newspaper entirely.

To date, there has been no authoritative analysis of the causes of the sex abuse crisis. Such a report could include the observation that all organizations that work with children and adolescents have an abuser rate of roughly two percent to five percent as noted elsewhere in this volume. The report would have to address why bishops in some dioceses transferred priests from parish to parish without informing the new parishes. Most importantly, the report would have to describe specifically what is being done to prevent abuses by priests—or by bishops—in the future. Writing a "final report" is obviously more complex due to the canonical independence of individual bishops. Imposing a national standard has proven nearly impossible as some bishops resist the auditing/reporting process the national office has attempted to impose.

PRINCIPLE #10—REMOVE INDIVIDUALS WHO ARE RESPONSIBLE

Reestablishing credibility in the institution after a crisis involves more than diagnosis and preventing future incidents. It involves removal of individuals who are perpetrators and those who failed to deal adequately with the scandal.

In the accounting and financial scandals that have engulfed corporate America since 2001, it was necessary to remove anyone who had participated in the falsification of accounting statements. It was also necessary to

remove anyone in the auditing or accounting organization who had knowledge of the fraud and did not blow the whistle, on the basis that anyone in
these organizations had a special responsibility for the integrity of the
financial statements. Finally, executives who supervised these groups
were often removed because they had failed to create a system that prevented fraud.

It is very clear that abusive priests must be removed from their assignments and from active ministry. The more difficult cases are those of
priests against whom there is only a single credible accusation from many
years before. Given the uncertainty over rehabilitation of sex offenders
and the possibility that other changes may yet appear, removal is clearly
the prudent choice.

The case of negligent bishops is harder. It was clear early in the process
that Cardinal Bernard Law had to resign. His oversight and management
of priest abusers had led to the worst pattern of abuse in the country. Reassignment of priest abusers to new parishes and the neglect of accumulat-
ing information regarding abuse required his removal. Similarly, the
National Catholic Reporter (NCR) is now arguing that Law's auxiliary
bishops who were actually closer to the decisions on reassignment should
also resign from their current posts (*NCR,* 2003). John Allen, in another
contribution to this volume, argues that the removal of bishops at times of
scandal runs counter to a Vatican norm that would force a bishop to stay
and clean up the mess he created. Perhaps this clash of traditions led to the
reluctance to remove Cardinal Law and some bishops, but the result is a
substantial loss of confidence among American Catholics and other members of the public that bishops, too, will be held accountable.

As the auditing system created by the American bishops rolls out in late
2003 and 2004, the National Bishops Conference will have to decide what
to do about bishops who resist the reforms. There will clearly be calls for
the removal of recalcitrant bishops whose resistance taints the confidence
in all bishops and in the Church itself.

PRINCIPLE #11—PREVENT VICTIMIZATION OF PLAINTIFFS IN LIABILITY SUITS

Many American bishops were criticized for the harsh tactics of their
lawyers in liability suits brought by victims of priest sex abuse. This is a
problem well known to corporate crisis managers. Lawyers are incited to
seek court victories or, failing that, minimal settlements. Delay, obfusca-
tion, refusal to release information, intimidation, and threats to reveal inci-

dents in a victim's past life are all tactics employed by some lawyers—and apparently by some lawyers defending diocese and their insurance companies.

Bishops are in a position to prevent such abuse, just as CEOs of companies are similarly positioned to prevent this second victimization of victims who sue the company. Unfortunately, encouraged by the attitude of some in the Vatican that the sex abuse crisis was the creation of trial lawyers, some bishops believed they were justified in using harsh tactics.

While acknowledging that some suits are brought by cynical trial lawyers trying to extort large amounts from corporate or Church institutions, most crisis managers would argue that an institution must do everything it can not to appear harsh and punitive toward the victims. The newly named Boston Archbishop, Sean O'Malley, was given high marks for settling cases in Fall River, Massachusetts, earlier in his career when he and his lawyers met directly with the plaintiff's lawyers to work out a settlement. CEOs and bishops need to give direct orders to their lawyers not to challenge victims' credibility unless there is very strong evidence that the charge is false.

PRINCIPLE #12—CONTINUING PUBLIC REPORTING ON PROGRESS IN IMPLEMENTING SOLUTIONS

Once an issue has moved from the front pages to the back pages of the newspaper by good investigation and preventive efforts, there is still the need to report progress periodically in implementing solutions to the crisis. Such reports may themselves be buried on the back page, or even ignored by the press, but they are still critically important. Ongoing openness and reporting predisposes the press and the public to believe future statements by the institution and to give the institution the benefit of the doubt when new accusations emerge.

The media itself will initiate follow-up stories on a regular basis. Good reporters keep files on dates to do follow-up stories, for example when dioceses have promised to have certain reforms installed. News editors keep a list of anniversaries that trigger follow-up review stories. The July 2003 first anniversary of the passage of the Sarbanes-Oxley Act addressing corporate scandals led to many feature stories reviewing the scandals and steps the government and companies themselves have taken to clean up. Each year's anniversary of 9-11-01 produces a spate of articles reviewing the war on terror, steps to build a monument at ground zero, and the

plight of particular victims of the tragedy. Anniversaries of the initial disclosure of the Boston priest cases in early 2002, the June 2002 bishops
meeting on the sex abuse crisis, and the resignation of Cardinal Bernard
Law will produce feature stories.

It is critical that the institution cooperate with such follow-up stories,
working hard to demonstrate how it has responded to the crisis in good
faith. Such stories will be written regardless of the institution's attitude,
but they are opportunities to continue to rebuild credibility by once again
telling about steps taken to make a recurrence less likely and to protect
possible victims.

A FINAL PERSPECTIVE ON CRISIS MANAGEMENT

Embedded in these practical principles of crisis management are several
core lessons that corporations and others offer very poorly, resulting in a
succession of crises.

Once an issue has hit the front pages, there are no secrets. Any fact, but
particularly damaging ones, will eventually see the light of day. An organization is always in a stronger position if it releases the bad news itself,
and does it before anyone else. Once several teams of investigative
reporters and tabloid journalists are working on a story, all facts and
charges will surface. Nothing can be hidden.

No leader and no institution is above scrutiny and above accountability.
The chief executive of Exxon was quoted as saying "Don't you people
know I have a company to run?" when asked repeatedly about what Exxon
was doing to clean up after the Exxon Valdez oil spill. He was widely
chastised for his comment and learned that he, too, had to be accountable
for oil spills, their cleanup, and for the safe handling of his company's
tankers.

Richard Nixon in 1974 learned that a president of the United States
could not flaunt the law and engage in obstruction of justice on the
assumption that he was above the law. The release of the Watergate tapes
showing him obstructing justice led directly to his resignation.

Bishops, archbishops, and cardinals are now learning this lesson for
themselves. No clerical official is above the law; no clerical official is
above being called to account for his or her handling of difficult situations.
There is no exemption for priests or bishops on the assumption that they
are "doing the Lord's work" or that religious institutions are somehow different.

A higher standard of behavior and accountability is required of orga-nizations that claim to be values-driven and that preach to others about ethical and responsible behavior. Companies that tout their social respon-sibility are being scrutinized more thoroughly than companies that make no such claim. Any behavior found to be inconsistent with company claims becomes news.

Churches will be held to an extraordinarily high standard in the contem-porary environment. The Catholic Church not only seeks to teach morality to its own members, but also to influence American public policy on ethi-cal matters. In the wake of the priest sex abuse scandal, the behavior of Catholic bishops and priests will be examined in much greater detail than ever in the past. Every incident of sexual misbehavior, financial misman-agement, or abuse of power by a bishop or priest will be reported widely. Given this reality, only a heightened sense of accountability, an effective system and review process at the diocesan and national levels and a will-ingness by bishops to share oversight with knowledgeable layleaders can sustain the credibility of the Church.

REFERENCES

Baron, D. (2000). *Business and its environment* (3rd ed.). Upper Saddle River, NJ: Prentice Hall.

Blythe, B. T. (2002). *Blindsided: A manager's guide to catastrophic incidents in the workplace.* New York: Portfolio.

Fink, S. (2000). *Crisis management: Planning for the inevitable.* Lincoln, NE: iUniverse.com.

Hanson, K. O. (1998). The case of the nutritional foods. *Issues in Ethics, 9,* (1), pp. 22–23.

Institute for Crisis Management. (2003). The essence of crisis management. http://www.crisisexperts.com/essence_main.htm.

Martinelli, K. A., & Briggs, W. (1998). Integrating public relations and legal responses during a crisis: The case of Odwalla, Inc. *Public Relations Review, 24* (4), pp. 443–460.

Mitroff, I. I., Pearson, C. M., & Harrington, L. K. (1996). *The essential guide to managing corporate crises: A step-by-step handbook for surviving major catastrophes.* New York: Oxford University Press.

Murray, E., & Shohen, S. (1992, February). Lessons from the Tylenol tragedy on surviving a corporate crises. *Medical Marketing and Media, 27,* (2), pp. 14–19.

National Catholic Reporter. (2003, August 1). Time for more bishops to resign [Editorial].

Phillips, R., & Freeman, R.E. (2003). *Stakeholder theory and organizational ethics.* San Francisco: CA: Berrett-Koehler.

Scharioth, J., & Huber, M. (Eds.). (2003). *Achieving excellence in stakeholder management.* New York: Springer-Verlag.

Svendsen, A. (1998). *The stakeholder strategy: Profiting from collaborative business relationships.* San Francisco, CA: Berrett-Koehler.

Chapter 16

CONCLUSION: WHAT DO WE KNOW AND WHERE DO WE NEED TO GO?

Thomas G. Plante

As mentioned at the beginning of this book, 2002 was *not* a good year for the Roman Catholic Church in general and in the United States in particular. The year began with a remarkable series of articles initially published by *The Boston Globe* that detailed sexual abuse perpetrated by priests in the Boston Archdiocese and the resulting cover-up by religious superiors including bishops and even Cardinal Bernard Law. By the end of that year, about 400 American priests as well as several notable bishops were accused of sexual misconduct with minors; large dioceses such as the one in Boston were threatened with bankruptcy; Cardinal Law and several other Church leaders were disgraced and resigned; donations to the Church were cut in half in Boston and elsewhere; and it appeared among many in the public that the last organization on earth to be trusted was the Roman Catholic Church. Many wondered if the exploits and both ethical and moral failings of the Catholic Church may have been far worse than the corporate scandals of Enron, Arthur Anderson, Tyco, and MCI WorldCom that dominated the news as well. The crisis in the Catholic Church continued during 2003 and perhaps will continue well beyond these tumultuous years. Curiously, it has been well known for centuries that sexual behavior occurs between clergy and either consenting adults or minors. Only very recently has this behavior dominated the press and resulted in such a remarkable scandal in the Church. The American Catholic Church has experienced an enormous earthquake and the continuous and sizable aftershocks continue to rattle the institution and those both in and outside of it.

While there have been countless reports and analysis of the crisis in the popular media, surprisingly few scholarly analyses based on solid research and scholarship have appeared. This edited book has sought to fill this void. The project brought together many of the leading minds on sexual abuse committed by Roman Catholic priests from across the United States, Canada, England, and Rome. The book project assembled these experts at Santa Clara University for several days during May 2003 to work together on this topic. In doing so, we sought to discuss, debate, and outline a state-of-the-art understanding of this important problem from multiple perspectives. Each chapter was read and discussed among the group and feedback was provided to the contributors for inclusion in their final drafts that appear in this book. It was hoped that the resulting book would be a thoughtful, civil, data-driven, and scholarly approach to a very hotly debated and discussed topic.

In this concluding chapter, I briefly highlight what we currently know about clergy sexual abuse in the Catholic Church and suggest where we might go with this understanding. I end the chapter by offering nine principles that could be considered and perhaps followed in the future. Material presented in this chapter reflects the discussion that the contributors to this book had during our May 2003 conference. It is important to point out, however, that these thoughts do not reflect an agreement among all of the contributors. We do not all agree about each issue articulated in this chapter and in this book. Many thoughtful voices are heard but they do not represent one voice. Furthermore, our journalist participants made clear that they cannot support future directions for research and policy. Their job is to report on news and not make the news or offer policy suggestions. The diverse voices in this book represent victim advocates, mental health professionals evaluating and treating clergy sex offenders or victims, moral theologians, ethicists, journalists, and both canon and plaintiff attorneys.

Sexual abuse of minors committed by Roman Catholic priests is a problem that has existed throughout the world and throughout the long history of the Catholic Church. Although a clear minority of all Catholic clergy (accounting for perhaps two to six percent with the majority of these offenders targeting postpubescent, adolescent boys), some priests have tragically chosen to become sexually engaged with children or adolescents. Most of these men who abuse minors experienced child sexual abuse when they were young and currently suffer from a variety of comorbid psychiatric problems including personality, mood, substance abuse, and organic brain disorders (Bryant, 1999; Lothstein, 1999). Some of these men are amenable to treatment while others are not (Markham & Mikail, this volume). Victims usually are especially vulnerable due to their age at the time of abuse, trust in the priest and the Church, and personal and family stresses that typically have occurred among victims who may seek out the spiritual and pastoral counsel of a clergy member (de Fuentes, 1999). The number of clergy sexually involved with consenting adults is impossible to know at this time. Although the problem of clergy sexual abuse is not new, the intense media attention, public outcry, and numerous lawsuits are new.

Sadly, we also know that the sexual abuse of children is not limited to Roman Catholic priests (Francis & Turner, 1995; Isley & Isley, 1990; Ruzicka, 1997). Although solid data are impossible to obtain, it is clear that sexual abuse perpetrated by clergy is found among Protestant, Jewish, Muslim, and other religious traditions. Best estimates suggest that the figure of two to six percent may likely apply to male clergy members from other faith traditions as well as other professionals who have regular and private access to children and teens (e.g., bus drivers, Boy Scout leaders, coaches, and teachers). Tragically, sexual abuse of children and adolescents can be found in every area of the world and in every profession that has access to minors. Furthermore, since persons of varying sexual orientations as well as non-celibate clergy choose to sexually abuse minors, blaming this problem solely on celibacy or on those who maintain a homosexual orientation is unreasonable. Celibacy and homosexual orientations cannot uniquely be blamed for the problem of sexual abuse committed by priests. Clearly, sexual abuse of minors by priests would likely continue even if priests were allowed to marry and if all homosexual clergy were banished from the priesthood. However, the conceptualization, practice, and administration of priestly celibacy may create an environment for problematic sexual acting out (Sipe, 1995; Sipe, this volume).

The high frequency of sexual abuse throughout the world does not excuse priests or the Catholic Church for this behavior. It would be a significant problem if only one priest sexually abused one child anywhere in the world. We rightfully expect much better behavior from clergy than from the general population of men. We expect priests and other clergy members to set an ethical, moral, and spiritual standard that is higher than what is expected of others. We expect priests to be closer to and more like God, bridging the gap between what is human and divine. Furthermore, since priests make a lifelong commitment to celibacy, we expect them to refrain from sexual behavior with anyone including children, adolescents, consenting adults, and even themselves.

Many may argue that if the percentage of priests who sexually abuse minors is not significantly higher than among male clergy from other faith traditions or from the general population of men, then why does the Catholic Church appear to be so plagued by this problem? While there are many possible explanations for this phenomenon, a few will be highlighted here. First, there are about 45,000 active priests in the United States while there have been about 150,000 during the past 40 to 50 years. Therefore, if the two to six percent figure of sex offending clergy is accurate, then we can expect to have between about 1,000 and 3,000 sex offending priests currently (or until recently) working in ministry. This number swells to between about 3,000 and 10,000 if we consider all of the priests working in ministry in the United States during the past half century. Research from the St. Luke's Institute that specializes in the treatment of sex offending priests suggests that the average number of victims per priest is about eight (Rossetti, 1996, 2002a, 2002b). Therefore, we could expect up to 100,000 victims of priest sexual abuse during the past 40 to 50 years. Of course, some of the most notable cases such as the one in Boston that received so much media attention had more than 130 victims (Rezendes, this volume). Thus, part of the problem in the Catholic Church, relative to other traditions, is that since about 25 percent of the American public are Catholic, and there are so many priests relative to clergy from other faith traditions, the percentage of offending clergy will result in much bigger numbers of offenders in the Catholic Church than among other faith traditions having much fewer clergy in their ranks.

More importantly, however, is how the Church structure manages these issues when they come to light. Most faith traditions have some kind of lay board of directors who hire, fire, and evaluate their clergy. In a nutshell, clergy from other traditions are on a shorter leash than Catholic clergy. If a particular Catholic religious superior such as a bishop does not manage a complaint or a problem with his clergy very well, then the virus of sexual abuse can spread rapidly. Moving problematic clergy from parish to parish without input from various lay boards of directors allows clergy sexual predators to continue to victimize vulnerable children and others. If someone doesn't like how a bishop or religious superior makes decisions, what recourse does one have? Bishops and priests are not elected to office and do not have contracts that are renewed with input from lay boards or congregations. So, while the percentage of clergy who victimize minors and others may not be significantly different across the various faith traditions, the number of victims and the ability to avoid intervention and potential prosecution can be quite different across the faith traditions.

Therefore, there may likely be more victims per perpetrator in the Catholic Church.

Perhaps many Church leaders have been in denial about this problem. Many have maintained a bunker mentality, trying to keep information from both the press and the laity and hoping that the problem would go away or at least remain hidden. Many Church leaders seek to protect not only the Church as an institution but the abusing priests who are their colleagues and friends. The priesthood is a brotherhood and family. When someone in the family is accused of misconduct, there is a likely impulse and desire to protect the family member and deny that significant problems exist. It is hard for a family that maintains an emphasis on compassion and forgiveness to "throw the book" at one of the family members for wrongdoing. Many Church leaders may also do little to control abusing priests or make public statements about their behavior in order to prevent others from questioning their own potential sexual indiscretions. The fact that priests (and especially bishops and other Church leaders) have historically experienced tremendous reverence, authority, and power as well as an almost demigod status in society may contribute to both narcissism and an abuse of both power and trust. This may at least partially explain not only the abusive behavior of some priests but also the behavior of many Church officials.

This type of defensiveness is typical of other powerful hierarchical organizations. Many have complained that business executives, physicians, police officers, and members of the military do little to protect and defend others from sexual or other types of abuse perpetrated by their members. Organizations that maintain positions of power, authority, prestige, and male domination with few checks and balances or accountability may set the stage for abusive behaviors to thrive (Conley, 1998). In many areas the behavior of executives, priests, doctors, police officers, and military personnel are not questioned very easily or are questioned without significant consequence.

It is easy to demonize sex offending priests, religious superiors, and Church hierarchy in general who have failed to deal with the problem of sex offending clergy effectively. It is easy to demand that civil authorities "lock them up and throw away the key." However, evidence suggests that many offending clergy can be treated and treated effectively (Bryant, 1999; Markham & Mikail, this volume; Rossetti, 2002a, 2002b) and that non-Church officials including secular mental health professionals and institutions must take some of the blame for their evaluation and treatment recommendations over the years. While there will always be some clergy who cannot be rehabilitated, data from hospitals specializing in the treatment of sexual offending clergy have found low rates of further abuse by treated clergy (Bryant, 1999; Rossetti, 2002a, 2002b).

More efforts to evaluate and screen applicants to religious life may be useful but only moderately effective. Since it has been noted that the majority of priests who choose to become sexually involved with minors do so after (and rarely before) ordination (Bryant, 1999; Plante, 1999), sexual abuse among this population rarely manifests itself at the time of these evaluations. However, at a minimum, vocation directors and consulting psychologists asked to evaluate applicants to religious life could be better attuned to some of the risk factors for sexual abuse such as a personal history of sexual victimization, impulse control and substance abuse problems, psychological and relational immaturity, and difficulties maintaining mature close adult relationships (Bryant, 1999; Markham & Mikail, this volume; Plante, 1999).

The Church could have done more over the years to prevent sexual abuse from occurring. Victims and their families could have been treated with more respect and compassion. Offending clergy could have been treated quickly and relieved from duties that placed them in contact with potential victims. Clearly, some bishops and superiors have made terrible and tragic decisions about managing clergy sex offenders when they should have known better. The current media spotlight on sex offending clergy has acted as an opportunity to examine this problem more closely and to develop interventions at both individual and institutional levels. The problem of sex offending clergy often lacks simple answers. However, it is also not rocket science. There are strategies and procedures that have been successfully used with other populations (such as mental health professionals) that can be used with the Church. We can perhaps never totally eliminate abuse of children among the ranks of clergy or any occupational profession but we can do much more to minimize the risk. At stake is the moral and spiritual authority of the Church as well as the well-being of countless priests and laypersons.

Ultimately, there are three fundamental questions to consider when thinking about sex offending clergy. First and foremost is what can the Church do differently to best protect current and future children from being harmed by a clergy member? Second, what can the Church (and others) do for the victims of clergy abuse? Finally, what should the Church do with their clergy (including both offending priests and religious superiors such as bishops) who have harmed others? Given these questions, where do we go from here? The following is a list of nine important principles to guide the Church into the future.

1. *Protect children and families.* The first priority must be the protection of children and vulnerable adults. It is inexcusable that members of the clergy can sexually abuse and victimize children, teens, and families in any way. Certainly, anyone who has a sexual predilection towards children does not belong in their company. It is prudent that an alcoholic, even if sober for many years, not work as a bartender. Similarly, a priest with a sexual predilection for children does not belong in a parish or school with children present. Even if they have been successfully treated for their sexual acting out behaviors, the risk is too high to give them access to children and vulnerable others. All efforts should be made to eliminate the risks of abuse of vulnerable others by clergy. There are effective models and best practices that have been applied to mental health professionals, teachers, and others that have included one-strike laws and policies to significantly reduce the risk of sexual abuse perpetrated by these professionals. In fact, the percentage of mental health professionals who had a sexual encounter with a client was reduced from about twenty percent to about one percent within one generation using a combination of education, training, and licensing legislation. What we have learned from these other populations can be applied to clergy members as well.

2. *The Church must be responsible and accountable.* Church officials must take responsibility and be accountable for their policies and procedures to ensure that their clergy do not victimize children. The question, "What did he know and when did he know it," which was often noted during the Watergate years in the mid 1970s, applies to religious superiors and mental health professionals involved with clergy abuse cases. Given research and practice guidelines since the mid- to late-1980s, it is inexcusable since those years for religious superiors and mental health professionals to have suggested that sex offending clergy return to unsupervised ministry among children. The Catholic Church as well as other institutions must use state-of-the-art information and best practices to properly screen, evaluate, and supervise their representatives to minimize potential victimization. If a police officer, soldier, schoolteacher, or other authority figure abuses power and influence and victimizes others, they (as well as their institutions) must answer to civil and criminal proceedings and be held accountable for their behavior. The Church is no exception.

3. *Attorneys and insurance carriers can only help so much.* Defense lawyers and insurance companies should not dictate the policies and directions of the Catholic Church. While attorneys and insurance carriers must be involved with helping the Church cope with an onslaught of lawsuits, the Church must answer to a higher moral and ethical authority and have much higher standards to uphold relative to secular institutions.

4. *The Church should not forget its spiritual and moral tradition.* The Church needs to provide genuine moral and religious leadership that is based on the wisdom of the Judaic-Christian tradition and, specifically, of the gospel story of Jesus. There is a gospel-based accountability to uphold religious, moral, and ethical standards and not to do what might be the most practical or expedient.

5. *Zero tolerance has some appeal although must be considered carefully.* While zero tolerance is a concept that has a great deal of popular support, there are many complex issues that make zero tolerance easier said than done. While a zero-tolerance policy might result in some potential injustices (e.g., someone who has an unsubstantiated accusation of sexual misconduct 40 years ago associated with an alcohol problem and who has had 40 years of a spotless record following alcohol treatment but is now expelled from ministry), they may need to occur in order for the Church to regain its place as a legitimate and believable spiritual and moral leader. Furthermore, many call for the defrocking of sex offending clergy. If the primary goal is to protect children from abuse, defrocking a priest may not be in the best interest of keeping children and vulnerable others safe. Sex offenders do get released from prison and probation and can often do what they want as long as they register as sex offenders with local authorities. The Church can use the vow of obedience to ensure that sex offending clergy stay far away from children and others forever. This level of control cannot occur in secular society once someone is released from the criminal justice system.

6. *Universality and clarity are needed in policies and procedures.* Policies regarding how to deal with accusations of sexual misconduct by clergy in terms of what the victims and accused can expect must be made clear across the land. These policies must be easy to understand. One shouldn't have to be a canon or civil lawyer to figure out the procedures and policies for making an accusation of sex abuse by clergy. The lack of universality and clarity as well as procedural due process is highly problematic for both victims and perpetrators of sexual misconduct. Some dioceses and religious orders are much further along than others in the development of state-of-the-art strategies for dealing with accusations of misconduct by clergy. Best practices and model programs need to share their methods with others to maximize the chances that good strategies and methods are used everywhere. It is unreasonable that some Church jurisdictions maintain excellent policies and procedures while others do not. Furthermore, other diverse institutions, companies, licensing boards, and so forth have accomplished this goal. Why can't the Catholic Church?

7. *Research is needed.* It is hard to solve important problems unless good data are available to help inform policy and procedures. It would be pro-

ductive to complete comprehensive research studies that can help us make decisions based on the best available data. The Church, the social science research community, the criminal justice system, the mental health professionals, victim groups, and others should work together to produce research that can inform application, practice, and policy. This is difficult to do since Church-funded research would be held suspect due to potential conflicts of interest. Other non-Church institutions may be reluctant to fund expensive projects that are focused on Catholic priests. Finally, Church officials must be comfortable releasing information that might challenge legal and moral issues of confidentiality before progress can be made.

8. *Keep the light on.* In the second chapter of this book, Michael Rezendes from the *Boston Globe* completes his chapter by stating that the *Boston Globe* Spotlight Team shed light on a very dark place and by calling for the continued keeping of this light on the darkness. This image is an important one and is worth repeating. Much good can ultimately come out of the crisis in the American Catholic Church if policies and procedures are developed to minimize the sexual victimization of minors in the present and future. If due to the attention the media and public have had on this problem, problematic and abusive clergy are treated in a way that can eliminate the risk of harm to others, if victims and their families are treated with compassion, respect, and care, and if the moral and spiritual authority and leadership of the Catholic Church can regain the respect and admiration of the people of God, much good can emerge. The Church has much to lose yet much to gain from the recent crisis. Furthermore, the light shed on the sexual victimization of children can be directed to all places where children are victimized both in and outside of the Catholic Church.

9. *Follow the example of Jesus.* The Catholic Church is a remarkable institution that encompasses 1 billion people representing almost 20 percent of the world's population and about 25 percent of the American population. It is an enormous organization that is about 2,000 years old. It would be productive for the Church and those involved with the Church to remember that it is a spiritual organization based on the life and teachings of Jesus. Lessons from the gospel should help inform all of the Church's actions. Common sense and compassion must be the order of the day rather than hysteria and rage. Perhaps we should consider the words of Jesus himself as quoted in chapter 5 of the Gospel of Matthew: "Be compassionate, therefore, as your heavenly Father is compassionate."

Responsibility, respect, integrity, competence, and concern for others (Plante, 2004) should be the principles used to best deal with the issue of clergy sexual abuse. This includes how we treat victims and offending clergy as well as how we best recover from the earthquake that has rocked the Catholic Church. The Church must do the right thing in dealing with past victims, potential victims, wayward priests, and bishops and other superiors who have mismanaged their subordinates, using the wisdom of the gospel and the best that the rich Catholic Christian spiritual and religious tradition can offer. To do otherwise is to sin.

REFERENCES

Bryant, C. (1999). Psychological treatment of priest sex offenders. In T. G. Plante (Ed.), *Bless me father for I have sinned: Perspectives on sexual abuse committed by Roman Catholic priests,* pp. 88–110. Westport, CT: Greenwood.

Conley, F. (1998). *Walking out on the boys.* New York: Farrar, Straus, and Giroux.

de Fuentes, N. (1999). Hear our cries: Victims-survivors of clergy sexual misconduct. In T. G. Plante (Ed.). *Bless me father for I have sinned: Perspectives on sexual abuse committed by Roman Catholic priests,* pp. 135–170. Westport, CT: Greenwood.

Francis, P. C., & Turner, N. R. (1995). Sexual misconduct within the Christian church: Who are the perpetrators and those they victimize? *Counseling & Values, 39,* 218–227.

Isley, P. J., & Isely, P. (1990). The sexual abuse of male children by church personnel: Intervention and prevention. *Pastoral Psychology, 39,* 85–98.

Lothstein, L. (1999). Neuropsychological findings in clergy who sexually abuse. In T. G. Plante (Ed.). *Bless me father for I have sinned: Perspectives on sexual abuse committed by Roman Catholic priests,* pp. 59–86. Westport, CT: Greenwood.

Plante, T. G. (2004). *Do the right thing: Living ethically in an unethical world.* Oakland, CA: New Harbinger.

Plante, T. G. (Ed.). (1999). *Bless me father for I have sinned: Perspectives on sexual abuse committed by Roman Catholic priests.* Westport, CT: Greenwood.

Rossetti, S. J. (1996). *A tragic grace: The Catholic Church and child sexual abuse.* NY: Liturgical Press.

Rossetti, S. J. (2002a). The Catholic Church and child sexual abuse. *America, 186,* 8–15.

Rossetti, S. J. (2002b). The Catholic Church and child sexual abuse. Paper presented at the 21st Annual Conference of the Association for the Treatment of Sexual Abusers, Montreal, Quebec, Canada.

Ruzicka, M. F. (1997). Predictor variables on clergy pedophiles. *Psychological Reports, 81,* 589–590.

Sipe, A. W. R. (1995). *Sex, priests, and power: Anatomy of a crisis.* New York: Brunner Mazel.

APPENDIX:
CHARTER FOR THE PROTECTION
OF CHILDREN AND YOUNG
PEOPLE, REVISED EDITION

PREAMBLE

The Church in the United States is experiencing a crisis without precedent in our times. The sexual abuse of children and young people by some priests and bishops, and the ways in which we bishops addressed these crimes and sins, have caused enormous pain, anger, and confusion. Innocent victims and their families have suffered terribly. In the past, secrecy has created an atmosphere that has inhibited the healing process and, in some cases, enabled sexually abusive behavior to be repeated. As bishops, we acknowledge our mistakes and our role in that suffering, and we apologize and take responsibility for too often failing victims and our people in the past. We also take responsibility for dealing with this problem strongly, consistently, and effectively in the future. From the depths of our hearts, we bishops express great sorrow and profound regret for what the Catholic people are enduring.

We, who have been given the responsibility of shepherding God's people, will, with God's help and in full collaboration with our people, continue to work to restore the bonds of trust that unite us. Words alone cannot accomplish this goal. It will begin with the actions we take here in our General Assembly and at home in our dioceses/eparchies.

The damage caused by sexual abuse of minors is devastating and long-lasting. We reach out to those who suffer, but especially to the victims of sexual abuse and their families. We apologize to them for the grave harm that has been inflicted upon them, and we offer them our help for the future. In the light of so much suffering, healing and reconciliation are beyond human capacity alone. Only God's grace, mercy, and forgiveness can lead us forward, trusting Christ's promise: "for God all things are possible" (Mt 19:26).

The loss of trust becomes even more tragic when its consequence is a loss of the faith that we have a sacred duty to foster. We make our own the words of our Holy Father: that sexual abuse of young people is "by every standard wrong and rightly considered a crime by society; it is also an appalling sin in the eyes of God" (Address to the Cardinals of the United States and Conference Officers, April 23, 2002).

The Conference of Bishops has been addressing the evil of sexual abuse of minors by a priest and, at its June 1992 meeting, established five principles to be followed (cf. Ad Hoc Committee on Sexual Abuse, National Conference of Catholic Bishops, *Restoring Trust,* November 1994). We also need to recognize that many dioceses and eparchies did implement in a responsible and timely fashion policies and procedures that have safeguarded children and young people. Many bishops did take appropriate steps to address clergy who were guilty of sexual misconduct.

Let there now be no doubt or confusion on anyone's part: For us, your bishops, our obligation to protect children and young people and to prevent sexual abuse flows from the mission and example given to us by Jesus Christ himself, in whose name we serve.

Jesus showed constant care for the vulnerable. He inaugurated his ministry with these words of the Prophet Isaiah:

> The Spirit of the Lord is upon me,
>> because he has anointed me
>> to bring glad tidings to the poor.
>> He has sent me to proclaim liberty to captives
>> and recovery of sight to the blind,
>> to let the oppressed go free,
>> and to proclaim a year acceptable to the Lord. (Lk 4:18)

In Matthew 25, the Lord made this part of his commission to his apostles and disciples when he told them that whenever they showed mercy and compassion to the least ones, they showed it to him.

Jesus extended this care in a tender and urgent way to children, rebuking his disciples for keeping them away from him: "Let the children come to me" (Mt 19:14). And he uttered the grave warning about anyone who would lead the little ones astray, saying that it would be better for such a person "to have a great millstone hung around his neck and to be drowned in the depths of the sea" (Mt 18:6).

We hear these words of the Lord as prophetic for this moment. With a firm determination to resolve this crisis, we bishops commit ourselves to a pastoral outreach to repair the breach with those who have suffered sexual abuse and with all the people of the Church. We renew our determination to provide safety and protection for children and young people in our church ministries and institutions. We pledge ourselves to act in a way that manifests our accountability to God, to his people, and to one another in this grave matter. We commit ourselves to do all we can to heal the trauma that victims/survivors and their families are suffering and the wound that the whole Church is experiencing. We acknowledge our need to be in dialogue with all Catholics, especially victims and parents, around this issue. By these actions, we want to demonstrate to the wider community that we comprehend the gravity of the sexual abuse of minors.

To fulfill these goals, our dioceses/eparchies and our national conference, in a spirit of repentance and renewal, will adopt and implement policies based upon the following.

TO PROMOTE HEALING AND RECONCILIATION WITH VICTIMS/SURVIVORS OF SEXUAL ABUSE OF MINORS

ARTICLE 1. Dioceses/eparchies will reach out to victims/survivors and their families and demonstrate a sincere commitment to their spiritual and emotional well-being. The first obligation of the Church with regard to the victims is for healing and reconciliation. Where such outreach is not already in place and operative, each diocese/eparchy is to develop an outreach to every person who has been the victim of sexual abuse* as a minor

---

*Sexual abuse of a minor includes sexual molestation or sexual exploitation of a minor and other behavior by which an adult uses a minor as an object of sexual gratification. Sexual abuse has been defined by different civil authorities in various ways, and these norms do not adopt any particular definition provided in civil law. Rather, the transgressions in question relate to obligations arising from divine commands regarding human sexual interaction as conveyed to us by the sixth commandment of the Decalogue (CIC, c. 1395 §2, CCEO, c. 1453 §1). Thus, the norm to be considered in assessing an allegation of sexual abuse of a minor is whether conduct or interaction with a minor qualifies as an external, objectively grave violation of the sixth commandment (USCCB, *Canonical Delicts Involving Sexual Misconduct and Dismissal from the Clerical State*, 1995, p. 6). A canonical offense against the sixth commandment of the Decalogue (CIC, c. 1395 §2; CCEO, c. 1453

by anyone acting in the name of the Church, whether the abuse was recent or occurred many years in the past. This outreach will include provision of counseling, spiritual assistance, support groups, and other social services agreed upon by the victim and the diocese/eparchy. In cooperation with social service agencies and other churches, support groups for victims/survivors and others affected by abuse should be fostered and encouraged in every diocese/eparchy and in local parish communities.

Through pastoral outreach to victims and their families, the diocesan/eparchial bishop or his representative will offer to meet with them, to listen with patience and compassion to their experiences and concerns, and to share the "profound sense of solidarity and concern" expressed by our Holy Father in his Address to the Cardinals of the United States and Conference Officers. This pastoral outreach by the bishop or his delegate will also be directed to faith communities in which the sexual abuse occurred.

ARTICLE 2. Dioceses/eparchies will have mechanisms in place to respond promptly to any allegation where there is reason to believe that sexual abuse of a minor has occurred. Dioceses/eparchies will have a competent person or persons to coordinate assistance for the immediate pastoral care of persons who claim to have been sexually abused as minors by clergy or other church personnel. Dioceses/eparchies will also have a review board

---

§1) need not be a complete act of intercourse. Nor, to be objectively grave, does an act need to involve force, physical contact, or a discernible harmful outcome. Moreover, "imputability [moral responsibility] for a canonical offense is presumed upon external violation...unless it is otherwise apparent" (CIC, c. 1321 §3; CCEO, c. 1414 §2 cf. CIC, cc. 1322–1327, and CCEO, cc. 1413, 1415, and 1416). If there is any doubt about whether a specific act fulfills this definition, the writings of recognized moral theologians should be consulted and the opinion of a recognized expert be obtained (*Canonical Delicts,* p. 6). Ultimately, it is the responsibility of the diocesan bishop/eparch, with the advice of a qualified review board, to determine the gravity of the alleged act.

The document *Charter for the Protection of Children and Young People* was developed by the Ad Hoc Committee on Sexual Abuse of the United States Conference of Catholic Bishops (USCCB). It was approved by the full body of U.S. Catholic bishops at its November 2002 General Meeting and has been authorized for publication by the undersigned.

Msgr. William P. Fay

General Secretary, USCCB

Charter for the Protection of Children and Young People is available in a print edition and may be ordered by telephoning (800) 235-8722. Ask for publication number 5-540.

that functions as a confidential consultative body to the bishop/eparch. The majority of its members will be lay persons not in the employ of the diocese/ eparchy (see norm 5 in *Essential Norms for Diocesan/Eparchial Policies Dealing with Allegations of Sexual Abuse of Minors by Priests or Deacons,* 2002). This board will advise the diocesan/eparchial bishop in his assess- ment of allegations of sexual abuse of minors and in his determination of suitability for ministry. It will regularly review diocesan/eparchial policies and procedures for dealing with sexual abuse of minors. Also, the board can review these matters both retrospectively and prospectively and give advice on all aspects of responses required in connection with these cases. The pro- cedures for those making a complaint will be readily available in printed form and will be the subject of periodic public announcements.

ARTICLE 3. Dioceses/eparchies will not enter into confidentiality agreements except for grave and substantial reasons brought forward by the victim/survivor and noted in the text of the agreement.

TO GUARANTEE AN EFFECTIVE RESPONSE TO ALLEGATIONS OF SEXUAL ABUSE OF MINORS

ARTICLE 4. Dioceses/eparchies will report an allegation of sexual abuse of a person who is a minor to the public authorities. Dioceses/eparchies will comply with all applicable civil laws with respect to the reporting of allega- tions of sexual abuse of minors to civil authorities and will cooperate in their investigation in accord with the law of the jurisdiction in question.

Dioceses/eparchies will cooperate with public authorities about report- ing in cases when the person is no longer a minor.

In every instance, dioceses/eparchies will advise victims of their right to make a report to public authorities and will support this right.

ARTICLE 5. We repeat the words of our Holy Father in his Address to the Cardinals of the United States and Conference Officers: "There is no place in the priesthood or religious life for those who would harm the young."

When an allegation of sexual abuse of a minor by a priest or a deacon is received, a preliminary investigation, in harmony with canon law (CIC, cc. 1717–1719; CCEO, cc. 1468–1470), will be initiated and conducted promptly and objectively. If this investigation so indicates, the diocesan/ eparchial bishop will both notify the Congregation for the Doctrine of the Faith and apply the precautionary measures mentioned in CIC, canon 1722, or CCEO, canon 1473—i.e., relieve the alleged offender promptly of his ministerial duties. The alleged offender may be requested to seek, or urged voluntarily to comply with, an appropriate medical and psycho-

logical evaluation, so long as this does not interfere with the investigation
by civil authorities. When the accusation has proved to be unfounded,
every step possible will be taken to restore the good name of the priest or
deacon.

When sexual abuse of a minor by a priest or a deacon is admitted or is
established after an appropriate process in accord with canon law, the following will pertain:

- Diocesan/eparchial policy will provide that for even a single act of
  sexual abuse (see Article 1, note *) of a minor—past, present, or
  future—the offending priest or deacon will be permanently
  removed from ministry, not excluding dismissal from the clerical
  state, if the case so warrants. In keeping with the stated purpose of
  this Charter, an offending priest or deacon will be offered professional assistance for his own healing and well-being, as well as for
  the purpose of prevention.

- In every case involving canonical penalties, the processes provided
  for in canon law must be observed (cf. *Canonical Delicts Involving
  Sexual Misconduct and Dismissal from the Clerical State,* 1995; cf.
  Letter from the Congregation for the Doctrine of the Faith, May 18,
  2001). For the sake of due process, the accused is to be encouraged
  to retain the assistance of civil and canonical counsel. When necessary, the diocese/eparchy will supply canonical counsel to a priest
  or deacon.

- Also provided for in canon law are the following: a request by the
  priest or deacon for dispensation from the obligation of holy orders
  and the loss of the clerical state or a request by the bishop for dismissal from the clerical state even without the consent of the priest
  or deacon (cf. *Canonical Delicts*).

- If the penalty of dismissal from the clerical state has not been
  applied (e.g., for reasons of advanced age or infirmity), the offender
  ought to lead a life of prayer and penance. He will not be permitted
  to celebrate Mass publicly or to administer the sacraments. He is to
  be instructed not to wear clerical garb or to present himself publicly
  as a priest.

- At all times, the diocesan bishop/eparch has the executive power of
  governance, through an administrative act, to remove an offending
  cleric from office, to remove or restrict his faculties, and to limit his
  exercise of priestly ministry. Because sexual abuse of a minor is a
  crime in all jurisdictions in the United States, for the sake of the
  common good and observing the provisions of canon law, the

diocesan bishop/eparch shall exercise this power of governance to ensure that any priest or deacon who has committed even one act of sexual abuse of a minor as described above shall not continue in active ministry.

ARTICLE 6. While the priestly commitment to the virtue of chastity and the gift of celibacy is well known, there will be clear and well-publicized diocesan/eparchial standards of ministerial behavior and appropriate boundaries for clergy and for any other church personnel in positions of trust who have regular contact with children and young people.

ARTICLE 7. Each diocese/eparchy will develop a communications policy that reflects a commitment to transparency and openness. Within the confines of respect for the privacy and the reputation of the individuals involved, dioceses/eparchies will deal as openly as possible with members of the community. This is especially so with regard to assisting and supporting parish communities directly affected by ministerial misconduct involving minors.

TO ENSURE THE ACCOUNTABILITY OF OUR PROCEDURES

ARTICLE 8. To assist in the consistent application of these principles and to provide a vehicle of accountability and assistance to dioceses/eparchies in this matter, we authorize the establishment of an Office for Child and Youth Protection at our national headquarters. The tasks of this Office will include (1) assisting individual dioceses/eparchies in the implementation of "safe environment" programs (see Article 12 below), (2) assisting provinces and regions in the development of appropriate mechanisms to audit adherence to policies, and (3) producing an annual public report on the progress made in implementing the standards in this Charter. This public report shall include the names of those dioceses/eparchies which, in the judgment of this Office, are not in compliance with the provisions and expectations of this Charter. This Office will have staffing sufficient to fulfill its basic purpose. Staff will consist of persons who are expert in the protection of minors; they will be appointed by the General Secretary of the Conference.

ARTICLE 9. The work of the Office for Child and Youth Protection will be assisted and monitored by a Review Board, including parents, appointed by the Conference President and reporting directly to him. The

Board will approve the annual report of the implementation of this Charter in each of our dioceses/eparchies, as well as any recommendations that emerge from this review, before the report is submitted to the President of the Conference and published. To understand the problem more fully and to enhance the effectiveness of our future response, the National Review Board will commission a comprehensive study of the causes and context of the current crisis. The Board will also commission a descriptive study, with the full cooperation of our dioceses/eparchies, of the nature and scope of the problem within the Catholic Church in the United States, including such data as statistics on perpetrators and victims.

ARTICLE 10. The membership of the Ad Hoc Committee on Sexual Abuse will be reconstituted to include representation from all the episcopal regions of the country.

ARTICLE 11. The President of the Conference will inform the Holy See of this Charter to indicate the manner in which we, the Catholic bishops, together with the entire Church in the United States, intend to address this present crisis.

TO PROTECT THE FAITHFUL IN THE FUTURE

ARTICLE 12. Dioceses/eparchies will establish "safe environment" programs. They will cooperate with parents, civil authorities, educators, and community organizations to provide education and training for children, youth, parents, ministers, educators, and others about ways to make and maintain a safe environment for children. Dioceses/eparchies will make clear to clergy and all members of the community the standards of conduct for clergy and other persons in positions of trust with regard to sexual abuse.

ARTICLE 13. Dioceses/eparchies will evaluate the background of all diocesan/eparchial and parish personnel who have regular contact with minors. Specifically, they will utilize the resources of law enforcement and other community agencies. In addition, they will employ adequate screening and evaluative techniques in deciding the fitness of candidates for ordination (cf. National Conference of Catholic Bishops, *Program of Priestly Formation,* 1993, no. 513).

ARTICLE 14. No priest or deacon who has committed an act of sexual abuse of a minor may be transferred for ministerial assignment to another diocese/eparchy or religious province. Before a priest or deacon can be transferred for residence to another diocese/eparchy or religious province, his bishop/eparch or religious ordinary shall forward, in a confidential manner, to the local bishop/eparch and religious ordinary (if applicable) of the proposed place of residence any and all information concerning any act of sexual abuse of a minor and any other information that he has been or may be a danger to children or young people (cf. National Conference of Catholic Bishops and Conference of Major Superiors of Men, *Proposed Guidelines on the Transfer or Assignment of Clergy and Religious,* 1993).

ARTICLE 15. The Ad Hoc Committee on Sexual Abuse and the Officers of the Conference of Major Superiors of Men will meet to determine how this Charter will be conveyed and established in the communities of religious men in the United States. Diocesan/eparchial bishops and major superiors of clerical institutes or their delegates will meet periodically to coordinate their roles concerning the issue of allegations made against a cleric member of a religious institute ministering in a diocese/eparchy.

ARTICLE 16. Given the extent of the problem of the sexual abuse of minors in our society, we are willing to cooperate with other churches and ecclesial communities, other religious bodies, institutions of learning, and other interested organizations in conducting research in this area.

ARTICLE 17. We pledge our complete cooperation with the Apostolic Visitation of our diocesan/eparchial seminaries and religious houses of formation recommended in the Interdicasterial Meeting with the Cardinals of the United States and the Conference Officers in April 2002. Unlike the previous visitation, these new visits will focus on the question of human formation for celibate chastity based on the criteria found in *Pastores Dabo Vobis.* We look forward to this opportunity to strengthen our priestly formation programs so that they may provide God's people with mature and holy priests. Dioceses/eparchies will develop systematic ongoing formation programs in keeping with the recent Conference document *Basic Plan for the Ongoing Formation of Priests* (2001) so as to assist priests in their living out of their vocation.

CONCLUSION

In the midst of this terrible crisis of sexual abuse of young people by priests and bishops and how it has been dealt with by bishops, many other issues have been raised. In this Charter we focus specifically on the painful issue at hand. However, in this matter, we do wish to affirm our concern especially with regard to issues related to effective consultation of the laity and the participation of God's people in decision making that affects their well-being.

We must increase our vigilance to prevent those few who might exploit the priesthood for their own immoral and criminal purposes from doing so. At the same time, we know that the sexual abuse of young people is not a problem inherent in the priesthood, nor are priests the only ones guilty of it. The vast majority of our priests are faithful in their ministry and happy in their vocation. Their people are enormously appreciative of the ministry provided by their priests. In the midst of trial, this remains a cause for rejoicing. We deeply regret that any of our decisions have obscured the good work of our priests, for which their people hold them in such respect.

It is within this context of the essential soundness of the priesthood and of the deep faith of our brothers and sisters in the Church that we know that we can meet and resolve this crisis for now and the future.

An essential means of dealing with the crisis is prayer for healing and reconciliation, and acts of reparation for the grave offense to God and the deep wound inflicted upon his holy people. Closely connected to prayer and acts of reparation is the call to holiness of life and the care of the diocesan/eparchial bishop to ensure that he and his priests avail themselves of the proven ways of avoiding sin and growing in holiness of life.

By what we have begun here today and by what we have stated and agreed to,

We pledge most solemnly to one another and to you, God's people, that we will work to our utmost for the protection of children and youth.

We pledge that we will devote to this goal the resources and personnel necessary to accomplish it.

We pledge that we will do our best to ordain to the priesthood and put into positions of trust only those who share this commitment to protecting children and youth.

We pledge that we will work toward healing and reconciliation for those sexually abused by clerics.

We make these pledges with a humbling sense of our own limitations, relying on the help of God and the support of his faithful priests and people to work with us to fulfill them.

Above all we believe, in the words of St. Paul as cited by Pope John Paul II in April 2002, that "where sin increased, grace overflowed all the more" (Rm 5:20). This is faith's message. With this faith, we are confident that we will not be conquered by evil but overcome evil with good (cf. Rm 12:21).

This charter is published for the dioceses/eparchies of the United States, and we bishops commit ourselves to its immediate implementation. It is to be reviewed in two years by the Conference of Bishops with the advice of the National Review Board created in Article 9 to ensure its effectiveness in resolving the problems of sexual abuse of minors by priests.

INDEX

ABOUT THE SERIES EDITOR
AND ADVISERS

J. HAROLD ELLENS is a Research Scholar at the University of Michigan, Department of Near Eastern Studies. He is a retired Presbyterian theologian and ordained minister, a retired U.S. Army Colonel, and a retired Professor of Philosophy, Theology, and Psychology. He has authored, coauthored, and/or edited 72 books and 148 professional journal articles. He served 15 years as Executive Director of the Christian Association for Psychological Studies, and as Founding Editor and Editor-in-Chief of the *Journal of Psychology and Christianity.* He holds a Ph.D. from Wayne State University in the Psychology of Human Communication, a Ph.D. from the University of Michigan in Biblical and Near Eastern Studies, and master's degrees from Calvin Theological Seminary, Princeton Theological Seminary, and the University of Michigan. He was born in Michigan, grew up in a Dutch-German immigrant community, and determined at age seven to enter the Christian Ministry as a means to help his people with the great amount of suffering he perceived all around him. His life's work has focused on the interface of psychology and religion.

ARCHBISHOP DESMOND TUTU is best known for his contribution to the cause of racial justice in South Africa, a contribution for which he was recognized with the Nobel Peace Prize in 1984. Archbishop Tutu has been an ordained priest since 1960. Among his many accomplishments are being named the first black General Secretary of the South African Council of Churches and serving as Archbishop of Cape Town. Once a high schoolteacher in South Africa, he has also taught theology in college, and holds honorary degrees from universities including Harvard, Oxford, Columbia, and Kent State. He has been awarded the Order for Meritorious Service presented by President Nelson Mandela, the Archbishop of Canterbury's Award for outstanding service to the Anglican community, the Family of Man Gold Medal Award, and the Martin Luther King Jr. Non-Violent Peace Award. The publications Archbishop Tutu has authored, coauthored, or made contributions to include *No Future Without Forgiveness* (2000), *Crying in the Wilderness: The Struggle for Justice in South Africa* (1982), and *The Rainbow People of God: The Making of a Peaceful Revolution* (1994).

LeROY H. ADEN is Professor Emeritus of Pastoral Theology at the Lutheran Theological Seminary in Philadelphia, Pennsylvania. He taught full-time at the seminary from 1967 to 1994 and part-time from 1994 to 2001. He served as Visiting Lecturer at Princeton Theological Seminary, Princeton, New Jersey, on a regular basis. In 2002, he coauthored *Preaching God's Compassion: Comforting Those Who Suffer* with Robert G. Hughes. Previously, he edited four books in a Psychology and Christianity series with J. Harold Ellens and David G. Benner. He served on the Board of Directors of the Christian Association for Psychological Studies for six years.

DONALD CAPPS, Psychologist of Religion, is William Hart Felmeth Professor of Pastoral Theology at Princeton Theological Seminary. In 1989, he was awarded an honorary doctorate from the University of Uppsala, Sweden, in recognition of the importance of his publications. He served as president of the Society for the Scientific Study of Religion from 1990 to 1992. Among his many significant books are *Men, Religion and Melancholia: James, Otto, Jung and Erikson;* also *Freud and Freudians on Religion: A Reader;* also *Social Phobia: Alleviating Anxiety in an Age of Self-Promotion;* and *Jesus: A Psychological Biography.* He also authored *The Child's Song: The Religious Abuse of Children.*

ZENON LOTUFO JR. is a Presbyterian minister (Independent Presbyterian Church of Brazil), a philosopher, and a psychotherapist, specialized in Transactional Analysis. He has lectured both to undergraduate and graduate courses in universities in São Paulo, Brazil. He coordinates the course of specialization in Pastoral Psychology of the Christian Psychologists and Psychiatrists Association. He is the author of the books, *Relações*

Humanas [Human Relations]; *Disfunções no Comportamento Organizacional* [Dysfunctions in Organizational Behavior]; and coauthor of *O Potencial Humano* [Human Potential]. He has also authored numerous journal articles.

DIRK ODENDAAL is South African; he was born in what is now called the Province of the Eastern Cape. He spent much of his youth in the Transkei in the town of Umtata, where his parents were teachers at a seminary. He trained as a minister at the Stellenbosch Seminary for the Dutch Reformed Church and was ordained in 1983 in the Dutch Reformed Church in Southern Africa. He transferred to East London in 1988 to minister to members of the Uniting Reformed Church in Southern Africa in one of the huge suburbs for Xhosa-speaking people. He received his doctorate (D.Litt.) in 1992 at the University of Port Elizabeth in Semitic Languages. At present, he is enrolled in a Masters course in Counselling Psychology at Rhodes University.

WAYNE G. ROLLINS is Professor Emeritus of Biblical Studies at Assumption College, Worcester, Massachusetts, and Adjunct Professor of Scripture at Hartford Seminary, Hartford, Connecticut. His writings include *The Gospels: Portraits of Christ* (1964), *Jung and the Bible* (1983), and *Soul and Psyche, The Bible in Psychological Perspective* (1999). He received his Ph.D. in New Testament Studies from Yale University and is the founder and chairman (1990–2000) of the Society of Biblical Literature Section on Psychology and Biblical Studies.

ABOUT THE EDITOR
AND CONTRIBUTORS

JOHN ALLEN JR. is the prize-winning Vatican writer for the *National Catholic Reporter.* He is also a CNN analyst on Vatican affairs. His work has been featured in *The New York Times,* the *Boston Globe,* the *Washington Monthly,* the *Irish Examiner, The Tablet,* and *The Miami Herald.* His reporting is admired across ideological divides; liberal commentator Andrew Greeley calls Allen's Vatican analysis "indispensable," while conservative Richard John Neuhaus says possibly the best reporting on the Holy See published in the United States is Allen's "The Word from Rome" column. His biography of Cardinal Joseph Ratzinger (*The Vatican's Enforcer of the Faith, Continuum,* November 2000) was reviewed widely. His second book, *Conclave: The Politics, Personalities and Process of the Next Papal Election* was published in 2002.

CURTIS C. BRYANT was a Jesuit priest and clinical psychologist, licensed in California, who lived and worked at Loyola Marymount University and maintained an independent practice. Father Bryant was director of Saint Luke's Institute, a psychiatric hospital in Maryland for priests and religious, for seven years. He also served as Consultant to the Vicar for Clergy in the Los Angeles Archdiocese for two years. Father Bryant's writing and reflection had focused on the intersection between spirituality and the healing arts with an effort to create a dialogue between the criminal justice and mental health systems. Father Bryant died following cancer surgery on November 18, 2003.

DAVID CLOHESSY has been the national director of SNAP, the Survivors Network of those Abused by Priests, the nation's largest and oldest support group for clergy abuse victims for the past 12 years. He has helped establish self-help SNAP chapters in all 50 states and has counseled hundreds of women and men hurt by spiritual leaders. He has worked in marginalized communities as an organizer of neighborhood groups and as a community relations staffer for a school district.

GERALD D. COLEMAN is a Sulpician priest, President/Rector and Professor of Moral Theology at St. Patrick's Seminary, Menlo Park, California, and a member of the Catholic Theological Society of America. He has published widely in the areas of moral and pastoral theology, as well as medical ethics. He has served on the Board of Directors and ethics committees of several Catholic hospitals. He is the author of *Human Sexuality: An All-Embracing Gift* (1992) and *Homosexuality: Catholic Teaching and Pastoral Practice* (1996). He has consulted widely with the National Conference of Catholic Bishops and Catholic clergy regarding his work in the areas of moral, pastoral, and medical questions.

NANETTE DE FUENTES is a licensed psychologist in independent practice in Glendale, California, specializing in sexual abuse recovery, sexual compulsivity disorders treatment, and integrating spirituality in therapy. Since 1991, she has provided psychological consultation, evaluation, and program development services to the Los Angeles Roman Catholic Archdiocese and St. John's Seminary and Seminary College in Camarillo. Dr. de Fuentes has also worked with over 10 national and worldwide Catholic religious orders, as well with Buddhist and Hindu religious groups. She is a founding member of the L.A. Archdiocese Clergy Misconduct Oversight Review Board and is herself a survivor of clergy sexual exploitation.

THOMAS P. DOYLE is a Dominican priest, canon lawyer, addictions counselor, and U.S. Air Force officer and chaplain. Formerly a secretary-canonist with the Vatican embassy in Washington, D.C., Father Doyle coauthored a detailed report on the impending disaster of clergy sexual abuse in 1985. Since then he has been an active advocate for victims and survivors of clergy sexual abuse. He has been an expert witness and consultant in several hundred civil cases throughout the United States, Canada, the United Kingdom, Ireland, Australia, and New Zealand. He has been recognized internationally as an expert on the clergy sex abuse issue and has lectured extensively and published several articles on the subject. His most recent articles include "Roman Catholic Clericalism,

Religious Duress and Clergy Sexual Abuse" published in *Pastoral Psychology* and "Abrogation of Trust in the Catholic Church," published in the *Association of Humanistic Psychology Journal.*

KIRK O. HANSON is Executive Director of the Markkula Center for Applied Ethics at Santa Clara University (California) and University Professor of Organizations and Society. Hanson has been at Santa Clara since 2001, when he took early retirement from Stanford University after teaching business ethics in the Graduate School of Business for 23 years and serving as Faculty Director of The Stanford Sloan Program. Hanson specializes in organizational ethics in business, government, and public benefit institutions. He has consulted with over 50 leading corporations and organizations, speaks widely on corporate ethics, and has served as an ethics expert witness in many legal cases. Hanson has written a column on workplace ethics for the *San Jose Mercury News,* chaired the Santa Clara County Political Ethics Commission, and served as the founding president of The Business Enterprise Trust, a national organization created by leaders in business, labor, media, and academia to promote exemplary behavior in business.

JOHN C. GONSIOREK is a clinical psychologist and holds a Diplomate in Clinical Psychology from the American Board of Professional Psychology. He is a past president of American Psychological Association Division 44, and has published widely in the areas of professional misconduct and impaired professionals, sexual orientation and identity, professional ethics, and other areas. He is author of *Breach of Trust: Sexual Exploitation by Health Care Professionals and Clergy* (1995). He has provided expert witness evaluation and testimony regarding impaired professionals, standards of care, and psychological damages. He is in independent practice of clinical psychology in Minneapolis, Minnesota.

JOHN ALLAN LOFTUS, a licensed psychologist and independent health service provider, is the former President of Regis College at the University of Toronto, where he is also professor of psychology and the psychology of religion. For several years he held the John J. Wintermeyer Chair in psychology at the University of Waterloo, St. Jerome's College, and is also the former Executive Director of Southdown, Canada's large treatment facility for clergy and religious. He is the author of the best-selling *Understanding Sexual Misconduct by Clergy: A Handbook for Ministers* (Pastoral Press, 1994) as well as the director and coauthor of one of the largest empirical studies of priests and sexuality.

LESLIE M. LOTHSTEIN is Director of Psychology at The Institute of Living, Hartford Hospital's Mental Health Network, Hartford, Connecticut. He is board-certified and a fellow of the American Psychological Association, the American Board of Professional Psychology, and the Connecticut Psychological Association. Dr. Lothstein has published one book and over 100 articles, book chapters, and reviews in the areas of sexuality (paraphilias), group therapy, and issues related to clergy sexual abuse. He is on the editorial board of the *International Journal of Group Psychotherapy* and the Advisory Board of the Whiting Forensic Division of Connecticut Valley Hospital. Dr. Lothstein has worked with over 700 clergy with psychiatric and psychosexual problems and has consulted with the National Conference of Catholic Bishops.

DONNA J. MARKHAM is an Adrian Dominican Sister currently serving as Special Assistant to the President and Director for Leadership Initiatives at Georgetown University, Washington, D.C. For the past 10 years, she served as President of the Southdown Institute. Dr. Markham is a registered clinical psychologist and a Fellow of the American Board of Professional Psychology. She is particularly engaged in issues pertaining to leadership development, organizational transformation, group analysis, and depth psychotherapeutic treatment. She has served in leadership in her own religious Congregation and as President of the Leadership Conference of Women Religious. Dr. Markham has published articles in journals including *Human Development, Health Progress, Review for Religious, The Way,* and *American Psychologist.* In addition, she is the author of *Spiritlinking Leadership: Working through Resistance to Organizational Change* (1999). Licensed to practice in Ontario, Michigan, and Nunavut, Canada, she established a clinical outreach program to serve the Inuit in the northeastern High Arctic.

KATHLEEN McCHESNEY is the Executive Director of the Office of Child and Youth Protection (OCYP) of the United States Conference of Catholic Bishops (USCCB). Appointed to this new office in December, 2002, Ms. McChesney is responsible for assisting U.S. Catholic dioceses/eparchies with implementing "safe-environment" programs for children and youth. The OCYP is also responsible for ensuring that U.S. Catholic bishops comply with the provisions of the *Charter and Essential Norms for the Protection of Children and Youth* through auditing and the preparation of an annual report. Ms. McChesney served in the Federal Bureau of Investigation for 24 years, retiring as Executive Assistant Director for Law

Enforcement Services, the third-highest position in that organization. Prior to her employment with the FBI, Ms. McChesney was a police officer and detective with Kings County Police, Seattle, Washington. She instructed courses at Seattle University and the Kings County Police Academy. Ms. McChesney is a recipient of the Presidential Meritorious Achievement Award, the Lifetime Achievement Award from the National Center for Women in Policing, the Illinois Security Chief's Association Public Service Award, the Anti-Defamation League's Community Service Award, and the Oregon Consular Corps's International Citizen Award.

SAMUEL F. MIKAIL is the Clinical Director of the Southdown Institute, a residential treatment facility providing comprehensive mental health services to church personnel. Dr. Mikail is a clinical psychologist registered to practice in the province of Ontario and the territory of Nunavut, Canada. He is a diplomate of the American Board of Professional Psychology, the Canadian Psychological Association, and the Section on Clinical Psychology of the Canadian Psychological Association (CPA). He has served as Chair of the Section on Clinical Psychology of CPA and as an executive member of the Canadian Council of Professional Psychology Programs. He has been a board member of the Canadian Psychological Association, the Canadian Pain Society, the Council of Provincial Associations of Psychology, the Canadian Register of Health Service Providers in Psychology, and the CPA Foundation. He is currently chair of the Accreditation Panel of CPA. He was a founding member of the Ottawa Group Psychotherapy Training Program and served on the training committee of the Canadian Group Psychotherapy Association Toronto Section Training Program. He is actively involved in research and clinical practice.

THOMAS G. PLANTE is professor of psychology at Santa Clara University, California, adjunct clinical associate professor of psychiatry and behavioral sciences at Stanford University School of Medicine, and consulting associate professor of education at Stanford University. He is a fellow of the American Psychological Association, the Society of Behavioral Medicine, and the Academy of Clinical Psychology. He has authored, coauthored, edited, or coedited six books including *Bless Me Father for I Have Sinned: Perspectives on Sexual Abuse Committed by Roman Catholic Priests* (1999), *Faith and Health: Psychological Perspectives* (2001, Guilford), *Do the Right Thing: Living Ethically in an Unethical World* (2004), and *Contemporary Clinical Psychology* (1999, Wiley). He has also published over 100 scholarly articles in professional journals. He has evaluated or treated more than 150 priests and applicants to the priesthood and has served as a consultant for a number of Church dioceses and religious orders. He maintains a private practice in Menlo Park, California.

MICHAEL REZENDES is a member of the *Boston Globe* Spotlight Team that won the 2003 Pulitzer Prize for Public Service for reporting on sexual abuse in the Catholic Church. A staff writer and editor at the *Globe* since 1989, Rezendes has worked as a political reporter covering presidential, state, and local elections, and was a weekly essayist, a roving national correspondent, and city hall bureau chief. Rezendes is also a coauthor of *Betrayal: The Crisis in the Catholic Church* (2002).

A. W. RICHARD SIPE spent 18 years in a Benedictine monastery; 11 of those years he was active in the priesthood. He was trained to deal with the mental health problems of priests and religious. In tandem with his private practice of psychotherapy, teaching in major seminaries, and lecturing in a medical school, he conducted a 25-year study on celibacy and sexuality in the priesthood. The results were published under the title *A Secret World: Sex, Priests, and Power: The Anatomy of a Crisis* (1995). *Celibacy: A Way of Loving, Living, and Serving* (1996), and *Celibacy in Crisis: A Secret World Revisited* (2003) have been published since. He is engaged full-time in the research of subjects related to sexuality and the priesthood.

WILLIAM C. SPOHN is Augustin Cardinal Bea SJ Distinguished Professor of Theology and Director of the Bannan Center for Jesuit Education at Santa Clara University, California. He is a moral theologian and writes on Scripture and ethics, spirituality and ethics, war and peace, and American religious ethics. From 1978 until 1992 he taught at the Jesuit School of Theology in Berkeley and the Graduate Theological Union. His latest book is *Go and Do Likewise: Jesus and Ethics* (Continuum, 1999).

MICHAEL WEGS is an alumnus of St. Thomas Aquinas High School Seminary, Hannibal, Missouri, where Anthony J. O'Connell, the former bishop of Palm Beach, Florida, served as an educator, spiritual director, and rector for 25 years. O'Connell resigned his Palm Beach post in March 2002, after former students came forward with sexual abuse allegations and secret cash settlements were disclosed to the public. Mr. Wegs is a survivor of O'Connell's victimization. Mr. Wegs is an award-winning journalist and corporate communications professional in Minneapolis, Minnesota.